Sites of Dissent

Creative Interventions in Global Politics

Series Editors: Shine Choi, Cristina Masters, Swati Parashar and Marysia Zalewski

The landscape of contemporary global politics is complex and oftentimes violent. Yet the urgency to provide solutions or immediate practical actions to this violence oftentimes leads to inadequate knowledge. This is despite the abundance of theoretical, conceptual and methodological tools available – much of this produced through conventional academic disciplines, notably International Relations, Political Theory and Philosophy. But the constraints imposed on these traditional disciplines profoundly limit their ability to incorporate and make effective use of more creative and innovative methodologies found in other disciplines and genres.

This series provides a unique opportunity to offer creative intellectual space to work with an eclectic and rich range of disciplines and approaches including performative methodologies, storytelling, narrative and auto-ethnography, embodied research methodologies, participant research, visual and film methodologies and arts-based methodologies.

Titles in the Series
Sites of Dissent: Nomad Science and Contentious Spatial Practice
Alissa Starodub

Sites of Dissent

Nomad Science and Contentious Spatial Practice

Alissa Starodub

ROWMAN & LITTLEFIELD
Lanham • Boulder • New York • London

Published by Rowman & Littlefield
An imprint of The Rowman & Littlefield Publishing Group, Inc.
4501 Forbes Boulevard, Suite 200, Lanham, Maryland 20706
www.rowman.com

86–90 Paul Street, London EC2A 4NE, United Kingdom

Copyright © 2021 by Alissa Starodub

This book is the published version of a PhD thesis at Ruhr University Bochum, 2018.

British Library Cataloguing in Publication Information Available

Library of Congress Cataloging-in-Publication Data Is Available

ISBN 978-1-5381-4633-0 (cloth)
ISBN 978-1-5381-8785-2 (paper)
ISBN 978-1-5381-4635-4 (electronic)

Contents

Acknowledgements

The page of acknowledgements is a special space. Here the people who have helped to give this book its present shape, direction and texture are appreciated and mentioned to the reader. The reader has already encountered some of these people on the pages of this book – my co-researchers and others involved in struggles on sites of dissent. A few lines of text would not be an adequate expression of my thankfulness to you. At different stages of making this book some of you made requests for what to put in the acknowledgements.

To thank all of you for going with me on a strange journey, all of your requests and suggestions are in here.

Kelly, right in the beginning of this research project, you asked me to promise that it will be written in a way that everyone could understand – not only academics. I hope I lived up to this expectation (I tried my best) and I am incredibly grateful for the time you took to discuss this book with me.

Martí, once we took notes for one of the stories on the roof of the house where you lived, you asked me to put this in the acknowledgement: "Without Martí this research project would not have been possible." Definitely.

And for Rolf who made jokes about the research method in one of the final collective discussions: "Rolf wrote all this."

I equally remember to thank Professor Hans Mainusch, Frau Schlonk, Puv Love, Mattusch, J. and my sister Kata as well as Andy for sending hordes of invisible pixies from the chaos dimension to keep me working during the hard times.

Massive thanks to my two incredible supervisors, Sabrina Zajak and Sara Motta. Without your support this book would have never come into being.

Introduction

Figure I.1   **Artwork by Kata.** *Source*: Author's own.

ON THE BIKE

My friends Angelo, Brian[1] and I were cycling away from the environmental action camp in the early hours of the morning. We feared that the cops would invade the camp and arrest everyone in revenge for the blockades of the gold extraction mine and mass trespass that took place the day before. We had taken our tent down really quickly, packed our stuff into bicycle bags and took off in the direction of our hometown. Later, we would take a train. Now, we were cycling towards the next little village whilst the sun was rising. The demonstration, the cops, the assemblies in the camp . . . all this was filling our heads in addition to the tiredness. None of us has said a word for a long time. After a few kilometres our pace slowed down.

"Do you think the action camp was an inclusive space?" asked Brian suddenly.

"Why do you say this?" I replied.

"All these different people – older people and young student-people, people who refuse to work and those who probably have an ordered life . . . do you think we created a space of resistance together, or do you think there were people left out – out of the actions, out of the social relationships – like it is always the case almost everywhere. So do you think we created some kind of better alternative?"

"I would say so," replied Angelo, "I think that all together we created a resistive space. Or, even several. A space that resists against capitalist environmental destruction, a site of dissent. The infrastructure that we have set up with all its facilities, showers, collective kitchen, kid's space . . . and everyone was somehow involved. On the other hand, even our utopias might reproduce some kind of exclusions."

"Well, I just think we have a lot to learn – because we are so different, different people. We have to study how we can find a collective ground for taking action and transforming the world. How can we find a shared language? How can we communicate *why* we do resistance?"

"We have to study ourselves, the movements, in different situations," I said, "Collect information, observe carefully and then exchange our experiences in a structured way. This is exactly what I want to do with this research project – you know, the book that I am writing now," I said happily.

"Can we take a break soon?" asked Angelo, "I am half dead."

"Sure. But how can you study 'ourselves, the movements'? I don't think it is possible. Nobody can say what 'the movements' actually is. And if it is, it will be some kind of academic thing that none of us will understand because it is written in an inaccessible language and applies some complicated research design to find out about 'the truth' about us."

"Basically, Brian is saying that you have to include *us* into your research, otherwise it's crap. Can we please take a break and discuss this when we are off the bikes?" Angelo insisted.

We were approaching the next little village. On my bike I was becoming aware that we were about to *do* research already, that our discussion was already part of a collective process of creating knowledge.

"And the research has to be horizontal, it has to be able to include everyone who participates in creating these sites of dissent – even if they can't write and never went to university. Otherwise, you will have to take an external position as if you knew everything and say: I have analysed that and this, and that that or this is the truth about autonomous movements! And it will simply not be very relevant because there are tons of other valid perspectives which you have not brought together," said Brian.

"And it is impossible to do this in a research project," said Angelo.

"I bet there are possibilities!" I replied and put my fingers on the brakes. "We need to develop a new, horizontal way of doing research with diverse people, with diverse knowledges, experiential knowledge, practical knowledge, theoretical knowledge and academic knowledge and so on. Because otherwise the production of knowledge that is seen as valid will always be limited to only one set of methods. It will be locked up in the ivory tower of academia."

"And how will you bring diverse knowledges together in a research project? It's going to be academic thing," asked Brian provocatively, and I was left searching for words.

This book is thus an attempt to fill this moment of silence in our conversation with lived alternatives, practical experiences and theoretical reflections.

It is the story of a research project that takes the readers to self-managed social centres, protest camps and occupied sites of sociopolitical dissent. On these sites, it attacks the epistemological privilege of academic researchers and creates knowledge with those who are involved in struggles for a horizontal society.

A line of horizontality runs as a key concept through the book. Its logic, as opposed to the logic of vertical organisation of power and implementation of decisions, will be nurtured from various angles: knowledge creation, social relations and forms of organisation.

For me, as the narrator of this book, the person who pieced its fragments together, finding words for this story has been a long path full of obstacles. My relationship to academic writing and thinking evolved on the way. When starting to write, I have not been treating different ways of thinking about, or "knowing" the world as equal to each other. I was focused on producing knowledge as an individualised researcher. Getting confronted with the critical voices of my friends and allies on sites of dissent and immersing myself in the theoretical realm of epistemology, I got convinced that *another* way of writing was possible; one that guides me away from the reproduction of academic norms and towards a bricolage of different ways of knowing, towards the refusal of science that silences different, *other* ways of knowing. I first began to look for ways to break out from academic writing and thinking. And then, somewhere along the path through sites of dissent, I decided to come back to the realm of academic "science" to turn it into a battleground. This was a tactical decision not to flee from this space, but to stay here in order to expand it and to let different others participate in its creation. Instead of inventing new words for a process of knowledge creation that horizontally involves many different ways of knowing, I have decided to occupy and squat the words "science" and "research." I have decided to continue to use them, although I am breaking their rules and confronting their meaning and the exclusions that it brings about.

On the journey through these chapters, I am thus also searching for a voice with which I can articulate and put into practice the beginnings of a horizontal approach to research. I will create space for self-reflection on this voice and its positioning within the research process. Compared to other voices participating in this research, it is the privileged voice of a doctoral student living off a scholarship – with lots of time to read, travel and write. Of course my subject position, like the subject positions of all the other people who have participated in this research, also encompasses much more.

  Whilst writing these chapters I have been living in different places, most of them were sites of dissent. I have been working on these chapters in even more places, surrounded by different people who were co-researchers and participants in this research project. My voice thus evolves as I learn to put it in relation to the voices of other participants – the voices of those who saw me writing these chapters, who read and discussed parts of the text, who made critical comments and made fun of me, who encouraged me and who are the protagonists of the stories that I am telling, those who created the material of this research. Their presence on these pages is as constitutive of the research process as my own voice. This text is thus written with and from the perspective of people struggling for horizontality, on and for sites of dissent. It is written *with* the people whom I have encountered on these sites. When Angelo, Brian and I start reflecting on the contentious spatial practices that we have witnessed and co-created in the camp, we enter into a knowledge-creation process about spatial practices of autonomous social movements, the movements who "see their everyday experiences and creations as the revolution they are making" (Sitrin, 2011, 271).

EXPANDING THE EPISTEMOLOGICAL SCOPE

"Extraordinary claims require extraordinary evidence" (Sagan, 1979, 62). This dictum was made popular by the astronomer and science communicator

Carl Sagan regarding the outlaw areas of science. How can I provide evidence for the claim that a horizontal and collective knowledge creation process can successfully replace "objective," "impartial" science that divides people into knowing subjects and objects of knowledge? How can I show that it is "possible to transform these relations of power through doing research, through subverting how knowledge is produced?" (Dadusc, 2014, 48).

The research project that runs as a storyline through the book is speaking through forms of collective inquiry. It tries to overcome the isolation which afflicts most researchers in rejecting the top-down way of creating knowledge by a researcher talking about an observed world. It escapes from this way of thinking wherever possible. The narrating voice is not an isolated voice, but a voice that beckons other voices near to construct something together: it participates in discussions, gets involved in situations, has arguments with co-researchers. . . . It is also failing several times on the way, yet, staying on the move, in motion towards a utopian vision of horizontal, collective and inclusive knowledge creation.

Is there a way of doing research that transforms relations of power between academic researchers and the researched? After my conversation with Angelo and Brian I set out to write the first chapter of this book alone, sitting in between piles of texts. I started to excavate concepts from the writings of those who offered to use them as theoretical components for own constructions of horizontal thinking (Deleuze and Guattari, 2010). In the first chapter, I appropriate the concepts of "royal science" and "nomad science" by Gilles Deleuze and Félix Guattari (2013) to set epistemological foundations that allow us to differentiate between a royal science enforcing a "valid" vision of the world through academic epistemological privilege and a nomad science which is travelling through different places, piecing together a collage of different but interwoven knowledges. Although these concepts gave me words to speak about horizontal and collective ways of creating knowledge in and about practices such as the action camp that Brian, Angelo and I had been part of, it was not enough. To create knowledge *with* rebellious others instead of *about* them, I needed a conception of places of encounter, a conception of sites on and for which the research could be leaving the realm of theory and turn into practice. Focusing on the spatial dimension of sociopolitical dissent in the first chapter thus sets the ground for the attempt at a collective theorisation of *practices* of social movements – those social movements that strive to put horizontal social relations into practice.

In the second chapter, I am gradually engaging in collective learning about the ways autonomous social movements transform and create space. Autonomous social movements are defined as movements which reject and try to separate from capital, the state and other forms of social authority, including dominant institutions and categories of identity (Day, 2004; Katsiaficas, 2006; Leinius, Vey and Hagemann, 2017), for example, anarchists, autonomous Marxists, autonomous feminists and radical ecologists. These movements can also be termed "horizontal" (Sitrin, 2011), meaning, they relate point-to-point, between equals, rather than vertically, between bosses and followers, and further, they are "post-representational" (Motta, 2011), meaning they oppose and subvert forms of social organisation which represent people from the outside. But *who* are these autonomous social movements? How do they speak, argue, theorise, how do they conceive themselves? Parts of the second chapter are a stammering approximation to these questions, woven with the voices of those who refuse to be theorised and defined in a top-down way, refusing a rigid fixation of meaning, positions, identities and therefore assembling a collage of enunciations, dialogues and debates.

The third chapter extends the borderzone of royal science and nomad science in picturing a method of research which has the potential to transgress relations of power between knower and known and to include a diversity of knowledges, ways of speaking and knowing due to its *participatory* aspirations. It starts with Participatory Action Research – a qualitative, participatory methodological approach (Breda, 2015; Kindon, Pain and Kesby, 2007; cf. Temper, del Bene and Martinez-Alier, 2015) which opens a space for nonacademic participants of the research to become involved into its conceptualisation. From here it is possible to step through a window of opportunity to develop an approach to horizontal research – Horizontal Participatory Action Research. This possibility does not necessarily amount to better quality research in the sense that it produces more accurate knowledge than Western iterations of science. Yet, it is a practice which prefigures another way of producing knowledge in a social world that does not exist yet – one in which the power over knowledge is distributed horizontally across society.

In the fourth chapter, I am leaving the books and texts and also leaving the sofas of discussion. I am finally dislocating my own position as an academic writer and turning into one of many protagonists of the stories that compose my case studies in this chapter on sites of dissent. I am learning to pick up knowledge as it is created in situations of daily life in cycles of journeys putting the deformalisation of knowledge creation in practice through horizontal participatory action research.

Most stories that compose this chapter were written whilst I was travelling through diverse sites of dissent – urban squats and social centres, rural occupations, demonstrations and protest events. They invite readers to moments of reflection in different contexts, to collective drifts through a rural protest camp against environmental destruction, to shared observations on contentious spatial practices in the moment of occupying a square . . . in other words: to places where we, as readers and writers, will finally leave the habit of citation and reproduction of what there already is behind; where it is possible to develop new ways of thinking.

Instead of analysing the collected experiences of contentious spatial practices on sites of dissent alone and drawing conclusions as an individual expert in the field, the fifth chapter is the result of an invitation to a *collective* analysis – in the garden of an autonomous cultural centre and in its kitchen.

Chapter six draws the results of this collective analysis as *lines of flight* escaping the status quo and building new horizontal alternatives in the shell of the old, hierarchical world (cf. Deleuze and Guattari, 2013). They are practical reflections of movement-relevant knowledge (Bevington and Dixon, 2005) drawn within concrete spatial practices articulating sociopolitical dissent and creating spaces for horizontal social relationships. They are traced within everyday life as well as within (epistemological) practices of knowledge creation struggling for a new horizontal research.

At the end of the book, at the end of my journey, I am looking back at the way I came in evaluating the possibilities and impossibilities of collective and horizontal knowledge creation in research. Was it possible to occupy "science" and "research" in making knowledge production more horizontal,[2] to shift towards a more collective, accessible and inclusive practice? I am pointing at the places where I stumbled and failed and at those where I transgressed barriers in creating a dwelling place in the border zones of academic and nonacademic research, royal science with fixed structures and nomad science picking up knowledge here and there.

This book is a fragmented heretic utterance which transforms a researcher into a storyteller, inhabiting the epistemological margins of academic knowledge production and the knowledges created in kitchens and public squares. It switches between logics of knowledge production desperately trying to find points of interconnection, expanding the epistemological scope.

Chapter 1

Nomad Science and Sites of Dissent

PARTICIPATORY QUALITY OF ATTENTION
VERSUS SCIENTIFIC OBJECTIVITY

I remember how a researcher introduced herself at an activist[1] gathering that I attended some years before I had started to do academic research myself. She explained that her research was supposed to help the voice of the movements being heard. Yet, my friends were saying: "I would not like to be researched." We had a heated discussion then and concluded that reflection on our collective actions was important and that *somebody* had to do it.

Since I started to do academic research, I never felt that it alienates me from the people I take collective action with. Quite the opposite: we get passionately involved in discussions about academic research being elitist and therefore necessarily hierarchical. Not everyone that I know, have affinity with and consider part of the autonomous social movements, agrees with me that writing an academic reflection helps to achieve our shared aim of putting horizontal social relationships into practice or creating space to do so. Nevertheless, I am in a relation of affinity with some of those within the autonomous social movements who share the idea that voicing our imaginaries not only in actions but also in words written on paper matter. When I write "our" imaginaries or "our" practices, I am speaking of practices that I engage in with others. These *others* are in some cases my friends, with whom I plot and conspire, with whom I share daily life and political experiences. I do not aim to speak *for* anyone when I speak of "our" practices. And yet I cannot speak purely of "my" practices in this context – for these exist and emerge only because of a relation to these others.

Does this mean that I have to "tame" my subjectivity (cf. Penshkin, 1988)?
Like an ethnographer who admits to her or his readers: here are the subjective
parts of my research, here is my subject position and there are my objects of
research (cf. Heshusius, 1994, 16)? Which parts of my research are not subjective then? And, if there are not-subjective parts of my research, "are the not-
subjective parts objective? If that is the case, then are we able to be objective
after all, after we thought we had done away with it? If so, must I then assume
that we have a reliable and/or objective way of knowing our subjectivity?"
(ibid., 16). The educational researcher Lous Heshusius who worked on the
topic of inclusion and confronted us with this ontological dilemma argues
that "there is no ontological or procedural objectivity (. . .), neither is there
ontological or procedural subjectivity to guide the research process" (ibid.,
16). Lous Heshusius shows how empiricist methodologies exclude the known
object from the knowledge production. She argues that "the idea of distance,
the idea that the knower is separate from the known," as in "knowing through
constructing distance became the epistemological stance for the study of
human behaviour" (ibid., 16). She rejects that this distance could be regulated
by objective methodology "borrowed" from the natural sciences and later by a
methodological admittance of subjectivity to "come clean" of it. To bridge the
dilemma of the objectivity-subjectivity dualism in scientific research, the gap
between the researching self and the researched other, she suggests engaging
with the researched in a mode of *"participatory consciousness* (. . .) which
means to be and to know, however temporarily, in nondualistic terms" (ibid.,
17). What she describes as participatory consciousness, has similarities to the
concept of affinity: "a recognition of the deeper kinship between ourselves
and other, is the ground from which participatory knowing emerges" (ibid.,
17). This relationship to others, the recognition of deeper kinship with others
or affinity, cannot be managed, evaluated and controlled in a process of scientific research, "for it is *in* the attentive, nonevaluative movement of consciousness (. . .) a participatory *quality* of attention. The question is not whether we
have 'reached' something but whether we can let go of something" (ibid., 18).

When one forgets self and becomes embedded in what one wants to understand,
there is an affirmative quality of kinship that no longer allows for privileged
status [of the researcher]. It renders the act of knowing an ethical act. The other
you are studying is no longer someone you can bombard with questions, but
someone who may just "beckon you near." Mutuality and ethicality are at once
embedded in a participatory mode of consciousness. By legitimizing the equa-
tion of knowing with distancing and with having control over the distance, the
idea of objectivity masks ideologies of power, which have been abundantly ana-
lyzed by feminist scholarship, deconstructionist thought and critical pedagogy,
and other postmodern voices. (Ibid., 19–20)

Within the logic of science that works with objective methodology "borrowed" from the natural sciences (Heshusius, 1998, 16), the horizontal relationship of different types of knowledges is difficult to achieve. It is especially problematic because "Positivist or quantitative research (the two terms are often conflated) continues to be the gold standard for social science research" (Brown and Strega, 2005, 7). This type of research takes the view that there is one true and "objective" observation about social reality to be discovered scientifically through unbiased observation and rigorous measurement by an allegedly neutral observer producing "neutral information on which all rational individuals can agree. While acknowledging the existence of other research approaches, most positivists position quantitative methodologies as superior" (ibid., 7) because their definition of reliability of findings is based on whether they are replicable through a similar process of deductive thinking (Moosa-Mitha, 2005, 45). Thus in this logic of scientific research we are confronted with one "reliable" type of knowledge production that is methodically discovering one objective "truth" about social reality (cf. ibid., 58). The power figure of the researcher is the protagonist of this type of knowledge production. This figure is constructed as "the expert," "the appropriator," "the discoverer" of knowledge who "extracts and exploits knowledges, or constructs a partial knowledge that serves within the institutional containment of valued narratives" (Herising, 2005, 132). This scientific view on social reality has successfully positioned itself as the most legitimate way to view the world (Strega, 2005, 201). Within this type of research there is no way to legitimise the various knowledges of and about contentious spatial practices that are coming from within the autonomous social movements; from knowledges that emerge through the experience of a situation, knowledge from intuition or knowledge about relationships to other people, knowledge that is difficult to put into scientific terms because the knower prefers different modalities of self-expression.

This kind of knowledge is not "reliable" knowledge, not knowledge produced according to the rigorous methodological guidelines that an "objective" observer would have posited. It is knowledge that deviates from the form of the superior "scientific" narrative (cf. Breda, 2015, 3). This narrative gained its hegemonic position during the Enlightenment period in European thought when (positivist) "science" and "knowledge" began to have the same meaning and when this division between scientific knowledge and all other types of knowledge became hierarchical with science being the "best" kind of knowledge, "superior to various forms of unreliable and unverifiable non-scientific knowledge" (ibid., 202) offering one "true" path to knowledge: "the application of rigorous scientific methodology by a rational, neutral and objective subject to the study of an object clearly positioned outside of himself. (. . .) Objectivity is achieved by separating the 'knowing subject' from the 'object of knowledge'" (ibid., 202) and is supposedly unattached to ideology and power.

Within the confines of this strict separation of the *knowing subject* from the *object of knowledge* there is no space to collaborate and to exchange between different types of knowledges, to co-create knowledge together. This is solely the task of the power figure of the researcher who has qualities such as rationality, reason, objectivity and impartiality and maintains its position "by its capacity to define itself as a universal standard against which the subjective, the emotional, the aesthetic, the natural, the (coloured, classed) feminine must be judged" (Usher, 1997, 45). Within most scientific research the social position of the expert researcher thus holds the power to extract knowledge from nescient research objects. It holds the power to represent them in the correct scientific narrative as what they really are in the "true" social reality. In this conception of scientific research, there is no space for collective, horizontal and relational knowledge creation between different positionings, different types of knowledge and different modes of expression.

As the scholar Sheila Sen Jasanoff writes,

> What we know about the world is intimately linked to our sense of what we can do about it, as well as to the felt legitimacy of specific actors, instruments and courses of action. Whether power is conceived in classical terms, as the power of the hegemon to govern the subject, or in the terms most eloquently proposed by Michel Foucault, as a disciplining force dispersed throughout society and implemented by many kinds of institutions, science and technology are indispensable to the expression and exercise of power. (Jasanoff, 2004, 14)

Science then, with its power of knowledge production, according to Jasanoff, operates as a *political* agent (cf. ibid., 14). Questions of how we produce knowledge are also questions of the social distribution of power and therefore structures of social oppression. Knowledge co-produces social order and the oppressions and exclusions that go with it. It is not neutral, no matter how objective and rational it claims to be.

It is thus no coincidence that patriarchy, a line of power and oppression that traverses forms of social life and is inscribed in social order, is paralleled in scientific knowledge production:

> Feminists of all hues have clearly demonstrated the systematic exclusion of women from sites at which knowledge is produced (in respect of geography, see

Berman, 1977; Lee, 1990; McDowell, 1979; McDowell and Peake, 1990). In geography, this has been accompanied by critiques concerned with the absence or inadequate conceptualization of gender in much research. Recently, feminist theory has advanced this kind of critique still further by examining more closely the consequences of women's exclusion from, or marginality within, academic discourse for the philosophical foundations of knowledge. (Bondi and Domosh, 1992, 201)

We find the same relations of power/knowledge in "unbiased and impartial" science regarding the question of who produces knowledge and what forms of knowledge are seen as legitimate, when we turn to the issue of colonial oppression:

> Traditional ethnographic research did have strong political implication, as it was used as a source of knowledge aimed at understanding colonized cultures and to extend colonisation further (Gough, 2008). The first ethnographic studies addressed the populations, cultures and histories of colonies within the British Empire, but defined themselves as unbiased and impartial account of the actual state of affairs. (. . .) Therefore the problem does not lie in research as such, but in the ways "proper" research and "true" knowledge are defined by scientific (Western, white, male) standards which dismiss and silence different epistemological possibilities (Denzin et al., 2008), writes Deanna Dadusc. (2014, 49–50)

Gendered oppression and colonialism are not the only examples of the power/ knowledge nexus in scientific research and its complicity with the reproduction of structural forms of oppression. To resist the "relation between power and knowledge that is exercised through social research, it is necessary to subvert the rationality and truth formations at stake" (ibid., 49). This means to unlearn the traditional objectivity and impartiality of science that researchers are being taught to reproduce in academic writing. It is precisely this performed objectivity and impartiality which ascribes superiority to scientific knowledge gained with a fixed set of methodological rules. It places forms of knowing which disregard these methodological rules at the bottom of the hierarchy. In short: it creates power relations between skilled, academic, objective, impartial subjects of knowledge and unskilled, nonacademic, situated and openly passionate objects of knowledge in silencing different epistemological possibilities, different ways of knowing (Kincheloe and Steinberg, 2008).

KNOWING FROM WITHIN A HORIZONTAL PLANE

Neither me nor my objects of research can respond to the demands of objectivist and/or empiricist scientific research whose desired outcome it is to create one "correct" knowledge crafted by one individual researcher as a representational theoretical product extracted from the real world. I am neither separated from my object of study, nor am I impartial. At times, I am not even rational. My theorisations are not separated from the practices that I study – at times they are one and the same thing. In my research, my "research objects" are most of the time more knowledgeable than myself. Due to the diverse types of knowledges that they contribute to my research they are not even representative in one "true" social reality that I could demonstrate or discover. Does this mean we have to surrender to the "master's tools" (Strega, 2005, 1999), to the normative scientific empiricist methodologies, to produce "valid" knowledge about contentious spatial practices of autonomous social movements?

Instead of doing so, instead of submitting to the existing script, it is possible to theorise this logic of knowledge production and to revert to *another* logic. The concepts of royal science and nomad science as introduced by Deleuze and Guattari in *A Thousand Plateaus* (2013) help to illustrate these different logics of knowledge production in shifting the focus towards the question of *how* knowledge is created.

Gilles Deleuze and Félix Guattari describe two different types of "science" in *A Thousand Plateaus*. A possible starting point for this comparison is Deleuze and Guattari's outline of royal science as a state science with a methodology restricted to using templates which implies a model of reproduction of this type of knowledge production process (cf. ibid., 420–36). Deleuze and Guattari use the example of travelling craftsmen carving stone arches on construction sites of the twelfth century (ibid., 424–30). On this construction site, royal science would be manifested in the architect's master plan to produce a stable stone building, including mathematical calculations and precise technical directions for every work step exactly predefining how the stone carvers' work has to be fitted into the statics of a Gothic cathedral, for example. Royal science thus imposes a division of labour on the construction site: the architect has the knowledge of the master plan and thus controls and directs the movements of the travelling workers who were "building cathedrals near and far, scattering construction sites across the land, drawing on active and passive power (mobility and strikes) that was far from convenient for the State. The State's response was to take over the management of the construction sites, merging all the divisions of labour in the supreme distinction between the intellectual and the manual, the theoretical and the practical, modelled upon the difference between 'governors' and 'governed'" (ibid., 429). Nomad science in contrast, is not a "science" in the "royal or legal sense established by history" (ibid., 421). The functioning of its model is marked by affinity and affect. It is composed of approximative and situated movements of the travelling stone carvers who need no reference to an architect's master plan of mathematical formula to create a stable stone arch holding the roof of a cathedral (cf. ibid., 421 ff). In the logic of nomad science, the skill of carving a stone arch, the knowledge of how this arch is to be made, is developed through the movement of the worker's body, through experience and exchange with other workers composed of information gathered along the path of the journey, through the worker's life experience and the varied engagements on different construction sites. Its process of creation and composition is rhizomatic and horizontal, coordination with the knowledge of different workers is developed through the practice of their profession on the construction site, not predefined by any master plan.

Applied to the study of autonomous social movement spatial practices then, royal science would define a research interest, apply a theoretical lens to a phenomenon to be analysed. This is comparable to the architect's blueprint for the cathedral in the example of Deleueze and Guattari: the social movement researcher is the architect with a master plan about how autonomous social movements react to a specific issue. The researcher's hypothesis predefines how the practices of autonomous social movements fit into a complex set of predefined factors. The researcher would then "impress a plane of organisation" (ibid., 430) in proceeding to gather data to produce a scientific, objective knowledge suitable for giving a presentation at an academic conference about the movement's practices, defining them, measuring them, and thus producing the autonomous social movements as a known object. Nomad science, in contrast, does not impress any plane of organisation on the practices of autonomous social movements. Knowledge in its model is created relationally in meetings, informal settings, actions and daily encounters. The construction sites scattered across the land could be represented by different groups of people engaging autonomously with the topic of gentrification in different cities, in this example. It is dependent on the local context and on the different subject positions involved in it; it is connected through rhizomatic nodes of relations where "each node connects to every other node" (ibid., 144). This is facilitating a decentralised and horizontal sharing of information through the diversification of its modalities: in group meetings, private conversations, assemblies, or encounters.

I take recourse to nomad science when writing about spatial practices of autonomous social movements which turns my writing into one of the "borderline phenomena in which nomad science exerts pressure on State science, and conversely, State science appropriates and transforms the elements of nomad science" (ibid., 422). Yet, according to Deleuze and Guattari, there are no binary divisions between royal science and nomad science – just like there are no binary divisions between the inside or the outside of autonomous social movements. The relational creation of knowledge represents a logic of knowledge creation where ends and means are continuous with the autonomous social movement's horizontal political articulation. The epistemic authority of royal science, in contrast, is hierarchical; it is what an architect would use to calculate the plan for the construction of a cathedral. What kind of empirical observations are suitable for making such a master plan that contains statements about how reality should be, how a cathedral is to be constructed, and how to get them? In the hands of scientists "data" is selected and produced in the confines of a research programme following a chosen theoretical commitment. This theoretical commitment is based on a predefined set of assumptions about reality. Why not choose another one? "Anything" (Feyerabend, 1975, 19) seems to work behind the scenes of the rigorous methodology of royal science. Still, "method" is only for those who master the complex code, rituals and language of science. Only those can take part in an epistemic culture that defines when and for whom it is possible to claim to know something about the world. As a result, royal science creates a place of epistemological privilege which entitles it to make objective and value-free truth claims. In this logic of knowledge production, objectivity is a construct bearing absolute authority to define what there is in the world. It hierarchically imposes itself upon the different and situated experiences *of* the world (Haraway, 1988).

Nomad science is "operating in an open space through which things-flows are distributed, rather than plotting out a closed space for linear solid things" (Deleuze and Guattari, 2013, 421). This is a stark contrast to royal science produced in closed conference rooms, but this is not to say that nomad science cannot be created in closed conference rooms. It simply has no privileged habitus of speaking or writing or formal entitlement to do so in the context of a university; it prefers no predefined citation style. What distinguishes it from royal science is that no place of knowledge production is granted epistemological authority – be it an encounter at the bin of a supermarket or a seminar on sustainable activism (cf. Starodub, 2015). In the model of royal science, moments of relational knowledge creation through experience with others might seem too insignificant to call them a "science." They are diverse and interwoven in a complex network of experiences; they occur spontaneously and sometimes in stressful situations. It is challenging to recognise them as such when they occur: How to focus on the abstract functioning of the model of nomad science right in the middle of a planning meeting for an action whilst being critical towards a friend's latest proposal?

In stepping out of this logic and moving towards the model of nomad science, this text turns into an experience of what Sara Motta terms, "border dwelling" that is shifting between nomad science and royal science (2013, 11). Such an epistemological rebellion can lead to marginalisation in destabilising and reformulating my role as an academic. Doing research "on the border" is not an individual's endeavour to employ an adequate method to get to know something about the world. It is a collective task, based on relations and situated in social contexts. The types of relationships that enable me to participate in the creation of a nomad science about the spatial practices of autonomous social movements "challenge traditional conceptualisations and practices of theoretical knowledge creation" (Motta, 2011, 181) as well as the epistemologically hierarchical relationship between researcher and the researched.

BETWEEN ROYAL SCIENCE AND NOMAD SCIENCE

A border dwelling between royal science and nomad science requires to be present both – in royal science, the used theoretical concepts allows us to glue pieces of relational knowledge into a text which is saying something about spatial practices of autonomous social movements; in nomad science, it is the situatedness of my subject position which locates me in relation to spatial practices of autonomous social movements. This is the epistemological starting point. It is located on the border of two different logics of knowledge creation and production; it strives towards the possibility of an ongoing translation work between these different ways of knowing which enables to speak across epistemological borders and to transgress them, giving birth to an extended, inclusive and prefigurative epistemology.

Ontologically this means that what we can know of social reality is accessed from different locations *in* this social reality and can be known from a living relationship with the studied practices in this social reality.

On an epistemological level, this entails that when I am writing about spatial practices of autonomous social movements, I am drawing upon another type of knowledge. It is a knowledge created relationally: I know of these practices because I have experienced them with others, because I have created them in relation with others. Effectively, the knowledge that was never exclusively *my* knowledge, is de-privatised and its shared ownership is made visible.

Taking the relational aspect of knowledge creation in nomad science into account means moving in a complex network where everything is interconnected, influenced, intertwined, of which one can only grasp a part. Here royal science helps to sketch a clear structure, a line of procedures that can help in orientating oneself, in not losing the plot. Royal science offers tools and ways of knowledge production that help to keep one's focus and bearings, that offer something to push through a research project, something to keep its possibly disassociating different parts together. In order to allow for deviations whilst keeping the research project directed at an aim, in the borderzone there are concessions to nomad science as well as to royal science. Whilst picking up and assembling knowledge with lawless techniques of nomad science, I am thus also pushing two research questions through this project. These research questions arguably have something defensive: Look, what I am doing is not just a random wandering but "proper" research. I am reproducing the scientific, academic pattern of knowledge creation in pushing my research questions all the way through the investigation – without deviating.

The research questions provide a stringent guidance to follow through the research process. Yet, I confess they are merely a pretext. They are rather a technique to situate oneself within the field of scientific research, to grapple there in order to subvert and intrude the structures of the field later on. There are many possible ways of structuring a research project, ways of organising in order not to lose one's goals out of sight. Hunting answers to research questions is certainly one of them – a way set out by academic research. When beginning to engage in this research project, I did not know much about other possibilities. I suspected that they will get more tangible as I begin to explore hoping to become brave enough to deviate from already known and approved structures at some point.

The questions that I chose to pursue are consciously formulated as quite the opposite of narrow research questions. They do not aim at proving a certainty that one already has.

Research Question 1:
   In altering and inventing anew the rules of academic research methods and in transforming its linguistic expression into the language of everyday discourses accessible to as many people as possible, does one succeed in doing horizontal and collective research with diverse forms of knowing?

Whilst this first research question addresses the realm of methodological expression, the second question is derived from the disparity of what would be my object of research. It is Angelo's scepticism about defining the commonalities of "the movements" that pushes me to search for a shared political leitmotiv that is guiding the diverse political practices of "the movement." Is there something that is capable of unifying the practices that I am researching whilst foregrounding their diversity?

Research Question 2:
   What is the common leitmotiv of autonomous social movements' spatial practices of dissent – if there is any?

Of course, there is an assumption that pushes me to word this second research question: contentious spatial practices of autonomous social movements take place on diverse geographical terrains, they take different forms – on the countryside as rural occupations against the exploitation of environmental resources; in urban contexts, they take the form of squatting; they can be temporary events such as riots and demonstrations or permanent dwelling environments; they might stretch out over a larger geographical area such as a neighbourhood or a several hectares large rural territory and include hundreds of people, or, on the contrary, present themselves as small and experimental alternatives to the sociopolitical status quo such as a self-managed neighbourhood bar consisting of two rented rooms. Can these different spatial practices be driven by a shared political desire then and how is this desire expressed in the different material places? To compare these different sites, to put them in relation to each other, it is necessary to conceive of what they could have in common.

FROM SPACE TO SPATIAL PRACTICE

"How does writing about spatial concepts help to develop strategies and tactics for social movements, park squatters, antifascist activists, tree huggers and environmentalists and on demonstrations and so on? This is what you want to do in the end, right? Why do you then give so much attention to space?" my friend Gino[2] asked me after I presented him the idea of this book.

I reminded Gino of how we got evicted from a squatted social centre a few years ago. Four hundred police forces and the special police task force broke through the barricaded front entrance as well as through the roof of the squatted social centre. The police operation was the state-controlled suppression of our transgression of societal norms that materialised in a squatted house which temporarily belonged to no one. Here decisions about what is happening inside were taken in consensual meetings; here rules structuring our relations were daily negotiated instead of enforced. When the police physically broke into our squatted territory and was faced with our resistance – the whole situation was a spatial articulation of sociopolitical dissent. The people in the squat not only refused to leave a building but also attempted to refuse the destruction of the site which encompassed far more than the squatted building. They refused to obey the rule that unused privatised space should be left empty; they refused to accept that a noncommercial social centre would be crushed by the physical attack of the forces of order. They refused to believe that there was no space for horizontal self-organisation, no space for taking time to self-organise one's daily business without buying into a business relation to its spatiality.

I added,

> The political contention about the squatted social centre space was like an argument. It was an argument between different logics of building social relationships in space. And I want to word the social vision that is behind the concrete practice of the squatted social centre, for example. I want to understand how it is connected to other expressions of this vision.

Space is not the ultimate analytical dimension for researching sociopolitical dissent. It surely is a tactical field to articulate sociopolitical dissent though. Theoretical conceptualisations of spatiality provide an intellectual path to conceive a certain type of socio-spatial interaction as expression of sociopolitical dissent. They also help to *see* dissent in geographical locations and to carve out a shared understanding of it, before engaging with concrete practices of sociopolitical dissent. An understanding of contentious spatial practices articulating dissent in social and spatial order can be built on an understanding of spatiality. But there is not *one* understanding of spatiality – there is rather an intellectual history of different understandings of spatiality and their evolution to be traced before arriving at a point of analysing and understanding social relations in and through space.

So I begin with another concession to royal science. I begin with stepping on the terrain of academic thought about spatiality, with referencing, repeating what has been there before, building on a body of already existing literature.

Space cannot purely be conceived in analysing metric space with statistical devices as it was the case in the social sciences in the nineteenth century (Comte, 2009). Already the "social environment" of Durkheim that is actively *made* as a product of previous social activity (Durkheim, 1982) suggested that there are more promising ways to understand the construction of space as a social language materialising social relations (Halbwachs, 1992), that it is constructed in interactions of individuals and has an influence on them (Simmel in Frisby, 1992). The social environment is creating networked arrangements where the individual is situated in the spatiality of social power dynamics (Foucault, 1997). Michel Foucault showed that social power relations constitute themselves in spatialities, in the spatial order of societies and in their administrative buildings and institutions (Foucault, 1991). In the 1970s, the philosopher and sociologist Henri Lefebvre then inspired to see power not only in a few of society's spatial arrangements but everywhere in space (Lefebvre, 1976a). Lefebvre sees space as actively being produced and reproduced in everyday practices (1991), in the rhythms of daily life mapping space as a process (1992). He also pointed out contentious possibilities to create another just space, a self-made space where something else is possible (1968). It is fruitful to theorise the contention over different ways of making space as creative resistance to spatial mechanisms of control and exclusion (Deleuze and Guattari, 2013) that the geographer David Harvey sees as producing spatial injustice (Harvey, 1993). Fighting for another type of space is fighting for another type of life, if space is performed and experienced by people doing things in space and if, according to relational geographers, everything is in flow and interconnected, then the smallest micro-movement of a spatial practice can serve to challenge the power geometry of socio-spatial order (Massey, 1994). Feminist geographers outline space as contentious on every level in showing how the most private performances can *make space* in resistance to oppressive power dynamics (cf. Bondi and Domosh, 1992). After all, how specific places have been meaningfully constructed by capitalists, architects, urban planners, communities and institutions cannot be excluded from spatial analysis, nor can the reactions to these acts of spatial construction. Challenges or reinforcements of these constructions shape everyday social behaviour (Tuan, 1974). Behaviours that are "out of place" challenge the unspoken socio-spatial order. Repertoires of spatial contention are therefore saturated with place-specific social norms (Cresswell, 1996); they are situated and heterogeneous. If place is a moment of spatial flows, "the terrain where basic social practices (. . .) are lived out" (Merrifield, 1993, 522). A conceptualisation of space as a process of contention that is to be contextualised unveils simultaneous and potentially contradictory experiences of space.

Martin and Miller write, "Space is socially produced and constituted as it, in turn, dialectically constitutes social production and reproduction" (2003, 147). Inequalities can be seen as inscribed in the landscape of daily life – in poor housing situations juxtaposed to gated communities of wealth, in the allocation of schools, public services, police presence . . . in the geographies created by contemporary global capitalism. Contention thus arises from wherever it is possible to perceive and conceive such inequalities producing challenges to the existing spatial order in various forms. They offer new (imagined) spatial structurings or dismantle the old ones through ruptures. Lefèbvre explains,

> Sociopolitical contradictions are realised spatially. The contradictions of space thus make the contradictions of social relations operative. In other words, spatial

contradictions "express" conflicts between sociopolitical interests and forces; it is only in space that such conflicts come effectively into play, and in doing so they become contradictions of space. (1991, 365)

The field of research is thus focused on those places *where contentious politics take place*, where people take spaces, shape spaces, get expulsed and evicted from spaces, where space is threatened, transformed and contested, where dissent might turn into barricades.

SPACE AS CONTENTION

Contentious politics refers to concerted, counter-hegemonic social and political action, in which differently positioned participants come together to challenge dominant systems of authority, in order to promote and enact alternative imaginaries. (Leitner et al., 2008, 157)

Spatialities that result from the praxis of contentious politics provide a geographical location to focus our analytical attention. Contemporary geographers and other theorists have used and are using a range of different words to describe this kind of spatialities.

A number of contemporary geographers refers to these spaces as "autonomous geographies" – "those spaces where people desire to constitute non-capitalist, egalitarian and solidaristic forms of political, social and economic organization through a combination of resistance and creation" (Pickerill and Chatterton, 2006, 730). Elsewhere these spaces are termed "safe spaces" (Sewell, 2001, 69 in reference to Charles Tilly), "counter-spatialities" (Motta, 2014), "spaces of hope" (Harvey, 2001), "free spaces" (Evans, 1979), "geographies of resistance" (Pile, 1997) or "action spaces" (Peterson, 2001). Particularly useful for my research is how Peterson explains action spaces: "The temporal militant action space (. . .) is the action space of an *event*, either constructed by militant activists or a sociocultural event which is 'reconstructed' by militant social movement action. Militant political actions take *place*" (ibid., 2). The territorial action space is the action space of place or territory acted out through specific geographies: on the street surrounding a military base or in a squatted house. It is both constructed of actions articulating dissent and co-constructive of these actions (ibid., 5) in directly lived spaces which are both unstable and penetrable (cf. ibid., 10). This is because they are constantly in a process of becoming, transforming themselves by transforming their exterior environment and at the same time being subjected to change by it. Dwelling is intense, impermanent and mobile (cf. Urry, 2001, 14).

Abby Peterson describes action spaces as vast complexities of intercon-
nections, of links or openings between spatiality and social action. People
involved in creating, appropriating, defending, or maintaining a territorial
action space are engaged in a struggle against domination, appropriating
places in conjunction with cognitive maps of territory whilst acting in and on
spatiality. Peterson explains, "Consequently, the actions of militant groups/
action networks take place in the places controlled by practices of domination, but they nevertheless subvert these places," and whilst doing so "their
actions cannot be separated from practices of domination, they are "hybrid
practices" (2001, 6–7). Hence these spaces of resistance against domination
are conceived as unstable, always on the move and penetrable by the forces
and mechanisms of domination and control that they seek to escape. They can
be understood as *movement*, "a change from one 'place' on the cognitive map
of its social relations to another, which underlines its transformative power"
(ibid., 7). Peterson draws on Deleuze when invoking the multiplicity, difference and horizontality of these movements understood as journeys, micro-
movements of resistance, from a number of points on a number of paths and
travels towards many destinations.

In drawing on Gilles Deleuze and Félix Guattari's philosophical concepts of
territorialisation and de-territorialisation to theorise the becoming of "action
spaces," Peterson (and others who have done so, most notably in Non-
representational Geographies (cf. Cadman, 2009) emphasises the productive
effects of flows and interruptions in conceptualising space as contention. To
territorialise is "to claim spaces, to include some and exclude others from
particular 'places.' (. . .) However, both inclusion and exclusion tactics under-
lining spatial organisation – territorialisation processes – are fundamentally
bound up with the social construction of identities" (Peterson, 2001, 7–8).
De-territorialisation then, happens in "one-off actions" on "enemy territory"
(ibid., 8).

Chatterton, Featherstone and Routledge provide a good example. In 2009
the Klimaforum, an international gathering in Copenhagen provided a space
for articulations that were excluded from the official summit of COP15, the
United Nations Climate Change Conference, and "placed" the antagonism to
climate politics:

> Klimaforum (. . .) provided a space for the articulation of grievances, and antag-
> onisms concerning a range of climate justice campaigns. A diversity of narra-
> tives, especially from struggles in the global South, concerning the effects of
> climate change on communities were voiced. For example, a Tibetan delegation
> from the "Third Pole" network, gave a presentation in the Forum that discussed

the forcible relocation of Tibetan nomads by the Chinese authorities from the grasslands of the Tibetan plateau into fenced model villages. (Chatterton, Featherstone and Routledge, 2013, 8)

The space of the Klimaforum made other articulations, other silenced imaginaries of climate justice tangible.

Similarly, the occupation of Syntagma Square in Athens in 2011 created a space for another type of social relationships in transforming the public square in front of the Parliament into an encampment where interaction between strangers was a common pattern, where, as Marilena Simiti describes, "multiple working groups were established to support and sustain collective mobilizations (e.g., a nursery, a food and beverage rationing group, a media group, a cleaning team, an artistic team). The working groups operated horizontally according to the principles of grassroots democracy. Open discussions about the state of the economy and the possibility of alternative economic policies were held, enabling citizens to voice their opinion and concerns. (. . .) This participatory ethos also guided the proceedings of the popular assemblies, the main decision-making body of the movement. Every evening at 21:00 a popular assembly was held" (Simiti, 2014, 18). The possibility of relative autogestion in the square, as well as the provision of an "open space where citizens from all over the city could assemble" to participate in its experience (ibid., 6) turned it into an "other space" in direct and discursive oppositions to the Greek Parliament and the decisions taken there, prefiguring another type of collective self-management through the contentious spatial practice of square occupation.

These kinds of spaces not only facilitate another type of articulation through a less-exclusive logic of the voices being heard inside it but also open up a host of other possibilities for carrying out contentious spatial practice: "Occupied social centres (OSCs) turn unused or condemned public buildings and factories into self-organized cultural and political gathering spaces for the provision of radical social services, protest-planning and experimentation with independent cultural production of music, zines, art and pirate micro TV" (Hodkinson and Chatterton, 2006, 306).

To have some kind of linguistic referentiality, to be able to speak of these different, temporary and permanent localities, geographical areas and places of micro-movements, I propose to call them "sites of dissent" for now. I will not proceed to extract characteristics of sites of dissent here in order to measure or make comparative arguments about them.

Instead, in what follows now, I will turn my attention to the social relations that constitute sites of dissent and to the alternative social world that they are prefiguring and leave my comfortable working environment with its printed articles, book markers and citation programmes. The places that I will be writing and reflecting about will be empty and solitary theorisations without writing about the relations that constitute them, without *letting these relations into the text* – at least with an however awkward attempt of finding a plane of interaction that is situated horizontally within these social relations. The next chapter makes thus a first step towards horizontal and collective knowledge creation with those involved in sites of dissent.

Chapter 2

Studying Autonomous Social Movements

A Collage

AUTONOMOUS SOCIAL MOVEMENTS AS AN OBJECT OF RESEARCH

What are you writing about in this chapter, in this text? If I were confronted with this question by someone and prompted to set the grounds for my onto-logical choices, I would hastily answer that I am writing about contentious spatial practices of autonomous social movements. I am content with being able to give a short and concise answer and yet I know that it is not a com-plete answer – it is not as simple as that. In answering this fictitious question, I have defined my object of research: autonomous social movements and their spatial practices. Defining something, fixing its meaning, delimiting what something *is* from the position of a researcher is a hegemonic prac-tice carving out a conceptual territory, willfully excluding some things and including others. Making a definition, as in a conceptual operationalisation of an identity or a phenomenon to be able to subject it to further examination in a lockstep process of research, means pressing an object of research into a category, a classification. I am complicit with autonomous social movements who, as an object of research, deceive and refuse categories and classification. Nevertheless, in this chapter I will provide readers with several academic def-initions and theorisations of autonomous social movements – definitions and theorisations that speak about them, that seek to put into words *how autono-mous social movements are in the world.* I will not do this because I believe that these definitions and classifications are right but because I want to show how autonomous social movements have been treated as objects of research on the one hand and, on the other hand, because I cannot escape the linguistic need to convey meaning building on meanings that have been created before.

Richard Day theorises the practices of autonomous social movements as post-representational articulations of political desire (Day, 2005). This means that I am writing about the spatial practices of a kind of social movements that "see their everyday experiences and creations as the revolution they are making" (Sitrin, 2011, 271). The way political desire is articulated – through the use of horizontality as a tool of autonomous self-organisation and as a goal (cf. Azzellini and Sitrin, 2014) – already projects the desired social transformation of autonomous social movements into the present. It acts through a plurality of political *expressions* instead of representation. To give an example of post-representational practices of autonomous social movements, Simon Tormey relates Occupy Wall Street as "one kind of resistance that 'represents' in its post-representativity the response of those at the margins of wealthy countries of the metropolitan centre" (Tormey, 2012, 135) to the Zapatista insurrection described as "another kind of resistance, one characteristic of the needs and resources of groups at the global periphery. They are both concerned with the same issue (. . .). They resonate in different ways, they have different effects, but their concerns are very similar" (ibid.). Both movements resist institutionalised hegemonic, hierarchical power relations by using horizontal decision-making and social relationships as a tool and a projection of their desired outcomes.

Characteristics of autonomous social movements have been coined as a demarcation within social movement studies by writers such as Georgy Katsiaficas (2006), Richard Day (2005; 2001), David Graeber (2002), Marina Sitrin (2011), Saul Newman (2011). Hans Pruijt argues that in the writings of these authors the continuity between ends and means of autonomous social movements is defining their prefigurative politics of taking action and creating knowledge, of a self-shaping along the lines of their desired society with an emphasis on self-organisation and creation of lived alternatives in egalitarian and nonhierarchical social structures (Pruijt, 2014, 145–46). This can be seen as a contrast to institutionalised or more formally organised social movements, such as trade unions because "an institutionalized orientation is characterized by a clear division of labor and authority, a centralized organisation, and a loose coupling of ends and means" (ibid., 144). Within autonomous social movements the individual participates in organisations which are dispensable – they can be restructured any time and exist to serve the individual's desires and goals. In organisational politics, the individual is dispensable for the existence of an organisation – she performs a function within it and can be replaced by another individual performing exactly the same function (cf. Flesher Fominaya, 2007, 339). This reveals the opposition of autonomous social movements to a type of hegemony that is attributed to institutionalised and representational structures with a fixed group membership: the hierarchical division of labour and authority (ibid.). In his historical analysis of European autonomous social movements, Georgy Katsiaficas explains the rejection of fixed group identities by autonomous social movements with their opposition to the existing social order which reproduces exploitative divisions of labour and authority and couples it with group identities (Katsiaficas, 2006). This opposition emerges from an articulation of *individual* and collective needs fleshed out in an anti-oppressive critique of everyday life. Cristina Flesher Fominaya argues that the resulting "anti-identitarian" orientation of autonomous social movements can be seen as a further characteristic, enabling them to create a collective identity based on plurality, difference and multiplicity escaping the logic of representation (Flesher Fominaya, 2010, 399). Instead of resisting oppression as women, refugees, workers, poor or indigenous people, autonomous social movement's resistance is conditioned by decentralised, informalised and affinity-based organising (Day, 2001; 2004). Instead of subsumption under an identitarian politics which is representing demands advanced by a shared subject position, cohesion in autonomous social movements is defined by a post-representational collective practice of direct action. This action is prefiguring the fulfilment of individual and collective political desires; it is defined by the coming together of small groups connected through personal relationships of affinity. That is, through rejecting hegemonic goals and freeing oneself from oppression in reaching out to others in solidarity, in developing various shared goals to combat oppression in the multitude of its facets, including everyday life.

I am thus talking about movements that are horizontally organised through affinity that enables them to collectively engage in a plurality of contentious practices. It is impossible to find one fitting unifying definition. I can only give an insight into this horizontal plane of affect from a *position within* this plane. Every location on this plane is different, constituted of different identities, relationships and contexts.

Seen from within this plane, autonomous social movements are never completely horizontal – there are various degrees of formal hierarchies in different movements and informal hierarchies within groups can never be completely abolished. Also, social oppression and discrimination do not cease to exist for autonomous social movement participants since they can never form a completely closed bubble that is untouched by discriminations, hierarchies, painful experiences and exploitative relationships that exist in society. These things always get back into the social fields of autonomous social movements – through prior socialisation, through trauma, through events in personal lives. Horizontal self-organisation and a reliance on autonomous self-definitions in relation to society are within autonomous social movements attempts to prefigure a less oppressive world and never a fully achieved form of social organisation or relations.

To talk about these attempts at prefiguration, one has to take part in a relational process of knowing about spatial practices of autonomous social movements. This is a position that admits to know not *about* others but *with* others, a position that places itself amongst others within the practices that it studies.

Take the example of a barricade defending a social centre from eviction. Depending on from which side one is looking at it, the barricade can mean different things, and different things can be said or not said about it. How can you know why it is there? Is it there because you know that people discussed it in small groups or during an assembly, or because someone had simply set out to gather material for its construction? Is the barricade being built in this specific moment because people know that the cops will come? Maybe someone leaked the day of eviction? Is the barbed wire there to provide a spectacle for the media or is it there because of a heated discussion that took place between pacifists and proponents of militant action? If you can answer all or some of these questions about the construction of the barricade, you also know that the contentious spatial practice of defending a squat is a process of forming and transforming relationships. In contrast, if one is to assume that there is one fixed singular position within the squat that articulates dissent (such as "the squatters movement" or "the right to the city movement"), that this position has a goal (such as mobilising certain elements of the movement or take the political opportunity presented by the eviction to mediatise the struggle), one loses the attentiveness to the relations of different subject positions involved in the struggle and to the process of their transformation.

Entering into a relational process of knowing does not only allow us to *understand more* about autonomous social movements contentious spatial practices, it also brings responsibilities vis-à-vis emerging vulnerabilities.

Giving detailed information about contentious practices that prefigure horizontal social alternatives can also expose those who participate to the repression of those forces in society that strive to keep social order as it is (O'Sullivan and Zepke, 2008). This repression can take various forms: those who articulate dissent are arrested and filed on protests, experience political repression through trials and house searches (Gelderloos, 2011; Willful Disobedience, 2001). The more information is provided about articulations of dissent, the easier it is to repress them. But how is it possible to engage nevertheless in a reflection process that requires comparison beyond one's geographical scope of action? How can stories and strategies of different struggles be transmitted?

Here, a specific form of anonymisation figures as a collectively elaborated answer to these questions.

This means that to protect the researchers and participants of this participatory action research as well as all people who are involved in autonomous social movement's contentious spatial practices, everything told about the different sites of dissent will be anonymised. In doing so I am not only changing the names of people and places involved, I am also cutting characteristics of real people apart, then mixing them amongst each other and puzzling them together again in a different composition to avoid de-anonymisation even if readers have knowledge about my personal environment. This means that a real person whose name I have changed for anonymisation might appear in another story with another name, and vice versa, one and the same character can be used in different stories but represent the experience, reaction, or statements of different real people. The protagonists of this book, co-researchers and participants, will be listed in the appendices. Their names are invented and in some cases chosen by co-researchers and participants themselves. Yet, one or the other co-researcher might be able to recognise parts of themselves appearing in some of the chapters.

As for the sites of dissent that are depicted, I am not only changing the names of localities but also anonymise them by changing all the features of the distinct sites of dissent that can be obscured without changing their political context, keeping a comparative analysis possible despite the anonymisation. Only those features will be changed that allow tracking singular identities down and might expose them to political repression. Readers, especially those with political involvement in autonomous social movements spatial practices, will be familiar with the specific sites of dissent portrayed here without knowing their precise location. This format of anonymisation allows me to work with collected field material without losing hold of the details and to add a level of anonymisation that makes the reconstruction of identities more difficult although my identity as a researcher and participant is revealed.

COLLAGE, AND AND AND, BRICOLAGE

In the logic of social movement scholars, my friends and I doubtlessly fit into contemporary definitions of social movement participants. We see "the social order as contested and malleable rather than as natural and given" (Buechler, 2000, 5). We engage in collective actions to contest and transform social order even in the face of conflicts followed by repression (Singh, 2001, 30). Through our prior knowledge of and participation in social movements, interpersonal connections, friendships and bonds, we have become individuals embedded in a social network of shared ideological values which are also reflected in our organisational style of contentious politics stressing direct action and participatory decision-making (Dalton, Kuechler and Bürklin, 1990, 12, 5). We find ourselves in solidarity with the oppressed others in a struggle for autonomy (Scott, 1990, 21) because we feel that "under the existing social order, in particular under the existing economic and political institutions, we [they] do not have a full stake in society, (. . .) we [they] are not really *of* this society" (Heberle, 1995, 58). Pressed into categories used by most social movement studies, my friends and I are indeed "social movement participants." Yet neither social movement studies, nor autonomous social movements, nor the practices constituting our participation can be reduced to these categories. The latter include a multiplicity of features, biographies, motivations and identities that remain invisible if we are to restrict ourselves to a number of analytical terms.

To be able to speak of the spatial practices of autonomous social movements it was necessary to make ontological and epistemological choices in order to decide on the terms of representation of these spatial practices.

Refusing as Kevin Hetherington put it, "to get social theory to work holistically and represent the world as a single and simple picture" (1998, 9), I am starting to stammer: how can a post-representational object of research be denoted as "spatial practices of autonomous social movements"?

"Stammering" is an adding process of terms, where multiplicity is to be found between elements associated in a stammering of "AND, AND, AND" (Deleuze and Parnet, 1987, 34). In such a connotative adding process, the different elements still do not come together as a whole but their multiplicity denotes more than their sum.

"You don't have to be learned, to know or be familiar with a particular area, but to pick up this or that in areas which are very different," encourages Deleuze in an interview with his student Claire Parnet. "This is better than the 'cut-up.' It is rather a 'pick-me-up' or 'pick-up' – in the dictionary = collecting up, chance, restarting of the motor, getting on to the wavelength" (ibid., 10). Deleuze finds the power of the AND in encounters: his encounter with Félix Guattari, with Claire Parnet and with other people with whom he gave birth to words, stories, ideas, insights and theoretical concepts (ibid., 15 ff). In these encounters "something is produced which doesn't belong to either of us, but is between 2, 3, 4, . . . n. No longer is it 'x explains x, signed x,' but 'Deleuze explains Guattari, signed you,' 'x explains y, signed z.' Thus the conversation would become a real function" (ibid., 19). Parnet is picking up on the spaces in between the elements assembled in these encounters. For her, this connotative move invented by Deleuze is not opposed to binary divisions (she accuses Deleuze of creating new binary divisions instead of avoiding binaries in his theoretical concepts: "the rhizomes or grass against the trees; the war-machine against the state apparatus; (. . .)" [ibid., 34]), it is opposed to the holism of social theory instead: "It is not the elements of the sets which define the multiplicity. What defines it is the AND, as something which has its place between the elements or between the sets" (ibid., 34–35). The AND is neither the one nor the other. It builds into a line of flight escaping denotation in generating a rhizomatic set of associations (cf. ibid., 36–39).

Deleuze suggests connotation as an escape route from representative denotation of a research object. The capacity of the AND to glue different elements together is seductive: it seems to create a possibility for conceptualisation without creating a hierarchy of epistemological privilege; difference and multiplicity in the significations, appearances, shapes, forms, articulations of the elements that are placed on a horizontal plane do not arrest the flow of meaning between them. It is thus possible to pick up a concept here, a friend's story there, a memory, a theoretical insight and to arrange them on a horizontal epistemological plane. Yet, connotation can be exclusive. It requires the reader to be able to follow the connotative move in one line of meaning. What if the reader does not have similar experiences to those for whom a particular line of connotation works?

Deleuze and Guattari have encouraged their readers to *use* their concepts in practice, to modify, recycle and reinvent them. This means picking out the pieces that can be of use to recompose them giving birth to something else, something new (Deleuze and Guattari, 1994). Thus, I feel free to walk on the suggested escape route from denotation and to recycle the techniques of collage, AND AND AND and bricolage.

In the rest of this chapter, AND will be used as a glue as well – a tool for crafting a *collage* of spatial practices of autonomous social movements.

The advantage of collage is that it can be seen as a full image from many different points which are all connected. A collage works like a rhizome, whilst in a connotative move one would have to follow a train of thought, a path, and jump from one element to the next to get to the full image.

The process of making a collage has similarities with what Hakim Bey terms "cultural *bricolage*" (Bey, 2008, 86). Bey's theorisation is founded on an "ontological anarchism" (ibid., 2) which rejects any fixed categories and draws on expressivism instead. "I define my terms by making them more vague" (ibid., 85–86) writes Bey as he loots and loiters in different theories and traditions in an informational world. "The constellation of concepts involves 'breaking rules' of ordered perception to arrive at direct

experiencing, somewhat analogous to the process whereby chaos spontaneously resolves into fractal nonlinear orders" (ibid., 86). Bey wants his readers
to overcome barriers of perception and habits in seeing how theoretical elements can be recombined. A collage is similar in that sense: it also requires
those who look at it to open themselves to the differences of its elements and
to ask questions about them: What can we learn about the different elements
in this constellation? The collage, as opposed to denotation, gives something
more than a preformed concept. It can be unfinished, things can be added. It
seeks to inspire and speaks to imagination, it invites participation because not
everything is worked out. The collage is a process in progress. At best you
can still see pieces of adhesive tape, traces of scissors. The glue, the AND,
is invisible behind the elements, it acts (linguistically) as a process of adding
things, of putting pieces together.

In what follows, I will cut out and glue different elements of my collage to
carefully approach an image of spatial practices of autonomous social movements. Some of the different elements will be overlapping, some of them
might look incomplete whilst others will have amusing details. I will pick up
what I find on my path: field notes, a discussion with my friends in the living
room, contrasting bits of nomad science, theoretical concepts from royal science. The task is to disclose why these and not other elements fit with each
other. It is to show why these and not other elements form an assemblage
which is the spatial practices of autonomous social movements.

The first part of the collage is always where one starts to assemble it as a
person with relationships to others in the world. We might know where to
get a cheap canvas to start gluing things on it or a friend might have a spare
one. This is how the collage starts. My friends are present on every page. Our
relationship of affinity co-created many elements of this collage. Our voices
will resonate from the pages of the collage when we discuss the discomfort
of being represented and denoted in social movement theory. These conversations necessarily turn into conversations about who we are and why we
take contentious action to articulate sociopolitical dissent. The voices of my
friends will help to explain the necessity of deviance, the desire for an alternative starting point from which to embark on a discovery of contentious spatial
practices of autonomous social movements. They will demonstrate in practice
what canonical social movement theory could not offer to us and how it was
possible to fill these gaps by ourselves.

    I do not exclude myself as a participant from these conversations. I try to
speak with the same voice when I am talking to my friends and when I am
writing this text. I try not to perform an "ethnographic betrayal" that occurs in
royal science: "When our subjects read what we write, [they must be] startled

by the fact that our voices are newly altered so as to be measured and thoughtful, while their voices remain raw" (Young, 2005, 213).

My Friends AND Social Movement Theory

In the first move of adding something to something else in the collage, I take up the encounters of my friends with the underlying assumptions of "social movement theory" (Jasper, 2010, 965).

How did this encounter take place? Its beginning is shaped by my own reading and working with the body of literature that is in academia commonly referred to as social movement studies, including new social movement studies. Some parts of it were already familiar to some of my friends. The continuation of our encounter with social movement theory is shaped by our conversations about this chapter: it has been criticised and questioned, read and reread, discussed and rewritten again.

When revisiting social movement theory, my friends and I have seen that there is no such thing as one unified social movement theory but rather many paradigmatic perspectives on "social movements" as an object of research (van Stekelenburg and Klandermans, 2009, 18). This object of research could not be captured in one single agreed upon definition. We have seen how these paradigmatic perspectives each focus on different features of social movements seeking to answer questions about the "outcomes" of their collective actions (Staggenborg, 2011, 26), whilst it remains unclear whether they are really looking at one and the same thing or just subsuming different observable events under one contested term. And finally we have seen these paradigmatic narratives replace each other, collapse (Jaspers, 2010), melt together, collaborate (Canel, 1992), change over time (Staggenborg, 2011, 12) whilst sharply attacking and criticising each other (see, for instance, McCarthy and Zald, 1977; McAdam, 1982). This happens "for a number of reasons including historical changes, the accumulation of anomalies, the partiality of the approaches' central metaphors" (Jasper, 2010, 965), and incommensurability of underlying assumptions coming from different theoretical perspectives.

Some of these classical core assumptions made me and my friends shiver with unease: panics, mass movements, marches, riots, demonstrations are all analysed with the same analytical tools, within the theoretical paradigm of collective behaviour theories that had its peak of popularity amongst researchers from the late 1940s up to the 1960s (Buechler, 2000, 32). The direct causes for all types of collective behaviour – from spontaneous panic to planned revolutions (Melucci, 1996, 19) – are seen to be rooted in the psychological condition of individuals who are assumed to experience unease. Collective actions are thus something that falls out of the box of daily life, as abnormal reactions to stress or breakdown. They are primarily psychological not political and therefore to be regarded as dangerous and irrational. Of course the theoretical paradigm of collective behaviour theories is multifaceted, too. It experienced a variation and transformation of its underlying assumptions about collective action. Collective action was theorised with different degrees of depreciation. Whilst it was conceivable to use the metaphor of cattle to describe collective actions in the early versions of collective behaviour approaches in social movement studies (Blumler, 1951), later theorists brought the heritage of symbolic interactionism into studies of social movement's collective actions. They were seeing these as processes of communication, clarifying the difference between emotions and irrationality (Turner and Kilian, 1987). This still did not help to eradicate the status-quo bias towards social order and/or the political system in which social movements occur in later variants of collective behaviour theories based, for example, on a structural functionalism (Smelser, 1962). Nowadays, structural functionalism continues to define deviations from social and political norms as irrational, dangerous and extremist (Buechler, 2000, 28).

"It feels like collective behaviour approaches picture participants of autonomous social movements as badly integrated members of society," said Angelo with a grin on his face.

"Why are you laughing?" I asked.

"We are not integrated into *their* society! But we are perfectly fine inside an alternative community that they [the theorists] can not even *see*. I would describe myself as a perfectly 'integrated' individual. Also I don't think that I am generally perceived as an outsider."

Against the abnormality and incapacity that collective behaviour approaches seem to attribute to protest behaviour, Angelo holds that he is capable of shaping his social interactions in a self-determined way and implicitly rephrases "integrated" into "insider" and "not integrated" into "outsider." He keeps the autonomy to decide when he is to be perceived in which relationship to society.

Theoretical paradigms linking participants of social movements' relative deprivation to collective behaviour approaches (see, for example, Davies, 1962) make my friends and me feel equally uneasy about their attempt to explain the timing of revolutionary activity roughly which goes something like: when a prolonged period of social and economic development is followed by a sudden reversal, rebellion is more likely to occur. The relative deprivation of social movement participants was also used, together with the psychological concept of cognitive dissonance, to theorise the "causes" of contentious collective behaviour (Gurr, 1969). This happened through an attribution of psychological conditions such as an interconnection of frustration and aggression to social movement participants.

> The assumption here is presumably that people aspire to be better-off on existing terms. That there's some quantifiable scheme of things everyone wants, and people want or expect more or less of these, and people protest to get themselves higher up the ladder. But this is assuming that people want things that the system is offering, that can be quantified. What if someone wants things that are radically different from what the system can offer – qualitatively different? So in my case for instance, I value autonomy – not being pushed around and so on – and peak experiences, and compassion, and I much prefer to do things in nonhierarchical ways. In fact I don't just prefer it, I need things to be organised this way to feel part of the process. But the system always wants capitulation, or compromise, or inauthenticity, alienation. So, there's a kind of revolutionary desire which this theory is really missing. And this theory can't explain why people care about animals or the environment, or about groups they don't belong to – refugees for example. This feels like a theory that's being written by people whose heads are so deep inside the system that they can't even imagine that someone else might not have the same desires as they do. Also, it sounds a bit like they're [social movement researchers working with relative deprivation approaches] saying we're just jealous, or that our expectations are too high. It makes the problem about us, when the problem is with the system.

According to Gino, relative deprivation approaches in social movement studies thus fail to represent the motivations of autonomous social movement participants to engage in contentious political practices because they are incapable of accounting for a different kind of political desire – one that seeks to transform sociopolitical structures profoundly instead of participating in their stabilisation.

In the 1970s, social movement theory gave birth to new paradigmatic views, partly replacing the ones mentioned earlier. The theoretical assumptions underlying the approaches of resource mobilisation, political opportunity and political process to the study of social movement's contentious political expressions and actions emphasise the rationality of social movement participants (Schwartz, 1976). In this perspective on social movement action, participants rationally choose to become part of organisational dynamics within social movements which are described as "social movement organisations" within "social movement industries" (McCarthy and Zald, 1977) just like other people choose to become part of the political institutions because they benefit from this choice in one way or the other (Tilly, 1978). This economistic logic assumes that people act to maximise their personal gains. It places its ontological focus on relatively formal and publicly visible forms of self-organisation within movements. The people who act within such organisational dynamics raise funds, speak with governmental organisations, organise protests, are seeking to maintain a flow of resources in support for the movement's goals.

Reading about political opportunity approaches in social movement studies made Angelo laugh:

> We want increased access to political decision making power? This is like say-ing: As soon as the system gives us an opportunity we are taking it and become a "movement"? This [theory] is just talking about the supply side of the political system. It ignores the real, structural reasons [of our actions]. As if there would be a free slot for political [radical/autonomous] movements within the system. We do not make demands towards the existing political system. It is not our field of action, it is not whom we want to address with our actions.

Whilst political opportunity approaches hold that social movements take political opportunities given by or within the system of political represen-tation, contentious political practices that reject to address organisational structures of political representation, such as spontaneous or clandestine actions or contentious lifestyles, are made invisible. Instead, it is assumed that movements function like entrepreneurial companies: they calculate risks, costs, profits and opportunities.

Aims, political desires, or behaviours that are different from these catego-ries are still interpreted as if they are within these categories. This excludes a possibility of profound and radical transformation that not only simply adds new categories and subsumes everything new or radically different under its operational logic, but transforms the logic of operation instead, and makes aims, political desires and behaviours thinkable that leave a fixed conception of "political" and "imaginable" behind.

Not all theoretical currents within this paradigm of social movement stud-ies exclude the political directedness of social movements to challenge structural inequalities. Social movements are not always solely seen as taking political opportunities. They have also been studied with a focus on processes of communication and interaction between their participants, "movement leaders," politicians and civil society as well as under the aspect of a processual "cognitive liberation" of their participants, for example, in a change of consciousness of an oppressed group to form a movement (McAdam, 1982, 48).

In the 1990s, a new paradigm challenged the rational cast that prior theorisations had crafted for social movements (Johnston and Klandermans, 1995, 3–5). It shifted the focus towards concepts such as the expressiveness of social movements (Hetherington, 1998), and their prefigurative dimension of actions (Day, 2001; Motta, 2013). These "new social movement theories" as Buechler (1995) termed them are attempts to explain collective actions of social movements in looking at their political and ideological motivations for action as well as their identity and cultural background. They subscribe to a set of core assumptions about the social movements studied: "new" social movements are claimed to have replaced the old ones (which were directed at achieving a proletarian revolution). "New" movements are seen to be responding to the transformation of everyday life in post-modernity (Singh, 2001) with a carving out of post-materialist values such as autonomy and horizontal relationships connected to their way of self-organising. This posits "new" movements in sharp contrast to old social movements (Larana, Johnston and Gusfield, 1994). New social movement theories have been heavily critiqued that question the newness of the "new social movements" (Buechler, 2000, 49). They make big claims about the changing nature of society and social movements. Despite their more appreciative attitude towards the contentious politics of social movements, when my friends and I engaged with the body of literature of new social movement theories we remained suspicious. Yet, we do not necessarily disagree with the statements that this set of theories make about social movements.

Brian says:

> Identities have a role in social movements, but I'm not sure it's any bigger than in other fields of life. There's a style of activism which does that, which is kinda obsessed with identity, but thankfully it's not the whole movement. Actually I feel there isn't really an identity in autonomous movements, there isn't a single label which covers everyone, an organisation we all belong to or a code of norms we all subscribe to, it's more a sense of affinity of various degrees, which comes from hanging out with people, holding similar beliefs, and doing things together.

"I am, we are, probably their object of research, yes," admitted Brian in a discussion with Angelo, Gino and me about new social movement studies. I asked him: "You do not seem happy about this?"

Brian said: "Happy?! Hell, [my name], the cops are talking about us, the judges are talking about us, the journalists are talking about us and these dudes [social movement theorists] are talking about us, too. I say: Let them talk. They are not speaking about me anyway. They cannot speak about movements as long as they are not speaking from within movements. Because until then they don't know the movements."

Gino: "Surely this cannot be said about every person who does research on social movements. Probably some of them are in touch with the movements that they are studying. I think writing about autonomous social movements is complicated, though . . . everything is informal and presenting something *general* simply does not work out."

Angelo: "I can tell you what I think of some social movement theories, but they are not important to me."

"Why?" I asked then.

"I can give you an example, why," said Gino. "I have kept a newspaper article about a questionnaire that a group of social movement researchers asked participants of a Stop-G7 camp to fill out. I'll get it from my room."

We read the article together. It is about the answers that social movement researchers got from participants of a protest camp in 2007 regarding their motivation to engage in demonstrations and riots. The article contains some examples of the questions in a survey sample that was distributed and filled out during the camp. We laugh several times because the questions seem nonsensical to us. Gino commented at the end:

> They are just answering their own questions anyway in this research. It is not relevant to me because I am not interested in what they are interested. I am not interested if participants in a Stop-G7 camp are over thirty years old or not. And I do not even believe that they are going to find out anything about our motivations this way.

My friends do not feel represented by the way participants of the camp are constructed as an object of research, because they lack a relation to the knowledge production process of the researchers. As long as the knowledge is not created from within the movement, it cannot answer questions that have a relevance for the movement which develops these questions relationally. The knowledge production process of the researchers follows a logic of knowledge production that objectifies and denotes social movements and in doing so enforces a categorical identity onto participants of autonomous social movements contentious spatial practices.

In his book *Difference and Repetition*, Gilles Deleuze shows how the logic of categorical representation is connected to the logic of identity: for something to be representable in categorical terms, there is a logic of identity at work that seeks to annihilate differences in creating fixed, measurable categories of identities for beings that are always in a "flow of becoming" (Deleuze, 1994).

The problem with the "logic of identity" is that groups' natures are defined as essential and/or substantial (Young, 1995, 157). Iris Marion Young argues that group-based oppression and conflict is most extreme when they are based in a conception of difference as otherness between groups (ibid.). "For example, men and women have been stereotyped as rational or emotional, public or private and one group makes use of these essential or substantive differences to subjugate the other group. The obvious problem with the logic of identity is that whatever group tends to dominate, to have the most privilege and power, will represent themselves as active human subjects and represent everyone else as 'others,' not up to the level of the original, until and unless they find a way to conform to the definition of the individual or citizen established by the dominant group" (Olkowski, 1999, 12). According to Dorothea Olkowski, differences that *do not fit* must either be assimilated to one accepted category or denied.

To undermine this oppressive logic of identity, it must become possible to differentiate differences instead of representing them as merely specific differences belonging to a single genus. Representation, for Deleuze, is also a particularly restricted mode of thinking which represents at the same time the dominant model of seeing the world amongst western thinkers (Deleuze, 1994; 2003). He opposes representation to the logic of difference. In the logic of representation difference is thus allowed an existence in terms of identity only as a generic concept, only as long as it is representable by this generic concept. This is necessary to stabilise a system of hierarchical distribution, irrespective of the multiplicity of representable identities that it includes. They must all be subsumed under the generic concept that is capable of subordinating all differences. Representation thus organises different elements in a stable hierarchical form. This is a matter of taking something for an object, conceiving it as static and assigning it to a specific place in the categorical hierarchy. Representation is thus a politically motivated choice for stability over transformation, for hierarchical instead of horizontal organisation. Representation conditions the hierarchical distribution of power that characterises the "state apparatus" – the most static form of organisation (Deleuze and Guattari, 2013).

Due to the political rejection of representation as an organising principle, autonomous social movements do not even have an identity to be represented. My friends who are involved in post-representative movements can thus not be represented by social movement theories.

At this point, I am adding *post-representativity* as an element to the collage. It now reads as

My Friends AND Social Movement Theory AND Post-Representativity

The next step is now to investigate the relationship of these elements.

The articulations of my friends about social movement theory suggest that their refusal and rejection of representation by social movement research is not simply due to what they perceive as misrepresentations within specific theoretical approaches. My friends reject the function of representation and its production of organisational forms of social relationships. This does not mean that my friends reject knowledge creation. They would accept research that seeks to avoid representational hierarchies in making their knowledge production process accessible to the movement. Angelo gives an example:

> I am thinking of Occupy in 2011 in the camp in. . . . There was almost no representation of us to the exterior. I remember the assembly said, "If somebody wants to know something about us they can/have to come to our assembly." It's the same for social movement researchers.

Ernesto Laclau has argued that representation is hegemonic in the sense that it creates a structure between elements in which one element is placed above other elements which it is capable of subsuming in one way or another. This thus produces an unevenness in relations of power between elements (Butler, Laclau and Zizek, 2000).

Richard Day argues that in contentious political practices that are challenging oppressive power dynamics produced by hegemonic representation "the goal is not to create a new power around a hegemonic centre, but to challenge, disrupt and disorient the processes of global hegemony, to *refuse, rather than rearticulate* those forces" (Day, 2004, 730).

In this sense my friends' objection to being represented in what Sassen terms, "disciplinary knowledge" (2006, 379) is a political refusal – a refusal for the same political reasons that drive my friends to relate with contentious post-representational political practices of "social movements." Occupy is one example of such movements that challenge representation directly in telling us "that no form of representative politics, no political party, can change the basic coordinates of the liberal-democratic capitalist system" that they oppose (Tormey, 2012, 134). "In this horizon only a 'disorganised' repertoire of direct and immediate political actions enables people to be 'heard' as opposed to being subsumed within the machinic meta-mobilism of 'normal' politics" (ibid.). The refusal to being represented within the current status quo is in some cases of contentious political practices "an ideological choice or position – a rejection of the state or forms of hierarchical powers; but for millions of others it is the result of a lack of alternatives" (Azzellini and Sitrin, 2014, 9). In the context of what social movement researchers identify as collective practices of contemporary social movements, this refusal entails a "break with old forms of organization and social relationships" through "creation of new ways of being and organizing" (ibid.).

Marina Sitrin and Dario Azzelini have spoken to people who are organising and participating in direct decision-making processes in assemblies, who self-organise factories and health clinics without bosses and formal hierarchies, who take to the streets to occupy squares and engage in horizontal reflection processes about their needs and political desires to restructure societal deci-sion-making processes. For Debbie from the autonomous Solidarity Health Clinic in Thessaloniki (as for Deleuze and Guattari, 2013, 5–8 and 187–89), the rejection of representation is rather an organisational than an ideological question which entails autonomous and horizontal decision-making:

> We are very used to delegating responsibility to somebody else and giving them the power to make decisions over what is happening. We don't think of that as democratic. We don't want to have representatives, we want to represent ourselves. Of course, this raises several problems . . . how do you structure or organize decision making? As a process of decision-making it's much more useful to have all voices heard. It's interesting that when people gather they automatically, instinctively adhere to principles of direct democracy. This is because, essentially, when something is very important to you, you want to make the decision for yourself and not have somebody else to decide for you. (Debbie in Sitrin and Azzelini, 2014, 52)

Thus the rejection of representation is reflected in horizontal ways of self-organising and decision-making: vertical power structures in decision-making processes are replaced by a flat network, a "rhizome" (Deleuze and Guattari, 2013, 12–15), where every element of the network is connected to every other element on a horizontal plane without imposing a centre or hierarchy (Ravage, 1999). Within such organisational structures it makes a difference whether the rhizomatic assemblage of elements, its functions, desires and goals, is described from within the rhizome or from the outside. Everything that defines the rhizomatic organism is happening between its elements and is only visible in relation to these elements. "The rhizome makes us distinguish between the liminal and the subliminal, between what 'expert' commentary sees above, and what lurks beneath the surface" (Tormey, 2012, 133).

My friend Brian suggested that in theorisations about social movements, their denotation and the resulting function of representation depends on the type of relation that one element has with what there is to be denoted. In the context of Brian's post-representative political practices, representation can only take place through a relation of affinity between elements of a specific, local rhizome:

"Well, what all these approaches have in common is that they are saying something about social movements. But this works only well if someone knows us. The way you are doing it right now it works: you are speaking from within a situation that you know."

The relation between social movement theory and my friends draws a line to the issue of representation – some new social movement researchers are aware of the refusal to be represented and analyse it as a denotative characteristic of my friend's contentious political practices:

> this is a movement about reinventing democracy. It is not opposed to organization. It is about creating new forms of organization. It is not lacking in ideology. Those new forms of organization *are* its ideology. It is about creating and enacting horizontal networks instead of top-down structures like states, parties or corporations; networks based on principles of decentralized, non-hierarchical consensus democracy. Ultimately, it aspires to be much more than that, because ultimately it aspires to reinvent daily life as whole. (Graeber, 2002, 70)

Horizontality is a new element that now adds to the line of approximation, to the collage of autonomous social movements spatial practices. We can now trace this line as

My Friends AND Social Movement Theory AND Post-Representativity AND Horizontality

Social movement researchers have identified horizontal self-organisation as a defining feature of social movements (Diani and McAdam, 2003). Yet, within a denotative approach, acknowledging the importance of horizontal self-organisation does not always allow me and my friends to explore its political implications for social movements. Such categorical representations of what social movements are, are based on a denotation of "central aspects of social movements" (Fuchs, 2006, 108) which are again based on a collection of other denotations – often (diverging) definitions of social movements by social movement researchers (cf. ibid., 109). "A social movement" thus turns out to be "a social system that is characterized by a certain protest identity" (ibid., 129). This social system happens to be organised in the shape of a network (Diani, 2003). A network is nothing more than an organisational structure which is horizontal. It is perfectly suitable for being integrated into the logic of capitalism where businesses, enterprises and the internet, for example, are also organised as networks. Despite its antagonistic position to the sociopolitical system, the "protest identity" of a self-organised social movement simply enhances "the dynamic of the political system" (ibid., 115). Horizontal self-organisation is one of the functions of this "protest identity" which is representable as an oppositional element within social order that makes it more dynamic, more democratic and more modern (ibid., 115).

In such denotative definitions of social movements, horizontality cannot be thought as radically opposed to or outside of social order. In this example, representation in social movement studies has once again facilitated to deny "social movements" (as a unified object of research) their difference and rejection of the functioning of the current sociopolitical system.

If we refuse to see horizontal self-organisation simply as a characteristic of a certain protest identity, it might turn out to be much more than an organisational principle. It is nevertheless *also* an organisational principle – one that is based on the diversity and difference of the elements organised within it. Donatella della Porta uses the concept of a deliberative decision-making process to analyse horizontal self-organisation in autonomous social movements: the distribution of decision-making power amongst different subject positions that are not subsumed in one representable category is conditioned by a plurality of values and perspectives that are put in relation horizontally (della Porta, 2005). This excludes a single, united "protest identity" in horizontal self-organisation. When horizontal self-organisation is seen as a political refusal of representation based on the rejection of power hierarchies, it also turns it into a tool against these (Pickerill and Chatterton, 2006, 740).

Horizontal communication and relationships are a matter of people talking to each other, interacting and expressing their needs and desires openly (cf. Landstreicher, 2004, 4). Autonomous social movements have developed techniques of horizontal self-organisation such as affinity-groups (self-organisation to take action in small groups), spokescouncils and consensus decision-making (Pickerill and Chatterton, 2006; della Porta, 2008). The attempt to build collective processes whilst managing internal differences in a decentralised coordination building horizontal ties amongst diverse and autonomous elements, free and open participation and circulation of information and self-directed networking (Juris, 2009, 214) is often, within activist as well as academic circles, referred to as "horizontalism" or "horizontalidad" (Sitrin, 2006).

Felippa, Janinka and I started to debate whether the decision-making structures in a self-managed social centre where we just had organised an event were really horizontal. Noticing that the distribution of knowledge about how to organise things was distributed unevenly in the collective, Felippa said:

> Knowledge is not necessarily power. For example, if I know how to repair the toilet and you don't and I show it to you – do I really have power over you then?

I picked some broken glass from the floor trying to focus my participatory quality of attention and replied:

> In a big group with diverse people, for example, an open assembly like the one of this social centre, the accumulation of specialised knowledge is necessary. But it could also be several people who share this role. In other situations, I think you don't need this.

"I don't think that having people who sometimes tell other people what to do and how to do it is something that can happen within horizontal self-organisation. Because this is just not horizontality! I will still maintain that horizontality in decision-making and in interactions is an absolute goal to be attained at all costs! Even at the costs of efficiency," Janinka said energetically.

Felippa: "But this is not the same as a general who shouts at his soldiers! It all depends on the relationship we have with the people who tell us to move on, to turn off the water, to make our point as brief and precise as possible."

Felippa's comparison with a general giving orders to soldiers opposes an extremely hierarchical form of organisation to a horizontal plane of social relationships. The latter can only work in the absence of hierarchical decision-making structures which are decoupled from relationships of trust and affinity. Affinity between people can only exist without the oppression of hierarchical power over people.

Within autonomous self-organisation, decisions are being taken individually, whether they are associated to an appointed rotating decision-making task, or not. Taking part in autonomous contentious political practices is an individual decision which needs to be reaffirmed again and again. In horizontal self-organisation, there are no organisational structures which provide participants with a formal membership or ready-made reasons for their participation. Individual reasons, degrees and forms of participation in autonomous social movement, political practices are heterogeneous, just like the people that could take part in these practices.

The autonomy of different subject positions within a collective action or struggle conditions the horizontality of a decision-making process or organisational form in autonomous social movements. *Autonomy* thus continues the collage and traces an approximative line which now reads as this:

My Friends AND Social Movement Theory AND Post-Representativity AND Horizontality AND Autonomy

The individual-collective dichotomy is a key tension in autonomous social movement politics (Pickerill and Chatterton, 2006, 733). Although autonomy is a collective project carried out in collective practices, it still implies individual autonomy – the capacity to make choices in freedom, to self-legislate[1] (Robinson, 2010). In the context of European autonomous social movements, autonomy has a variety of meanings.

First, autonomy presupposes a horizontal social relationship between autonomous individuals in everyday life.

The historian George Katsiaficas gives an account of the autonomy of struggle of the 1970s autonomous feminist movement resisting patriarchy. The struggle was determined and led by women with the aim of self-empowerment. Here, importance was placed on "decentralization, autonomy of every single group. In existing groups, it means the self-determination of working structures and content, within which hoped for antihierarchical structures allow affected individuals the widest possible space for their autonomous development" (activist cited in Katsiaficas, 2006, 75). In autonomist feminism, the importance of the everyday is very visible: women's oppression is theorised and resisted through the politicisation of social reproduction, through a rejection of representational strategies reproducing the exclusion of reproductive sites of private spheres as opposed to the productive site of the public sphere (Federici, 2004).

Their resistance to patriarchy is thus autonomous from whatever male supporters might do since the autonomy of a struggle is a living practice of empowerment.

Within collective struggles autonomy implies that in the struggle against a specific oppression it is the oppressed who dispose of the knowledge that is necessary for the resistance because it is located in everyday experiences of oppression and resistance (cf. Scott, 1990). Autonomy is thus also the empowerment of the oppressed to fight oppression (eventually together with diverse supporters who respect their knowledge) in horizontal relationships. The goal of autonomous politics, as suggested by Katsiaficas, is the subversion of oppressive politics, not the conquest of power (Katsiaficas, 2006, 267). As such autonomous politics are anti-hegemonic, turned against hierarchised power structures and mechanisms of oppression between individuals. This is closely related to horizontal self-organisation.

"Autonomy" within social movements solves the individual-collective dichotomy that emerges when collective action is taken in horizontal self-organisation by individuals who relate as different identities. Yet in relation to social movements the word "autonomous" can mean much more.

Within social movements in Europe it is also used as a political label to draw distinctions, as in differences in ways of acting politically within the same issue (for example, within the antifascist movement in Germany *autonomous antifa* stands for collective antifascist actions of individuals who perform the action not as part of a political group with a label or a name or an organisation [Keller et al., 2013, 67–69]). For some social movement researchers, it is a word capable of describing a specific type of movement as autonomous social movements (Flesher Fominaya, 2007; Katsiaficas, 2006; Newman, 2011; Prujit, 2014 and others) because it brings so many social movement characteristics in relation to each other.

My friends Bill and Ian add more meanings to *autonomy*:

> For me, *autonomous* comes from the history of the antifa – people who said they want to fight fascism not along a pre-programmed institutional plan or together with the state or political parties but with their own hands. I have not been politically socialised within this movement. So, in the historical context, I am not autonomous. But my politics are politics of autonomy – doing things in a self-determined way, liberating myself and others from structural oppression and not waiting for labeled groups to come and to do this for me,

explains Bill and continues:

> To give an example: There is a campaign to stop the construction of some intensive industrial mass farming. People in the campaign make a petition and some demonstrations against the construction of this factory. They try to speak to politicians and get some NGO funding to raise awareness for animal exploitation. Maybe the campaign *is* an NGO. Other people get together and decide that they want to do something against the construction of this factory – independent from the campaign; because they have their own analysis why the construction should be stopped. What they will do is an autonomous action. They won't listen to a predefined narrative on *how* to resist industrial animal exploitation. They will develop an autonomous analysis of why to resist and how to resist.

Ian adds:
> Autonomous could stand for "self-defined." It means: we will not remain confined to a political role that someone or something gives us; we will be a

political actor on our own terms. And autonomous means to take the freedom to develop our own independent political practices, our own analysis of the situation. It means being uncontrollable.

Ian alluded to the long history of social movement struggles that the word "autonomous" is connected to – including diverse currents of thought such as Open Marxism, autonomous Marxism and anarchism (Böhm et al., 2010) and implications in diverse issues such as feminism and anti-patriarchy, student protests, squatting, anti-fascism, struggles against exploitation of labour and anti-colonialism, as well as struggles for territorial autonomy (Katsiaficas, 2006). Yet, for Ian in his present political practices "autonomous" is "a way of doing things."

"You said that 'autonomous' is a way of *doing* things . . ." I am trying to continue the conversation with Bill and Ian.

Ian: "I know where this is getting at! You want us to say something about the importance of direct action and so on. It's always the same: when academics write their books about 'ethnographies of direct action' they always want some activist voices to make their theory sound more 'true.' I read books, too – and I recognise the pattern. You want to theorise 'doing.' You can write about what we do and call it prefigurative politics, politics of the act."

Bill: "Don't be so hostile! This could be true direct action on paper," he giggles. "Taking direct action in theory in saying that pure theory is impossible without properly engaging in what we do. Because we *do* our theory. What a mess! . . . Maybe it is a different kind of theory, an anti-theoretical theory because it is not concerned with making a framework for our actions but our actions create the theoretical framework? You still need us to say something more about this to theorise it?"

Me: "No . . ."

Ian: "And you think you can do this with theory? Isn't this against the philosophy of congruence between ends and means? If you want to get to the point of *doing*, transforming the world – why theorise it?"

Me: "Theorising is also a way of doing. How we think of the world is at the same time reproducing the world in a certain way. And if we can change things here, this is also a battle won."

Ian: "As long as in your theory you manage to get to the point where the theory turns into action – then: yes, maybe."

Bill: "This would be a prefigurative theory. One that abolishes itself. Because it would say that the theory is where we get together to create alternatives or dismantle the status-quo to create space for these alternatives."

Ian: "Yes, but whatever she writes, there will always be one problem: the projection of our utopia into the present is always unfinished and always in contradiction with our utopian aims. Theory in contrast is most of the time something complete, something finished, something thought through. So theory about direct action has to be unfinished, too – to leave space for doing, for hopeless affirmative acts that seem nonsensical because we won't get to our utopian society. Because a politics of direct action, a politics of empowerment to actually change something with everyone involved, with many hands doing different things, simply escapes complete theorisation. You have to leave a gap in your theory for this."

Me: "That was my plan. But first I need to put what we do into a theoretical context. . . . It is just an approximative attempt to bring everything together anyway. Don't worry, it will remain incomplete."

Conceiving autonomy as something that has to be acted out in different aspects of self-determination adds another element to the collage since autonomy in its place in the collage relates to a new element: prefiguration/ direct action – as in *doing* autonomy. The collage thus reads as a longer lines of approximation to autonomous social movements' spatial practices:

My Friends AND Social Movement Theory AND Post-Representation AND Horizontality AND Autonomy AND Prefiguration/Direct Action

Bill and Ian have sought words for the incompleteness of the utopian projection of political desires for autonomy that are expressed through actions in autonomous social movements. There are a number of other attempts to find words for a politics of the act that is prefiguring its outcome through present practices whilst always being in contention with the present society. Saul Newman describes autonomy as "an ongoing project of political spatialisation rather than a fully achieved form of social organization" (Newman, 2011, 13). The spatialities that are created within this ongoing project "are based on the idea of 'prefigurative politics' (summed up by the phrase 'be the change you want to see')" (Pickerill and Chatterton, 2006, 738), on the idea of social transformation as an accumulation of small changes, creating alternatives outside of vertical power structures. They are thus taking concrete shapes as contentious spatialities and/or moments of utopian rupture with the present (cf. Gordon, 2008, 35–38).

In relation to the practices of autonomous social movements, the term "prefigurative politics" which was coined in the 1970s (see Boggs, 1977) is used to refer to "attempts to create tools and practices today that foreshadow the future society that is aspired to" (Flesher Fominaya, 2007, 339). This means that in prefigurative politics there is a clear and important link between means and ends. Horizontal organisational forms, decision-making processes, and forms of action are not just means to an end – they are ends in themselves.

My friends have made it clear that the "hopeless affirmative acts that seem nonsensical because we won't get to our utopian society" have a conceptual primacy over their theoretical conceptualisation that aims to bring them together as a whole "prefigurative politics." In everyday practices we can find the agency to empower ourselves to decide autonomously about the organisation of everyday life. This political desire has given up the "expectation of a non-dominating response from structures of domination" (Day, 2005, 95) in that it does not formulate demands towards apparatuses that organise everyday life. A politics of the act has given up the "fantasy (. . .) that the currently hegemonic formation will recognize the validity of the claim presented to it and respond in a way that produces an event of emancipation" (ibid.). Instead, it creates a moment of empowerment, a moment of rupture from the current hegemonic organisation of everyday life (Lefebvre and Levich, 2007). When taking direct action against the status quo, when faced with injustice produced by the status quo, "one is acting as if one is already free" (Graeber, 2009, 203). In his ethnography of direct action, David Graeber mentions that in discussions amongst activists the term "direct action" is used to refer to tactics of militancy as opposed to less confrontational civil disobedience (ibid., 204). This is because taking direct action includes a refusal of subjection to the executive and juridical response of the state apparatus. It is solely directed towards the utopian prefiguration of the action itself and is therefore necessarily confrontational in its content but not necessarily in its form.

> Direct action is not only a method of protest but also a way of "building the future now." (. . .) it is self-directed rather than a response to the activities of capital or state (. . .). We can define our own goals and achieve them through our own efforts. One of the most important aspects of direct action is the organisation involved in order for it to be successful. By organising to achieve our goal ourselves we learn valuable skills and discover that organisation without hierarchy is possible. Where it succeeds, direct action shows that people can control their own lives. (Sparrow, 1997, 7)

This is where the continuity of ends and means comes effectively into play and creates a living contention with the here and now:

> blockades, pickets, sabotage, squatting, tree spiking, lockouts, occupations, rolling strikes, slow downs, the revolutionary general strike. In the community it involves, amongst other things, establishing our own organisations such as food co-ops and community access radio and tv to provide for our social needs,

blocking the freeway developments which divide and poison our communities and taking and squatting the houses that we need to live in. In the forests, direct action interposes our bodies, our will and our ingenuity between wilderness and those who would destroy it and act against the profits of the organisations which direct the exploitation of nature and against those organisations themselves. In the industry and in the workplace direct action aims either to extend workers control or to directly attack the profits of the employers. (Ibid., 6)

Whether direct action takes the shape of autonomous horizontal self-organisation to grow and distribute vegetables, or whether it mobilises people to confront hegemonic formations of power through expressing sociopolitical dissent on the streets – it consists of hands-on transformations of reality pointing to an utopian projection of another social reality that dimly takes shape in the moment of the action.

The next addition to the collage therefore consists of actions that are *taking place*, disturbing, transforming and rupturing with reality to make space for something different, for desires and imaginaries that are in contention with reality.

The last element in the line of flight added in the process of "stammering" and composing a collage of spatial practices of autonomous social movements is *space*.

We have arrived at a collage of different elements that reads as:

My Friends AND Social Movement Theory AND Post-Representation AND Horizontality AND Autonomy AND Prefiguration/Direct Action AND Space

In the first chapter, I have concluded that fighting for another type of space is fighting for another type of life. If we conceive it as performed and experienced by people doing things in space and if, according to relational geographers, everything is in flow and interconnected, then the smallest micro-movement of a spatial practice can serve to challenge the power geometry of socio-spatial order (Massey, 1994). The repertoires of this struggle for another type of space, another type of life, are place-specific, situated and heterogeneous.

Gino: "You can use space to transform society for a moment. In the moment of a reclaim the streets rave, for example. We bring chairs and sofas out on the street, and a little sound system, too. And maybe someone bakes a cake and the neighbours are interested and come to join us. We distribute flyers and engage in conversations we would not have in normal life with them. Then we turn the music on and dance and no car can pass. Until the cops come. And then it is dissolved as if nothing ever happened. But *something* happened. The street will never be the same as it was before. We will never forget what happened here."

Ian: "In the city people sometimes occupy squares and make a tent village there. There would be a collective people's kitchen for donation and political discussions in the public space, and consensus decision-making circles. This would also be an autonomous zone against the cops, against the politics of gentrification, with a political agenda such as the right to adequate housing for refugees. And there would be an info point."

Felippa: "Being involved in a social centre is doing spatial politics. It is taking or occupying space and making something different; Outside someone or something else organises space for you. And you have to agree on how to use it and play by the rules – not go here, not play there, not do this or that or pay a fine. In the social centre everyone can make the rules of the space if it is self-organised. Maybe the social centre has been there before we started to get involved in this kind of politics, maybe it has been squatted decades ago. But if we are involved in it and we keep it as an autonomous space we are still making contentious space: without our involvement and the involvement of others it would simply cease to exist. The simple task of sweeping the floor after a concert is part of it. Outside the same task would be something alienating to do."

Gino: "The body in space is a tool that we can use to make contentious politics: if I sit on the floor in the underground instead on a designated seat; if I sit in front of the entrance to a chain shop to make a symbolic action against sweat shops or if I sit on the rail tracks to block a train full of fascists or nuclear waste."

Bill: "Defending a territory and trying to rip it out of the control of the state . . . like the Zapatista! Here space is really conflict. And also it is a conflict over space. And at the same time space is used to carry out the conflict between different ways of societal organisation – the horizontal one and the hierarchical one."

In my friends' examples of contentious spatial practices of autonomous social movements the space of a square, the space of rail tracks or the space of a social centre is the terrain in which political contestations of social order are expressed. Behaviours in space or the transformation of a space are at the same time the vehicle for articulations of dissent. The organisation of space and its dynamics of power is also what gives rise to the contention, it is where abstracts antagonisms become tangible.

If I want to learn about how, why and under what circumstances it is possible to transform socio-spatial order in creating utopian alternatives, I need to turn my sensitive attention to the already existing attempts to do so. In the first chapter, these attempts were conceived as sites of dissent created through contentious spatial agency in specific places and territories. In this chapter, I have outlined how the creation of sites of dissent is constituted through contentious spatial practices of autonomous social movements.

Another kind of space, a heterotopia is coming into existence though contentious spatial practices of autonomous social movements. These practices may be temporary, destructive, creative, permanent, taking place on the countryside or in the city, involve small territories or be composed of a single movement, a little action, or transform an entire street, an entire area, or several of these at once. In spatial practices of autonomous social movements, the experience of place is self-made and self-determined through an empowering spatial agency: the power to act upon spatiality and to transform it and the social relationships that it is composed of.

To illustrate this I will share field notes that some participants of the genderp@nks, an autonomous gender-queer[2] affinity group, and I made collectively about the subversion of a Christopher Street Day parade. We have experienced how contentious spatial practices of autonomous social movements transformed the street during the parade creating a temporary heterotopia with an empowering spatial agency.

Soon after the genderp@nks had designed their first flyer informing about the group, the local LGB[3] organisation started the preparation for a Christopher Street Day parade. The genderp@nks decided to issue a call out to show a not-only-lesbian-gay-bisexual gender presence on this parade and to welcome and visibilise "all genders," not only lesbian, gay and bisexual orientations. People that are not representable in any (fixed) gender category not only showed up and expressed themselves within the crowd of the parade in a "pink block" but also in speeches, chants, behaviours and performances on the street. The "pink block" consisted of many un-representable gender identities who had self-organised networking with other queers in different cities, to turn the Christopher Street Day into a day of deconstruction of gender categories during different events. The programme included discussions, talks and a self-organised queer party which provided a space to express one's difference in dissociation from gender norms – through ways of acting, dressing, dancing, communicating. The genderp@nks did not formulate a demand towards institutionalised gender politics of difference to include (more) multiple identities in their event but created an autonomous space to express themselves instead – on the streets during the parade and in the social centre where the queer party took place afterwards. "What matters here, are the experiences of the self that got created during this event," a genderp@nk told me, "what matters is the experience of being able to relate to other people beyond gender-normed communication in a space in which we can free ourselves from gender related oppression."

TOWARDS A PARTICIPATORY ACTION RESEARCH

I have been writing *about* autonomous social movements, what they are like (horizontal, prefigurative, anti-identitarian, etc.) and what they do (performing contentious spatial practices, articulating sociopolitical dissent). *Autonomous social movements* has emerged as a denotation. Before having started to craft the collage I had already established that escaping denotation completely is impossible – after all I will need to use words that fix the meaning of what I am writing about to make myself understood. Why have I been using the words "autonomous social movements" and not "newest social movements" (Day, 2005), a term that has been already coined in social movement studies and includes many elements of my collage?

I choose the less common term *autonomous* to describe the social movements that I am studying. *Autonomous* describes what these social movements do and how they do it; it is an element of the collage and thus inseparable from other elements such as *horizontal* or *prefigurative*. *Autonomous* is not a label that seeks to compare movements such as *new* social movements or *newest* social movements. *Autonomous* stands for a practice that relates horizontality to post-representativity and prefiguration/direct action. As such it serves as a linguistic compromise to describe the heterogeneous forms and practices of the movements.

In this chapter, a diffused "we" appears on an approximative line of flight towards an exploration of autonomous social movements spatial practices. It is the result of a collage and I am part of the picture. The collage of autonomous social movement spatial practices is not finished. It remains incomplete and further elements might be added in the process of exploration. There is no distance from which I can take a look at the collage like an art critic. This collage is an addition of relationships of affinity with my friends, a re-conceptualisation of our political identity in dissociation from representation through social movement theory.

It is now possible to ask *how* to research, explore and study post-representational, prefigurative, autonomous spatial practices with a method that maintains a continuity between ends and means, that allows for horizontal and collective knowledge creation whilst at the same time permitting to stay on the squatted field of "research." The relational dimension of collective knowledge production does not necessarily need to start from an already existing friendship. It can depart from any point of shared interest in creating knowledge horizontally on an issue that the co-researchers seek to explore. But how to surmount the barriers between academic and nonacademic ways of thinking and speaking? How to transmit narratives to theoretical concepts, how to add a structured research approach to direct actions articulating sociopolitical dissent? They appear irreconcilable and the only choice seems to travel back and forth between them.

This is what the epistemological figure of the travelling storyteller (Motta, 2013) does. The storyteller takes narrated knowledges from one place to a different place; she takes the narratives crafted in nomad science across the border into royal science where she can pick up the concepts of royal science and bring them back to the space of collective storytelling in nomad science when she speaks there about her research. "She dwells of necessity and choice in the margins. From here she develops a methodology of border-thinking that decentres dominant regimes and rationalities of knowledge to foster multiple grounds of epistemological becoming" (Lugones, 1992, 19).

To become a travelling storyteller, developing "a methodology of border-thinking" (ibid., 19) is the next task to take on. Such a methodology would be accepted as such in royal science whilst at the same time offering loopholes to escape into the logic of nomad science and returning with multifaceted knowledges, experiences and encounters from there to the orderly field of scientific research again. Such a methodology would then constitute a border zone, a dwelling place for the travelling storyteller, a place to live, to craft, create and construct with others.

The act of crafting the collage already shifted my attention towards *participatory* methods which not only allow a collaboration between researchers and participants but also help to transgress hierarchical divisions of labour. To do so, the scholar needs to unlearn a lot of what he or she has learned in his or her formal education (Kimpson, 2005, 90). A participant of the militant research collective *Precarias a la Deriva* describes this process of unlearning as "'starting from oneself,' as one among many, in order to 'get out of oneself' (out of one's individual ego and the radical group to which one belongs) and to encounter other resisting people" (Colectivo Situaciones, 2007, 87).

For a scholar "to unlearn oneself" means unlearning elements of knowledge production that are hegemonic, unlearning one's epistemologically privileged position and start learning with and from others whilst creating horizontal relationships with them (Motta, 2013b); Because research that is empowering to actualise desired social transformations "is not research on the marginalised but research by, for, and with them/us" (Brown and Strega, 2005, 7). In contrast to methodological claims to objectivity and neutrality which obscure the dynamics of power and privilege involved in the production and validation of knowledge, such participatory methodologies seek to make the location and political commitments of the researchers explicit (cf. ibid., 10).

Chapter 3

Horizontal Participatory Action Research

In a horizontal collaboration with other people, the researcher needs to learn to lose control since she is not producing one objective knowledge with one rigorous methodology any more. She is witnessing a messy networked process where different situated knowledges (Haraway, 1988) interconnect, form relationships, transform, fertilise each other and create new insights coming from different locations. The task of a participatory and horizontal research methodology is then to bring these differences together "elaborating a common plane" for their encounter (Colectivo Situaciones, 2007, 86), to make proof of a self-critical reflexivity which considers the extent of its own complicity in systems of domination. As Strega reminds us, reflexivity "highlights rather than obscures the participation of the researcher in the research process. It makes clear that interpretation is taking place and by implication calls into question the alleged neutrality and objectivity of the researcher/researchers (Strega, 2005, 229). Self-reflexivity in research thus offers an important political and methodological challenge to standard research practices.

When doing research on spatial practices of autonomous social movements *unlearning* means *participating* in contentious spatial practices of autonomous social movements. This means working, living, laughing, doing, experiencing, arguing, socialising – bringing research into one's life, the life that is shared with other people. With some of them I have closer relationships than with others, some are more involved in my research process than others. Doing participatory and horizontal research thus also means uncovering some of my personal relationships with those whom I will later introduce as co-researchers and participants.

This also means getting involved in collective action whilst putting horizontal social relationships into practice; and in the end, this means participating in forms of action and reflection that do not require the role of a professionalised facilitator because they emerge in multiple, diverse and uncontrollable relationships and interactions, through our collective reflections of varying forms.

In this context, my personal process of unlearning myself as a researcher is woven into the history of my political involvement with autonomous social movements. Sharing tasks of self-organisation in social centres, co-organising public events, disrupting master narratives, sitting in meetings for hours, having my friends arrested, participating in collective actions. My university training as a researcher runs parallel to this history of involvement. For a long time, it was a separate world – one that was disrupting the expression of my political desires and stealing time. Academic knowledge was an annoying thing, appearing as almost irrelevant for what I was doing. As an undergraduate student, I chose to do night shifts in our squatted social centre threatened by eviction rather than studying for exams. Only as a postgraduate student I started to explore ways of thinking theory and practice of autonomous social movements together, to engage with theorisations of prefigurative politics, to discover the many facets of the concept of autonomy, to learn about participatory methodologies. After finishing my studies, I nevertheless felt the urge to leave the university and the sphere of academic knowledge production, to have a life with more direct action and less institutional obligations. At some point here, the desire to connect action with reflection, to structure and explain thoughts, reasons and motivations, creeped in. If not for others, then at least for myself, I felt the need to connect theoretical reflection with political engagement and action. Whilst living in a collective that was involved in struggles against gentrification and squatting empty buildings, I restarted to read and write like I did in university. "Is it necessary to 'return' to university to give meaning to what I am doing?" I wondered whilst waiting if my recent book orders would arrive by mail at our barricaded front door or not. What would my reflections change in the world if I continued to keep them for myself and just share them from time to time with my friends? Was there a way to "speak back to research" collectively, to melt theory and practice to transform both? I wanted to give my theoretical reflections a structure, but was it necessary to rent a room, get a properly working computer, stop roaming the streets at night to get up earlier and start writing something that has consistency, something I could show to others? "You want to become a researcher?! Go to the stiff world of conferences and so on?" Some of my friends were first shocked when I told them that I was considering doing a doctoral degree. "This just shows how unsustainable this lifestyle is: never having any cash, never being able to put oneself in a good condition to do something in a structured way. Because all the energy is spent elsewhere. If you get a scholarship, you could share your resources with others and it would give more stability to the people around you," others said. With a lot of fear of getting sucked into "the stiff world of conferences," I then decided that it was time for a partial return to academia. I decided that it would stay as only one amongst many projects and things I was doing. It was to never determine my life completely.

When docking into a university faculty, I "learned" to become a researcher – through re-learning ways of academic speaking and writing, through learning how to communicate. I was first convinced that this was necessary in order to place the contents and subject matters I was planning to weave together with multiple knowledges in the academic sphere of knowledge production. This soon turned into a battleground to expand the epistemological scope of scientific research. As a result, I needed to start unlearning myself as a researcher again.

I cautiously started to relate my political desires to theory. Unlearning, for me, means to melt theory and practice together. With this perspective, I find myself situated within committed and horizontal participatory research as one of the researched. I am not cleverer than them; I do not have a specialised overview of their situation and practices due to my university training, nor am I a specialised instigator of action. I am simply one of many, creating knowledge relationally. I am an involved storyteller who travels from situation to situation collecting insights and experiences and retelling them, re-assembling them with other storytellers.

The epistemological status of research findings based on localised and situated knowledges does not provide the basis for generalisable claims – yet it transcends the level of a purely local experience: "It is a valid claim that other people in similar situations might recognise similar experiences of their own within the text" (Genat, 2009, 114). Research findings are a structured collection of particular phenomena at particular moments in time and yet they are much more than that. When situated knowledges are put in relation to each other, their differences account of processes, contexts, mechanisms and dynamics in the social world as experienced by those who inhabit it. Within research methodologies that seek to break away from the positivist dictum of conceiving the validity of research findings as based on their generalisability, a triangulation of different and multiple experiences has offered an alternative conception of validation. However, in socially committed research, the validity of findings is not solely limited to the convergence of perspectives.

It includes the situatedness of an analysis in a political, social, global, personal context – a movement "from personal experiences to social theorising" (Cahill, 2010, 186).

A BRIEF OUTLINE OF THE HISTORY OF
PARTICIPATORY ACTION RESEARCH

Research that is committed to the practice of horizontal social transformation has a long history in the course of which it gave birth to methods for working with different and diverse situated knowledges. Feminist research, Indigenous paradigms as well as participatory action research (PAR) are all allies in doing horizontal research (cf. Potts and Brown, 2005, 281).

In what follows, I will give a brief outline of PAR and its different takes to later introduce my own approach to PAR – Horizontal Participatory Action Research. I am showing how PAR opens a window of opportunity for a transformation of research practices; I am showing why and where these windows of opportunity pop up and how it is possible to step through them. At the same time, this has something defensive: I am showing how and what I will be doing later on, when travelling through sites of dissent, is "proper" research – a research that sticks to a research methodology, a specific scientific approach that exists already, that has terms, concepts, mechanisms, rules that can be designated in the terms of royal science and is accepted in this field. It is some kind of *I can stay here because I have the right to be here* and at the same time I am clinging on to a research method because it structures my thoughts and findings, and allows me to follow them through, not to get lost in the deviations offered through multiple encounters.

Currently, PAR enjoys great popularity within some academic communities especially in the social sciences over the last two decades (Breda, 2015, 2). The academic trend of putting the terms "participatory" and "action" before research brought about co-optation. Not every project labelled PAR is "participatory" research in the sense that the objects of knowledge are admitted to actually co-shape the research process, develop the research questions, choose a methodology, or "action" research in the sense that the knowledge created in the research process is not made to be acted upon by participants (Potts and Brown, 2005, 281). There are many definitions of PAR. They are centred around the idea that researchers and participants undertake a collective, self-reflective inquiry to improve and understand their practices and the situations in which they find themselves aiming at their empowerment to move towards social justice (Baum, MacDougall, and Smith 2006, 854).

This idea of PAR has many origins and traditions which have been practised since the mid-1940s (Kindon, Pain and Kesby, 2007, 9). PAR is "multidisciplinary and multiform" (Swantz, 2008, 31) – hence no form of PAR can claim authenticity for itself. It has been described as an "orientation to inquiry" (Reason, 2004) rather than a ready-made research method. PAR only turns into a method when responding to a specific context, research question or problem with methodological innovation making every research process unique (Kindon, Pain and Kesby, 2007, 13). Knowing the history of its evolving forms and emphases as well as their contexts is important to appreciate PAR and its potential.

In 1946, Kurt Lewin coined the term "action research" for an iterative research process in which the researcher and the researched cyclically shift between action and reflection (Lewin, 1946). At that time, Lewin was a psychologist working in industrial settings in the United States where he focused on creating democratic workplaces and emphasised empowerment through education in the practice of inquiry. Lewin who was involved in struggles for social justice believed that research should lead to social action improving intergroup relationships (Breda, 2015, 7) through "social engineering," a planned method for social change (Lewin, 1946, 35). Today, many contemporary principles of organisational psychology such as collaborative workplace improvement processes draw from his ideas. Lewin's research participants, the industrial workers, those to be educated, are still conceived as objects of research, albeit ones that the researcher strives to meet, get to know and encounter. Lewin's cyclical research strategy consisting of action and reflection phases can be pictured as a movement going from the researcher's office to the group of concerned "subjects" to collect data in the field and then back to the office inside the researcher's institution to introduce the "subject's" opinion; then back to the field with a modified strategy for action, back to the office again, and so on (Montero, 2000, 132).

In the late 1950s, a participatory application of Lewin's action research was put into practice by the Colombian critical sociologist Orlando Fals Borda. Fals Borda refused to allow an epistemological distance between the "subjects" of his research and his own position and referred to himself as a "participatory researcher" (Fals Borda, 1985). He believed that a participatory way of doing research requires the researcher to be positioned within an emancipatory movement and thus requires a critical position towards conventional research methods demanding a separation from "research objects" (Fals Borda, 2013). Fals Borda himself worked within existing structures of autonomous institutions, aligned himself with progressive political parties and took part in civic resistance linking PAR to political activism

(Breda, 2015, 6). His political desire was to establish a society led by the proletariat and hence to be marked in its thinking by a "popular science" with the exploited being able to place their interpretations of reality against a science of the bourgeoisie (Fals Borda, 1979; Rahman, 2008, 38). According to Fals Borda, action research was to give the researched an ownership of the inquiries, of the entire process of knowledge creation, to enable an autonomous development of their analysis of reality (Fals Borda, 1987). He defined the process of such collective examinations as "a praxiological experiment. Theory and practice, thinking-persons and life-experiences (vivencias), how they interact, fuse, and react in the search for explanations to understand realities and promote social progress" (Fals Borda in Wicks et al., 2008, 12). As such, the practice of horizontal research processes is a political action against injustice and oppression, just as much as practical hands-on resistance to it:

> Forms and relationships of knowledge production should have as much, or even more, value than forms and relationships of material production. The elimination of exploitative patterns at the material or infrastructural level of a society does not assure, by itself, that the general system of exploitation has been destroyed; it becomes necessary to eliminate also the relationship governing the production of knowledge, production which tends to give ideological support to injustice, oppression and the destructive forces which characterize the modern world. (Fals Borda, 1987, 337)

Of course, such a radical rupture with the conventions of scientific research caused contention. Alain Tourain (Touraine, 1988) issued a warning against the politically committed researcher and Anthony Giddens argued against a radical subjectivism in which research subjects were seen as beings capable of understanding the conditions of their actions and called for a "recovery" from the everyday in the sociological direction of modern philosophy (Giddens, 1987, 52–72).

The investigación acción participativa[1] of the educator Paolo Freire who can be traced as the originator of PAR in Brazil (Breda, 2015, 5), was situated outside of scientific debates about subjectivism when it was first put into practice. Orlando Fals Broda and Paolo Freire were contemporaries and both engaged in PAR at the same time. Yet, Freire chose to focus on the practicalities of developing community-based research processes to enhance people's participation in the creation of knowledge and liberating social transformation. He was rather interested in the process of "conscientisation" than in scientific discourses. Conscientisation is, according to Freire, a liberating transformation in which marginalised people develop an awareness, a heightened consciousness, for the oppressive forces in their everyday life which then informs their political actions (Freire, 1972). Freire spent his time developing anti-oppressive and empowering forms of education with poor peasants unable to read. He referred to it as an education for critical consciousness which was also producing new knowledge, a new strategy to teach each other to read, to empower each other against being tricked into signing exploitative contracts. In English, this educational method is termed "popular education" or "critical education" (Breda, 2015). It provides a dialogical active approach to the participation of those subjects, who in conventional research are usually left voiceless creatures described by the researcher (Montero, 2000, 133). In Freire's inquiries, they are active members of an analysis concerning themselves and their environment (Freire, 1964). Freire's works craft PAR as a methodological approach that is deeply informed by movements for liberation and struggles for transformation.

In academic accounts of the development of PAR, Kurt Lewin, Orlando Fals Borda and Paolo Freire are often referred to as the initiators of PAR. Some authors divide their approaches to research into a Northern and a Southern strand of PAR with the Northern strand of PAR associated to Lewin being "less radical and less political" than Southern PAR (Breda, 2015, 6; see also Breda, 2015; Montero, 2000). In the early 1970s, PAR proliferated around the world, particularly in Africa, India and Latin America. The Canadian scholar Budd Hall launched the International Network of Participatory Research in 1977, inspired by Fals Borda and the Participatory Research of Marja Liisa Swantz's work with communities in the coastal region of Tanzania (Hall and Kidd, 1978, 5). The 1980s saw PAR gain ground in community development and international development contexts with Rapid and Participatory Rural Appraisal (RRA and PRA) approaches aiming to involve people as agents of their own development. In the 1990s, PAR continued to gain popularity blending with strands of Action Research and critical social science (Kindon et al., 2007, 10). Anisur Rahman and his colleagues worked with the Bhoomi Sena (Land Army), "a political movement for self-determination of a very oppressed tribal people in Palghar Taluk in Maharastra, India" (Rahman, 2008, 39), on developing decentralised and horizontal decision-making methods. Rahman identifies research projects within the Participatory Organizations of the Rural Poor (PORP) global programme as manifestations of PAR in India, the Philippines, Zimbabwe, Hungary and Bangladesh (ibid). In short, the complex history of PAR, its emergence over time from a broad range of fields and disciplines makes it difficult to define PAR as *one* method (Brydon-Miller, Greenwood and Maguire, 2003, 10). Sara Kindon, Rachel

Pain and Mike Kesby distinguish twenty-one "schools" currently engaging with various forms of PAR around the world (Kindon et al., 2007, 12).

Kindon, Pain and Kesby write:

> While there remain considerable differences, methodologically, epistemologically and politically between these strands, there is also overlap between the terms researchers use to communicate their action-oriented research practice, and distinctions are becoming increasingly blurred. (Kindon et al., 2007, 11)

In current research publications, the word "Participatory" when added to Action Research is often used to signal political commitment and a collaborative process of knowledge creation. While Fals Borda held the view that "Action" in PAR is self-evident and naturally included and tended to write it as P(A)R (cf. Fals Borda, 2006), after the critique of PAR's de-radicalisation (Cooke and Kothari, 2001a), in newer PAR publications the word "Action" serves as an important reminder that "it is the participants own activities which are meant to be informed by the ongoing inquiry" (Kindon et al., 2007, 11).

The increase of PAR projects that are being carried out all over the world brings an increasing amount of academic writings *about* PAR. Many of these writings seek to carve out, define and precise the methodological steps of PAR. Michelle Fine recalls a conversation with Paolo Freire: "He confided that a great sense of sadness overcame him when he realized that his radical teachings were being converted into lockstep curricula, checklists and structured principles" (Fine and Torre, 2008, 337). Because PAR is conceived as an interactive, collaborative process that is unique in each context, it is impossible to produce a fixed list of PAR characteristics or to give precise methodological instructions about how to do PAR. And yet, there are numerous examples of such lists of "key characteristics of PAR" as well as lists of "key stages in a typical PAR process" (cf. Kindon et al., 2007, 14–18).

Maritza Montero writes that "PAR is not:

- Sporadic consulting of specific groups of persons of interest for the researcher.
- Calling and gathering groups of people interested in a particular research topic to give them guidelines, telling them the way to do things, where to go, what to do, when to do it.
- Listening to people and then decide what one is going to keep and what one is going to leave out of research." (Montero, 2000, 136)

Participation in PAR is not a process that can be controlled by professionals.

Taken from an ontological perspective, PAR is based on the acceptance of the Other in her or his full difference as completely separate from the *I* which creates the possibility of dialogue. It is the acceptance of the separate character of the Other which permits to create relationships in which the Otherness of the *I* and its unique situatedness becomes fully accepted. The Other cannot exist outside the *I* – not by reduction but due to the complexity of intersubjective relations (Buber, 2008). In PAR, relations between different Others is a source of knowledge – PAR is based on relations (Grant et al., 2008, 489).

Full participation of an Other perspective entails that the Other is in a dialogical relation with oneself when choosing the object of research and directing attention to problems and issues. Participation in PAR is based on a utopian vision of horizontal social relations. PAR research practices are thus an attempt to move towards this utopian vision and not its full achievement. PAR thus never erases power inequities in the research process between different subject positions, it can only help to reduce these power inequities (cf. Grant et al., 2008, 491).

DIFFERENT TAKES ON PARTICIPATORY ACTION RESEARCH

Since PAR is participant-centred, made by its participants and only exists because of them, it is through their personal experiences, crises, problems, relations, that PAR sheds a light on broader social issues. In the process of PAR, these dynamics between and within participants manifest in "key interactional moments" – during collective action, in moments of reflection (Denzin, 1989, 15–17). The task of PAR as a research methodology is to tease out these moments from within everyday life. Hence, no two PAR projects are the same, because no two PAR researchers are the same. No two PAR projects will comply with the same rules and procedures, neither can their trajectories be the same or predicted in advance nor can relationships between participants be the same – just as there are different degrees and varieties of distance, leadership and participation (Reason and Bradbury, 2008b, 351–354).

In what follows, I will briefly sketch different takes on PAR by talking through different PAR projects to situate my own take on PAR as a Horizontal Participatory Action Research in relation to these different approaches. I will start with the different relations to participants and co-researchers that can be developed in projects of PAR.

"I congratulated the young people on developing definitions to frame the project and then offered two suggestions about how they might capitalize on 'participation.' I suggested that they be consistent in their attendance at group sessions and that they actively engage in project-related activities" (McIntyre, 2008, 16). Alice McIntyre writes about her PAR project with young people in an inner city public school in Bridgeport, Connecticut. I would like to use this PAR project as an example to illustrate how very clear divisions between the role of researcher and participants can still exist within PAR projects, and to illustrate the difficulty of deconstructing power relations in the collective creation of knowledge. Alice McIntyre presents her PAR project:

> In 1997, I was introduced to Mrs. Leslie, a sixth-grade teacher at the Blair School. She invited me to present my idea about a PAR project to her 24 African American, Jamaican, Puerto Rican, Dominican and Haitian students (12 boys and 12 girls). I told the young people a little bit about myself: my experiences growing up and teaching in Boston schools, my journey from classroom teaching in a university, and my desire to collaborate with them in exploring what it meant for them to live in a Bridgeport community. After a lively discussion about how we would engage that exploration, the young people decided to participate in the project. (Ibid., x)

The schoolchildren that McIntyre has chosen to work with will make a photography project to communicate their experiences. After the university scholar came into their classroom to speak to them, they decided to take part in an activity that they could co-shape. Yet, in this moment, which marks the beginning of the schoolchildren's participation in a PAR project, the horizontality of the knowledge creating process had already encountered limitations. Would the schoolchildren choose to communicate their experiences in this framework without an academic coming into their classroom and taking an agenda-setting subject position in this space? An adult speaking in a classroom is structurally a figure of authority that is given the space to define how and what is spoken about. No matter how inclusive and voluntary the ways of a researcher to invite the participants in "their project" to choose a means of self-expression are – because of structural power relations between a scientist and "their" participants, such a process will have its difficulties to remain free of domination disabling horizontality of knowledge creation. The same structural problem speaks from the pages of various PAR handbooks (Chevalier and Buckles, 2013; Danley and Ellison, 1999).

Unlike her young participants, McIntyre is not going around the community with a camera making pictures of her daily life. In her PAR project, it is assumed that she, the researcher, is so different from the participants that they cannot take action together: McIntyre does not have the same experience of growing up in a deprived area. Thus her relationship to the daily life in the community that she is working with is not explored with the same means than the one of her participants. Instead she takes on the role of directing, staging and structuring this process of exploration turning into an instigator.

If PAR researchers are to make "participants" engage on demand in an activity which is alternative or additional to their existing practice of self-expression, this has the dangerous potential to override already existing practices of collective knowledge creation in exchange for making these visible to the eyes of the scientist (Cooke and Kothari, 2001).

There are other PAR projects in which researcher and participants are one and the same, that is PAR processes in which action is taken *together*, not instigated by an outside agent. *Precarias a la Deriva* is a PAR project of women living in precarious conditions in Madrid. These women self-organised their research horizontally and in autonomy from any formal institution in the Women's squatted Social Centre *Eskalera Karakola*. There is not one academic researcher who instigated the project in approaching the women and proposing them to do research in a certain way or on a specific topic. For *Precarias a la Deriva* the need to research was born out of their individual and collective needs as economically disadvantaged women to develop strategies of cooperation, collective knowledge and subversion through a feminist analysis of precarity (Casas-Cortés and Cobarrubias, 2007). Every participant shares the experience of female precarity, every participant is a researcher (whether she is trained in university or not, engaged in other research projects or not). In *Precarias a la Deriva*, an unemployed university lecturer can be taught to do research by a waitress with a temp work contract – the research project is designed to create alliances amongst diverse precarities. *Precarias a la Deriva* use the participatory method of the drift to carry out their research: "a device to disconnect the crazed and routinised space-times, of the totally mobilized corporation-city and its 'population' (trips to work, shopping, daily itineraries in public transport) and as a path to rediscovery with new eyes, of the circuits of precarity" (Toret, 2006, 3). The drift is a form of action (women spreading out into the city of Madrid to collect testimonies of female precarity on buses, in post office queues . . .), followed by collective moments of reflection (when the women get together in a physical space such as the squatted Social Centre or later on also in the *Agencia de Asuntos Precarios* for encounters to invent mechanisms of grassroots mutualism).

Here the research process is shaped by a micropolitics of self-transformation, by feelings of anger, dissent, indignation, by a politics of becoming that leads people to take action for larger social change. New subjectivities are cultivated in the process of conscientisation and taking action. For Paolo Freire, action and reflection are inseparably united in PAR – human conscientisation brings a reflection on material reality and critical reflection is already action (Freire, 1972).

There are thus currents of PAR in which engaging in knowledge creation leads the researcher to engage in "messy situations" (Brydon-Miller et al., 2003, 12), invites him or her to become part of the world of scientific heretics, to encounter the beauty of chaos in knowledge creation and to learn to appreciate constant changes and transformations. Whilst some variants of PAR attempt to tame the mess, others embrace it to the fullest in transcending methodological limitations. Some variants of PAR (especially those drawing from Kurt Lewin's action research) are applicable only in an ordered context, such as the workplace or an institution, whilst other variants focus to give space for the possibility of self-transformation of diverse subject positions. At times two approaches labelled PAR can have opposite meanings in the process of research and it is important to situate oneself in a particular location within PAR, to speak about one's own scientific heresy and whether it allows oneself to step off the road and to give space for self-transformation and readiness to work with unpredictability.

Some PAR projects work with a predefined strategic focus on the engagement of the "key group of research participants" which is defined as the "participant focus group (. . .) to whom the project is highly significant" which is recruited before the beginning of the research process (Genat, 2009, 104–106). In such PAR projects, the identity of the participants is fixed and constructed by the researcher and initiator of the project who decides which issues are "highly significant" to which subject positions and thereby fails to horizontalise an important part of the collaborative knowledge creation. Such approaches stand in stark contrast to PAR projects in which the variety of participating subject positions is explored in the process of research. For example, Jenny Cameron and Katherine Gibson's PAR project "in a poststructuralist vein" explored the variety of economic identities in post-industrial Latrobe Valley, Australia, together with its inhabitants who were not preselected but simply came to the project by themselves from diverse backgrounds (Cameron and Gibson, 2005). Together they embarked on an expressive and surprising discovery of invisibilised and hidden economic practices, difficulties in everyday life, and creative solutions (ibid., 321–24).

It is equally important to acknowledge the considerable differences in methodological designs between research processes labelled as PAR. Some of them follow a rigorous methodological design that is neatly separating action stages from reflection stages and proceeds step by step, in an orderly fashion reproducing exactly the "lockstep curriculum" that saddened Paolo Freire (cf. Fine and Torre, 2008, 337).

In Jennifer Mullett's PAR project on women's health in mid-life, to take it as an example, the "objectives of the project" (Mullett, 2008, 366) are set before the researcher encounters the actual participants of the research process. Action and reflection are neatly cut in "stages" (ibid., 366; 368–69) – the interaction with participants is structured according to these stages; every stage is seen as a separate task that produces an outcome to be analysed later on. In the first stage, participants get "identified" by the researcher (ibid., 366); then in the final stage the women sing, perform and dance on a stage (ibid., 370). The research process of this PAR project has a schedule, a curriculum, to be accomplished to successfully present results. Research stages do not fertilise each other in the making, and the research process is not open to uncertainty, to a questioning of the intended outcome whilst it is being put together.

Other PAR approaches tend to think of action and reflection as inseparably intertwined in the research which is an uncontrollable process. This process peels away from pre-set structures and decentralises the places, times, people involved and settings in which decisions about the PAR project are made. Within such approaches, PAR does not only happen "in the four moments of action research, namely reflection, planning, action and observation" (Hughes and Seymour-Rolls, 2000). The research happens all the time in real life without getting structured into a research programme. Hughes and Seymour-Rolls write that "reflection in PAR is that moment where the research participants examine and construct, then evaluate and reconstruct their concerns (. . .). Action happens when the Plan is put into place and the hoped for improvement to the social situation occur. This action will be deliberate and strategic [citations removed]" (ibid.). Moments of reflection do not have to be a product of a research process which defines "a PAR project only as research when proper scientific methods are used to collect and examine data" (ibid.). Such a conception of PAR would still assume the existence of one legitimate "proper" recipe for knowledge creation and thus fails to be horizontally inclusive to different knowledges. Instead, moments of reflection can take place in all kinds of situations *related* to the research process. In a horizontal approach to PAR, the task is to discover, develop and experiment with suitable methods to include, make visible and value these moments of reflection. Action can happen spontaneously in between reflections, planning processes and observation. It may interrupt these phases, reorient them, stop them, mix the spirals or cycles of PAR, and the plan for the action may change in the course of action. It is not surprising that conceptions of PAR that take the shape of a lockstep curriculum (cycle one, step one: reflection – the group and its thematic concern is identified; step two: plan – the group plan to undertake an examination of the thematic concern and the social situation, in order to define and describe both accurately; step three and four: action and observation – the plan is put into action and the group collects their observations to reconvene; cycle two, step one: . . .) are mostly applied to environments with formalised social relations in institutionalised contexts such as workplaces. Here, a "large number of staff [are] dissatisfied with the roster" can be identified as research participants. The aim that is attributed to them is to develop a better roster as a successful PAR outcome (cf. ibid., table 2). This entails a pre-conceived definition of their empowerment: being empowered means to be able to develop a better roster. The staff is not given the opportunity to co-develop or question this definition of their empowerment in the workplace and the underlying reasons for being dissatisfied at one's workplace are not explored in depth.

In other currents of PAR the task is, in contrast, not to occupy a vanguard position that claims to have the unique capacity to improve a situation but to be attentive to transformations, to provide space for critical self-reflection within the struggle for empowerment that it is involved in. Accordingly, Kemmis and McTaggart define the "success" of a PAR project by the transformative, empowering processes that it triggers within participants – not by the accomplishment of a fixed curriculum of phases, steps and cycles with scientific methods that takes place independently of participant's inner individual evolvement (Kemmis and McTaggart, 2007, 277).

CO-RESEARCHERS, PARTICIPANTS AND MESSY SITUATIONS IN A HORIZONTAL PARTICIPATORY ACTION RESEARCH

How is my horizontal approach to PAR situated within these different takes on PAR and what does this situatedness imply for my research practice? When working with post-representative subject positions outside of institutional contexts, facing complex, multi-causal social problems, it is impossible to define a fixed group of co-researchers because relationships are tied to networked relations of affinity. Richard Day defines relationships of affinity as "non-universalizing, non-hierarchical, non-coercive relationships based on mutual aid and shared ethical commitments" (Day, 2005, 9). Each participant's affinity structure is different and yet affinity is a mutual relationship between people. By definition, relationships of affinity take the form of horizontal networks without a core or unified centre (ibid.). As such, a horizontal

PAR group is a node in the network of relations coming together in the PAR project.

My co-researchers are my friends and at the same time they are more than that. We share a political desire for the research questions raised in this project: How can we create knowledge horizontally? How can we create and maintain sites of dissent?

What is it that transforms me and, for example, all those friends of mine who were speaking in the previous chapter into *co-researchers*?

We share a praxis that brings us to co-create many different situations where we find each other sharing action and reflection: next to each other on a demonstration, next to each other in a discussions about horizontal knowledge creation in a living room; and our affinity between each other grows as we get to know each other's perspectives and points of view.

My friends give me feedback on my texts. They have read this text and helped to reshape it, rewrite and rework it. In everyday life we are inviting each other to participate in practices of autonomous social movements whilst at the same time being involved in different types of reflection *about* autonomous social movement practices. Some of these actions and reflections are part of this research process. Actions are happening independently of this PAR project and not only *because* of it. I find my co-researchers in their involvement in contentious spatial practices of autonomous social movements, not in identifying them as a specific social identity that I want to engage with for the sake of the PAR project.

But what about the *participants* of this research?

This PAR engages with people in different localities – different sites of dissent all over Europe. Yet, not all of these people are co-researchers. Participants of this PAR project might be the people who are doing the bar in an autonomous cultural centre, they might engage with the co-researchers in reflections on spatial practices of autonomous social movements, they might have taught us important things and we might also share specific political practices or articulations with research participants. Although they participate in co-shaping the research process at certain points, participants are different from co-researchers in that they do not feel part of all the different and overlapping research phases that this specific PAR project is composed of.

Whilst participants join the research process for specific moments, co-researchers are a node in the network of affinities that came together over the research process – and disassembled again.

Relationships of affinity are always in the process of becoming, always subjected to transformation through experience. Thus also the relationships of affinity that structure this group of co-researchers and their participation might transform during the process of research and people's relationship to this PAR project might change: Some co-researchers can turn into participants as they disengage from collective reflection processes at a certain point, for personal or other reasons; participants who have been contributing to the research process might turn into co-researchers in the course of action as our affinities grow. And this is exactly what happened.

Participants and co-researchers will appear as protagonists of the PAR. Some of them have started to speak in the previous chapters already and took part in theoretical reflections. The following schematic figure explains how the voices of co-researchers and participants are placed in the text. I have also included an appendix of all participants and co-researchers of this PAR project including myself.

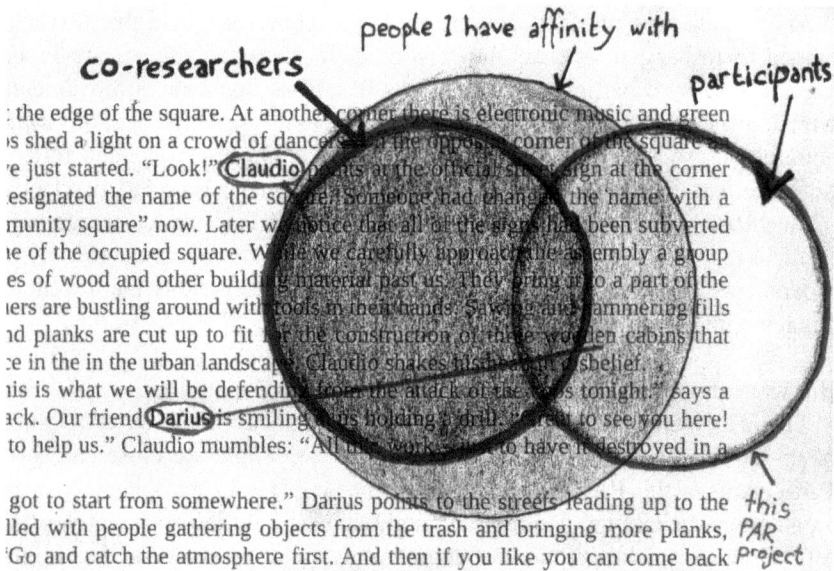

Figure 3.1   Participants and Co-Researchers. *Source*: Author's own.

"We hold that participatory action research is best conceptualized in collaborative terms. Participatory action research is itself a social – and educational – process" (Kemmis and McTaggart, 2007, 277). PAR is not facilitating, ordering or cleaning up messy relational knowledge creation, but learning to empower oneself with others in a messy social situation.

When PAR is not imposing a fixed number of steps in a fixed sequence but tracing, discovering and co-shaping the entangled process of relational knowledge creation and its obscure relationship to practices – whilst carefully paying attention to what we have learned in the process – it buys in to the beauty of chaos (Brydon-Miller et al., 2003). Horizontal PAR is letting participants discover methods that are suitable to their situation. Its research process is flexible and open enough to combine them and to put them into a dialogue with each other. At the same time, it abandons to control and shape a research curriculum and turns into a messy process.

The challenge of dealing with a messy research process is not unique to the method of horizontal PAR, yet it is one of its most important challenges: the mess appears in actions, in reflections, in the construction of relationships, in the direction of the research process.

How to know when one is actually doing *research*, being situated within an interrelated mess of relations, processes and events as a participatory action researcher? The *take-off moment* for when daily life becomes horizontal PAR can only be determined in hindsight, when it becomes possible to identify specific moments or interactions after which it was clear that collective experiences are now elements of a PAR process. Take-off moments might take very different shapes: Sometimes a take-off moment can be made very explicit in a conversation; sometimes it might be during a preparation meeting for a political action that decisions entail practices that form into a horizontal PAR.

Getting into a mess of processes, relations and differences, horizontal PAR turns into a chaotic, opaque method that operates on the border of "royal science" and "nomad science" (Deleuze and Guattari, 2010). In operating through a relational "logic of science" based on association and collective imagination, it moves towards nomad science: Nobody can tell what is actually happening, everything takes place at once and there is no master plan of how to bring everything back together (Deleuze, 1990; Deleuze and Guattari, 2013). Every master plan will fail and only convey a fraction of what really happened. As a research method, horizontal PAR can at the same time stay in the field of royal science. It can have a research design if someone is taking on the task of bringing order into the research process at a point in the course of the research. It can be structured, divided into sections, chapters and steps. It can then appear much more ordered and structured than it actually was in the course of the research, observation, action and reflection.

This tension on the borderzone of royal science and nomad science turns horizontal PAR into a methodological heresy, a scientific provocation. In this horizontal PAR, the experience that it was all a chaotic mess of travelling to places, losing things, getting into eventualities, ending up living somewhere and not knowing for how long, will be barely visible on the pages. Hence uncovering the messiness of its making is one of the loopholes to nomad science. Structuring, ordering, presenting and writing about these experiences is a permeable border to royal science.

Participation is sharing the experience of defending a house or a forest or an occupied territory, it is my friends and companions reflecting on actions and choosing actions to reflect on, taking place during discussions, when the research process is shaped. *Action*, this is involvement in contentious spatial practices of autonomous social movements – having an assembly, building, maintaining, or contributing to the existence of a site of dissent with practices, with observations, with plans and ideas, or other forms of contributions. *Research* is the collaborative free-floating process of bringing all this together: It is my self-reflection, the reflections of those involved in action, collective reflections of varying collectives, groups, encounters, that congregate in the action or find each other in relations of affinity or shared political desires. Research – this is all of us learning by doing and getting conscious of the process of relational knowledge creation. It takes place in my journal that I keep of various contentious spatial practices; and also when my friends are talking to me about my research activity; research is the knowledge I share, evaluate and conceive with my co-researchers as well as all the elements of its process of becoming.

Borderthinking – this is an attempt to settle on the border of royal science and nomad science, however temporarily. The border is that space in which royal science is almost not royal science anymore and nomad science has almost ceased to be nomad science but is just about to become something else. In this borderzone, there is not one clear methodological or totally intuitive way of thinking, researching and learning that leads to the right or to better results.

Borderthinking allows broadening the epistemological horizon in a way that it reaches beyond the practices of royal science (such as fulfilling a productive and logical lockstep curriculum of research phases), as well as beyond the epistemological scope of nomad science (as in: doing more than creating knowledge in spontaneous encounters, during the practices that are under investigation, going beyond the creation of a random patchwork of different findings).

Borderthinking in research is thus not (only) about finding a combination of practices of royal science and nomad science that 'works' but also about creating (sometimes) dysfunctional incoherences that provoke further learning, development and experimentation.

Borderthinking thus does not aim at creating ways of producing knowledge that are better or more efficient, it does not aim at presenting itself as a final, perfect development of epistemological practice, but as a research practice which can be developed further from multiple perspectives. Here, borderthinking aims at inaugurating new ways of collective learning on sites of dissent about the articulation of political desire as well as at treading new paths in researching dissent in a way which includes the researched.

BORDERTHINKING THE RESEARCH

This section places the focus on the dysfunctional incoherences in the encounter of royal science and nomad science. The tension of dwelling in the border zone between royal science and nomad science will be audible in my voice being responsive to how knowledge is created in nomad science on the one hand, and on the other hand also succumbing to the techniques of royal science in attempting to craft a methodological design.

To gain an understanding of the kind of dissent that is articulated through contentious spatial practices, to be able to understand the utopian social vision, that takes shape through a politics of direct action, it is necessary to be able to develop a broad vision of the phenomenon. That is, it is necessary to be able to see many of its ways of turning into material reality, the plethora of its forms.

What kinds of phenomena are going to be compared, and along which criteria are they selected? Whenever I started speaking about my questions with friends and accomplices during the research, I was left alone with my thoughts relatively soon.

Me: "If we compare different sites of dissent, we first have to find out in what they are different. Are they different because they are squatted or rented, or are they different because they are directed something concrete, like a mining project, or are they different because people live there full time? Then we would have to define what 'living full time' means. Or should we maybe construct a grid of comparison that is simply based on the visible, tangible, perceivable characteristics of the different sites of dissent . . . ? Like their geographical size and whether they take form in the urban material tissue or in fields and forests?"

Gino: "Just take everything that is a site of dissent. If it is described in the research, then people know what it is."

Me: "But how do we know if 'it' is a site of dissent? We need to think about how we turn 'site of dissent' into something we can use to create units for the comparison."

Gino: "I think this is not very interesting. And I don't really see why we need to build some kind of comparative methodological design that you mentioned earlier. You have already tried to explain it and I felt extremely bored."

Although I did not use the scientific words like "to operationalise" sites of dissent when trying to win over those I was seeing as research companions to think with me about a methodological design, my researcher's voice did not succeed in creating a participatory dimension of the narrative at this point.

Convinced of the necessity to be able to articulate what a site of dissent actually is, and to compare many of its different forms of materialisations in order to learn about the social vision that is articulated through them, I was left alone with this task. It would be possibly correct to say, that my inability to find the words that would inspire other people to participate in this part of the research bears the blame. Yet, a perfectly horizontal research would possibly not rely on the responsibility of individuals to motivate and inspire others but start as a collective project from the very conception of its idea. On the other hand, the conception and sharing of an idea relies on individuals being capable to transmit their thoughts to other individuals in a way that these could be picked up and developed further.

I have thus continued alone to craft a comparative analysis of different sites of dissent. In doing so, I have reproduced elements of royal science to structure the research in a way that allows us to explore the differences and similarities of sites of dissent in depth.

This decision was accompanied by many doubts: Am I being exclusive because my voice is left alone in this part just a voice of an individualised researcher? Have I been inviting co-researchers into "my" research project at this point and overriding other possibilities to structure the material? Why was leaving my field notes unstructured not also a solution? It was not a solution because "the material" did not exist as such. It is a composition of field notes in my own hurried handwriting, notes that someone typed up leaving comments, recordings of discussion without date, memory notes on flyers and numerous occasions on which I had to ask co-researchers: "Do you remember what we said about . . . ?"

What I identified as "material" from the field needed a lot of work to become presentable as a body of stories collected with the dissipated, fluctuating and explorative techniques of nomad science.

"I am not interested in keeping an overview. You have to structure it yourself somehow. I think you are the only one to whom it matters," said Ian, grinning at me.

I decided to bring the strong aspects of royal science into play: *to arrange the comparison of field-work material in a way that permits a deep analysis of reasons for differences and similarities*, in order to combine it with the strength of nomad science which lies in the way the material was gathered: *diving into the field in creating encounters between participants of the research, combining their knowledge in situative flows of storytelling and discussions.*

"Ok, what about this: Sites of dissent are the, however temporary, concrete places born from the exercise of contentious spatial practices of autonomous social movements. They are contradictory spaces that are never fully free, never fully autonomous, because they exist as physical spaces within a geographical materiality that they oppose. And they are composed of multiple micro-movements challenging the socio-spatial order," I said to Ian.

Ian: "If you want . . . "
Me: "They can be big and small: large squatted territories or neighbourhoods or small gardens of only a few square metres, a few rented rooms for a self-managed cafe. They can be an urban building or setting or an occupied forest, a camp in a field. They can be temporary settlements or actions like tent villages or demonstrations or they can be permanent, inhabited structures, homes of many people. . . . What else is there to add?"
Ian: "I think that's it. I will go out now. You can come with me if you want – or stay here with your computer."

I decided to "stay here" and to simply take the exterior material appearance of sites of dissent (large or small, temporary or permanent, urban or rural setting) as a comparative starting point to create a structure first.

"Why do we need to *compare* sites of dissent?" Ian shouted at me when he was half out of the door.

"To be able to make a comparison between *different* sites of dissent, to find out about the differences that exist between them – as well as about the similarities in their articulation of political desire."

Ian: "I think this can be quite rigid. You would get stuck in a rigid methodological approach and miss out on the reality on sites of dissent. And this reality cannot be squeezed into a box." The door shut and I continued to write:

Intentional methodological thinking can be both – a strength and a weakness when studying social movements. Indeed as Haiven and Khasnabish wrote in *The Radical Imagination*, a book that contains an account of a collective research process: "Methodological thinking is a weakness because it often leads to mechanical patterns and approaches to exploring social realities, approaches that are often bound up with the hubris of the researcher who, imagining him- or herself as situated outside of history and society, uses sophisticated tools to 'look in.' The strength of a focus on method lies in a more thorough and systematic way of putting the pieces of the world together" (2014, 209–10). I want to put intentional methodological thinking at the service of this purpose and turn it into a strength of this research carried out on the border of royal and nomad science. To develop a "systematic way of putting the pieces of the world together," I will use a comparative methodological design.

To compare spatial practices of autonomous social movements in different and specific sites of dissent, it is necessary to find reasons for differences and similarities within different types of sites of dissent. Materiality of sites of dissent, the imaginaries running through them as well as the spatial agency within them are heterogeneous and diverse due to their socio-spatial situatedness. It would be possible to find an infinite number of distinctions of differences within sites of dissent. Yet, comparing different entities with each other is such an intrinsic part of knowledge creation that it cannot be methodologically classified, as Faure argued (Faure, 1994). Nevertheless, to make an in-depth comparison between a larger number of different entities a structured approach is necessary. To facilitate the comparison, I will thus work with three axes of distinction of sites of dissent. I will assimilate to the practices of royal science and use its vocabulary: axes of distinction, sets of case studies . . . after our discussions with Gino, Felippa, Ian, Janinka, Angelo and Brian, these words have become alien objects and it requires a lot of borderthinking to imagine them in relation to lived practices.

As shown in figure 3.2, the three axes of distinction in my methodological design of case studies run along the dimensions of urban/rural, temporary/permanent and concentrated/large-scale sites of dissent.

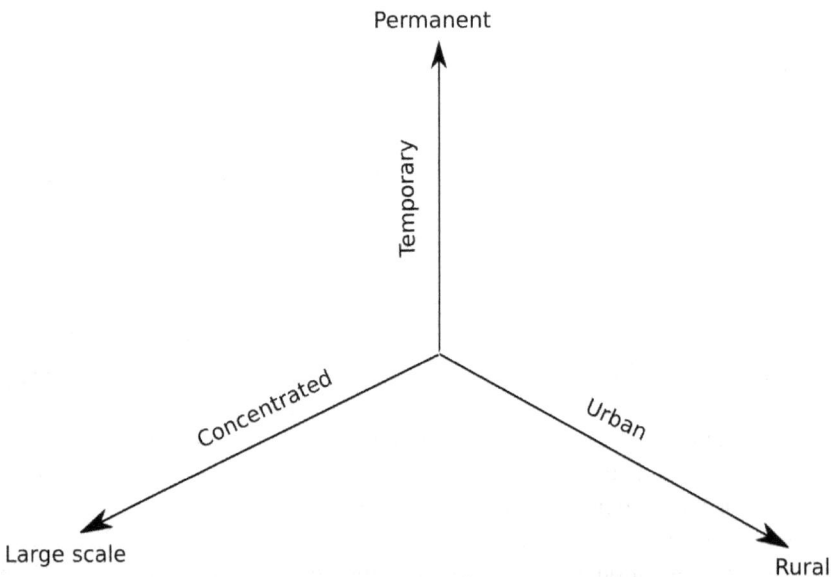

Figure 3.2   Three Axes of Distinction for Case Studies. *Source*: Author's own.

The combination of each end point of an axis with every other end point on the other two axes results in eight sets of case studies.

The methodological design thus structures the research as a comparative analysis of autonomous social movement's spatial practices: case studies of sites of dissent are situated on different ends along three axes of distinction. The choice of these axes aims at taking into account the structure of the environment of spatial practices (urban/rural) as well as their orientation on a temporal (temporary/permanent) and territorial (large-scale/concentrated) perspective.

The three axes of distinction are not conceived as binary divisions classifying sites of dissent but as a continuum where a particular site of dissent can be situated closer or further away from an imagined extreme point.

In the logic of royal science, the methodological design facilitates an exhaustive comparison: a *Most Different Systems Design* in the eight sets of case studies and a *Most Similar Systems Design* within the distinct sets of case studies. In royal science, a Most Similar Systems Design (MSSD) is used to compare similar cases assuming that the more similarities there are amongst the cases, the more it should be possible to find the factors that are responsible for differences between them. A Most Different Systems Design (MDSD) compares as contrasting cases as possible in seeking to find reasons for their similarities. In comparative research, MSSD and MDSD are most effective when combined together (Anckar, 2008).

When comparing spatial practices on sites of dissent that are within the same set of case studies, such as urban/temporary/concentrated for example, we can be particularly attentive to why spatial practices that we discover are nevertheless different from each other.

As Ian noticed, the reality on sites of dissent cannot be squeezed in a box. Not even with a methodological design. Sites of dissent are dynamic and constantly in motion, just like sociopolitical conflicts arise and lose intensity, transform and adapt to their context. My gaze is partial, fragmented, situated and directed by personal movements, physical movements, epistemological movements. The reality that I am trying "to squeeze in a box" is deboarding this box as there is no singular all-encompassing movement of putting-it-into-a-box but rather many chaotic journeys of different kinds between sites of dissent and research design, between nomad science and royal science. figure 3.3 is illustrating these journeys of research with which I attempted to gather something that could figure as "case studies" for a research design. The arrows of movement are figurative – they do not point at specific geographical locations.

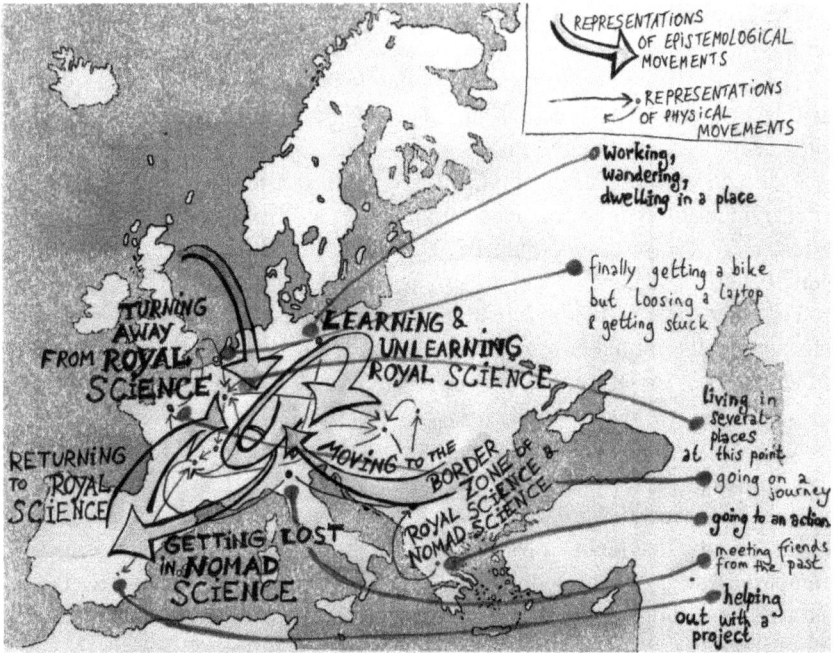

Figure 3.3 Journeys of Research. *Source*: Author's own.

How am I performing this movement of collection of case studies and what counts as case studies?

All case studies are located on the grid of urban/rural, temporary/permanent and concentrated/large-scale sites of dissent. I have a relationship and a history with all of these sites of dissent, but these relationships are varied. I know some of them much better than others. In some of them, I have been involved for a long time and there are others I have just visited for a few days. Some experiences of sites of dissent have been more intense than others. These differences are weighted out as much as possible in combining several case studies in one set of comparison.

Travelling between nomad science and royal science *site of dissent* gets translated into *story* and stories translate into *case studies*. The story of a site of dissent is thus the method of translation, the method of dwelling in the border zone. Each story is told with the voices of those who create and maintain the borders, rhythms, imaginaries of a site of dissent. It also contains descriptions of situations and spatial arrangements, barricades and open doors.

For the social movement scholar Eric Selbin the telling and retelling of stories constitutes a shared experiential structure which visibilises relational processes of transformation. Stories are narrative genealogical tracings of this transformation (Selbin, 2010, 46). Selbin contends that "a systematic return of stories to social science methodology" would help to make collective and horizontal knowledge creation of social movements articulating sociopolitical dissent more visible when doing research (ibid., 3). Stories are capable of illustrating affective relationships and transport emotional reactions of protagonists to the reader of the story.

"The story of one cannot be told without unfolding the story of many," writes Devi Dee Mucina about the story as a research method (Mucina, 2011, 1). The speed and intensity of a story can vary just like the style of the narration and the voice of the storyteller – all this allows to perceive more than the sum of the words composing the story. Storytelling thus allows for the "translation" of affective experiences which are key for the prefigurative political practices of autonomous social movements (Motta, 2013b).

Each of the stories that compose the next chapter will be an account of the horizontal PAR process that took place on a site of dissent. It will be composed of field notes, memories and discussions gathered together with a different composition of co-researchers and participants each time. In every case, we chose a suitable method for doing research in the situation on a specific site of dissent. In some cases I was doing research alone, using the method of psychogeographic wandering (dérive) whilst in other cases I was part of a group of co-researchers that chose the method of a collective drift to create knowledge about a site of dissent (just to give examples).

The following chapter is an invitation to embark on a journey through different sites of dissent. It is structured in five cycles of travel, reflection and encounters. I will narrate two of these cycles of journeys in full length to invite readers to a rural action camp against a planned gold extraction site, to an occupied square, to a tiny social centre and several other places to dive into the practices on these sites of dissent. When going into these sites of dissent I will get very close to the logic of nomad science and transgress the border of royal science in developing the voice of a storyteller, one of many on the sites. I will just briefly sum up the other three cycles of journey to give an idea about the structure and extensiveness of the comparative analysis and of the places it has taken me to inbetween.

Figure 3.4 Artwork by Kata. *Source*: Author's own.

Chapter 4

Sites of Dissent

FIRST CYCLE OF JOURNEYS: MOVEMENTS, PATTERNS AND SCATTERED COMPONENTS

The first cycle of journeys runs through a rural action camp against a planned gold extraction site, through an anti-racist camp on a squatted wasteland, through two weeks of a rebellious convergence against a summit in the metropolis, through urban unrests around an occupied square and through reflections on riots after the eviction of a social centre. The five case studies presented in the first cycle of journeys are all temporary sites of dissent. They have either been planned as a temporary gathering (as it was the case for the two camps and the convergence) or consisted of spatial practices that could only be sustained for a short duration of time.

The two camps and the convergence were intentionally designed for a fixed duration of time: a programme of events and the availability of a basic infrastructure had an end date that was set in advance. Kitchen collectives had been asked to cook meals, sleeping spaces had been provided for a large group of people only up to a date that was communicated in advance. As for the occupied square and story about the evicted social centre, the contentious spatial practices were carried out only for a short duration of time. The positioning of these five sites of dissent on the continuum between urban and rural locates the camp against the gold mine clearly as a temporary rural site of dissent, whilst the four remaining ones are urban sites of dissent. Except for the camp on a squatted wasteland, all of them have taken place in city centres. The camp on the squatted wasteland was located in an urban district that was not exactly central but still within the city which facilitated a constant movement between the site of dissent and the city centre (for protest actions and demonstrations).

Collective Conclusions

My memories of the action camp start with the journey that Brian, Angelo and I made on our bikes to get to its rural location. After hours of cycling through the countryside, something that looks like a car park attracts our attention. Next to some random rural road in a depopulated area, we see suddenly lots of caravans, buses with stickers and some really old trashy cars. Brian, Angelo and I instantly know that this is the entrance to the place that we have been looking for. A woman with courageously styled hair smiles at us and a young person standing next to a bus says "Hi!" as if we had met before. Brian, Angelo and I then know that we had finally joined the people we wanted to be with. We have found them on a meadow in the spacious scenery of rural fields.

The narrow parking corridor leads us to the corner of a little hand-made village: tents – big and small, banners, sculptures, a wooden stage and people bustling around. Everything is in motion – too many micro-movements to capture at one glance.

The landscape of our city where we came from is much more still than this: We are used to seeing almost empty streets where nothing is happening except for the traffic of cars. Here the cars stand still and the people move. We start to make a move as well and become part of the picture. One of the first tents near the only access to the camp has a sign: "Info Tent." There are several people behind a desk and lots of leaflets, hand-written posters with announcements and stickers. "Hey, we just arrived. Is there something we should know? Where can we set up our tents?" It is the right place to ask these questions – the action camp's welcome area for new arrivals like us.

In the area where the action camp took place, an international company is planning a gold mine. Upon arrival, my friends and i heard that this company had put pressure on local farmers not to let the protesters camp on their fields located near the mine. The planned extraction of 400 tonnes of gold requires the company to flatten three mountain tops, destroy one of the last natural reserves in the region, expropriate and re-settle hundreds of families, and leave behind a waste lake of 215 million cubic metres of dammed water containing cyanide – a toxic chemical commonly used in the process of gold extraction. The camp protest camp takes place to contest these projects of environmental destruction.

We set up our tents and spend the next days within the round shape of the camp between the workshop tents, the kitchen and child play area, the big meeting tent, information and welcome tent and at the bar, and within a "neighbourhood" of camp participants who have their tents next to each other and get collectively involved in decision-making processes and reproductive tasks in the camp. The area where we perform our movements during these days is maybe only as big as a farmhouse. Workshops and political discussions are taking place every day and when we are tired of processing new information or reflecting, we help in the kitchen, climb a tree, speak to other people, or enjoy the vegan meal prepared by the big kitchen collective that came to support the camp. Lots of affinities get created during these days through collective decision-making, discussions and simply getting to know each other.

On the last day of the camp Angelo, Brian and I are already cycling back home. It is the day after the "action day." Demonstrations, sit-ins, lock-ons, trespassing and some arrests on the ground of the planned gold mine – all this had happened yesterday. It is still very fresh in our memory. After a few hours of cycling, we take a break and start talking about what had happened in the camp and outside of it. During this break, a take-off moment of our collective reflection takes place: still high on adrenaline, me and my friends start to share our observations.

Angelo: "Now it feels like we are coming out of a nest."

Brian: "A nest?"

Angelo: "Yes, a place that is safe, where there's food all the time and showers – all you need to have head-space to focus on building relationships with the other people in the nest. And at the end of the breeding time, all collective energy erupts out into the world and directs itself against something we all wanted to oppose."

Me: "Maybe you are right: when we first came here, I had no clue what could happen on the action day. I did not know what action I was ready to do in this context and with whom. Having spent so much time with the people in the camp, and especially with you two, I felt empowered to act, to be part of a protest action. Because I became convinced of the fact that there is some kind of collective support structure behind me – people who organise lawyers, who fetch other people from prison if they have been arrested, people who give information to the rest of the camp at 3:00 a.m. in the morning, all this."

Angelo: "And also knowing what the others think. I mean: you can never know what *all* the others in the camp think, but the workshops provided me with an idea of who these people are. We had space to articulate our ideas there, to share what it means to be against environmental destruction for us personally – and to recognise ourselves in the motives and ways of rationalising of other people. This helped to build relationships based on political affinity with some people."

Brian: "If you are going to write something about this, then you should mention how the camp turned into an organism at some point. I don't really know when this happened. Maybe it happens for different people at different points in time. All I know is that yesterday night, on the last night of the camp, we were all one – all one organism. Remember how everyone who was back from actions or who was waiting for their friends was sitting in the dark near the info tent? Nobody wanted to sleep because we knew there are still people out there. And every time a different person took the microphone to speak to the camp. There were no organisers, just different people giving updates on the protest situation at the gold mine; if the police was still there or not; how many arrests were made . . . I observed that all the different people who used the mic said 'we' when they spoke about people from the camp."

Having left the camp in the very early morning hours after the action day, we cycle another 50 kilometres before we decide to put our tent down near a little creek. Angelo had asked us to leave early because he feared that the police might raid the camp in the last night. He said that this thought made him too excited and nervous to sleep anyway. Brian and I had agreed in thinking that we wanted to take good care of each other and to avoid stressful situations in each one of us where possible.

Now, after cycling we are all dead tired. Brian takes a bottle of wine out of his backpack with a conspirational smile.

"Relax and talk. What's on your minds? I see you are still in the protest camp with your thoughts. Let's share our reflections about what we just experienced together. I feel much closer to both of you after this experience. I want to continue thinking and acting with you," he says.

Me: "Something you have said before, Brian, made me think a lot. You said it was important to trace how we became an organism through the camp or because of the camp."

Brian: "Ok, an organism in the sense that we reproduce ourselves as what we are together. It is not only the simple fact that we all cook together and give donations for buying new ingredients. It is more about the way how the camp works – that everyone can participate in it: even in the more complicated tasks like sharing information! If you look at the info tent, you notice that it is all the time different people. Everyone can take the megaphone and make announcements, everyone can organise a workshop. There is not one person who is responsible – people seem to know that we are all responsible to the same degree, that this is all DIY."

Angelo: "If you say that we were all one organism, it is important to point out that we are not a peaceful organism that fits well into its surroundings. We are at war with what is around us. This is why the camp was in this specific spot near the gold mine. But we also fight within ourselves. Certainly there are many great people in the camp and we try to have no leaders who tell us what to do, but there are still conflicts and hierarchies. A lot of conflicts!"

Brian: "Like the anonymous discussion about the effects of sexual violence that people had with markers on the wall of the compost toilet?"

Me: "Or like when some people got angry because they did not want people from the political party of the Greens to participate in one of the assemblies?"

Angelo: "Yes, like this. But still – when people come together to have these fights, it seems worth it – because it is worth it to fight together with these people and to get along well with each other. So we need to have those fights to make it even better next time. After all, this camp is not about the action at the gold mine but about forming new collectivities that are ready to fight against environmental destruction."

Square Memories

"We come back to the square!"

"We meet at the square!"

These shouts cut through the soundscape of the demonstration and ring in our ears. Claudio and I exchange glances and decide to follow that part of the demonstration which will leave the authorised route. The square in the city centre that is occupied since almost two months now will be our point of reference. Cops have been lining along the sides of the demonstration since its departure. They will try to prevent us from walking our own route. There will be confrontations and it is unclear whether the demonstration will really arrive at the square. The city is under voltage: since the government announced to enact an unpopular law about housing rights, spontaneous demonstrations, riots and the occupation of a square shook daily urban life regularly. Claudio and I had hitchhiked several hundred kilometres to be here for this moment: The people occupying the little square right in the city centre at the crossroads of three large streets had announced not to leave their encampment for the night.

The part of the demonstration that had spontaneously decided to draw its own route across the city towards the occupied square gets dispersed and regroups several times, runs through clouds of tear gas whilst singing and shouting about the people's rights to the city.

At nightfall, Claudio and I arrive at one of the edges of the occupied square. I hear drum beats and I see a fire show just beginning on one of the corners of the square. At another corner there is electronic music and green and blue blinking lamps shed a light on a crowd of dancers. On the opposite corner of the square, an assembly seems to have just started. "Look!" Claudio points at the official street sign at the corner of the road that had designated the name of the square. Someone had changed the name with a stencil – it is the *Community Square* now. Later, we notice that all of the signs had been subverted to display the new name of the occupied square. Whilst we carefully approach the assembly, a group of people drags big piles of wood and other building material past us. They bring it to a part of the square where many others are bustling around with tools in their hands. Sawing and hammering fills the air here. Boards and planks are cut up to fit for the construction of three wooden cabins that seem totally out of place in the urban landscape. Claudio shakes his head in disbelief.

"Don't be so sceptical," says an amused familiar voice in our back. Our friend Darius is smiling at us holding a drill. "Great to see you here!" Darius says and Claudio mumbles quietly in response: "All this work – just to have it destroyed in a few hours by cops."

"Probably. But you've got to start from somewhere." Darius points to the streets leading up to the square – they are all filled with people gathering objects from the trash and bringing more planks, boards and furniture. "Go and catch the atmosphere first if you have just arrived," he suggests.

The tiny square is extremely crowded. Banners are covering the statue in the middle: "This is a space of resistance!" The surroundings are covered in paint: pictures on benches, spray paint on walls. Claudio and I walk past a little library and a big canteen where food is given out for free. The sides of the square that are separating it from the road are filled with all kinds of stalls lined up next to each other – student groups, trade unions, artists are displaying books and pamphlets. Even a team of lawyers has installed a tent on one corner of the square. "Let's join the assembly," I suggest to Claudio and we both sit down on the ground like about two hundred other people. Different people take turns speaking through a megaphone. If somebody wants to say something they get up and start queuing to wait for their turn to speak. The people sitting on the ground make signs with their hands if they agree with something that one of the speakers says. This is how it is visible whether a suggestion finds approval or not. The assembly takes place every evening.

One day later, Darius, Claudio and I are sitting in a tiny apartment that Darius is renting. The square has been evicted last night. Only a pile of trash reminds of the life of the *Community Square* that had attempted to settle here. The site of dissent had been destroyed by the riot police and the occupiers had been forced to leave by clouds of tear gas and police batons. The square is empty now. "The cops have destroyed a community of resistance," says Darius. "It is now deprived of its place."

Claudio asks him: "It has been a *community* of resistance?" and he answers: "It was an open community of resistance. Whoever was there could participate in the decision-making to form it. You have been at the last assembly, too. So you have been part of it as well and you can answer this question, too. The last assembly was the moment when the people present in the square took the decision to stay there."

"What formed the community of resistance, do you think?" I ask them.

Darius: "As far as I remember, there were quite different positions in the discussion. The person whom I heard speaking first, said he was a trade union member. He also suggested to form an organisation that would keep fighting together against unjust housing laws after the square was evicted. He was talking as if it was already sure that the square was going to be evicted, as if it was not there anymore."

Claudio: "And he said that his trade union would support an 'organisation' that would be the follow up of the self-organisation on the square. I think he imagined something more formalised, some kind of group that could meet in the rooms rented by his trade union."

Me: "And I remember that not many people agreed with this proposal. The second speaker that I remember talking through the mic was much more emotional and passionate and she got much more hand signs of agreement. Quite a lot actually! She invited everyone to stay on the square overnight and to continue building the huts and the barricades instead of sitting and talking in the assembly."

Darius: "She said that the square was 'our home' and that we should not be forced to quit it because so many things had been constructed collectively. I don't know what she means exactly because I wasn't there since the beginning but probably she meant the 'home' of the movement that came up in this square."

Claudio: "I think I remember the next speaker saying in a dreamy and reflected way that there will be lots of squares like this in the future."

The three of us remembered vividly that one of the speakers who was from a collective of lawyers expressed his solidarity for the people who were going to attempt to keep the square. He gave the number of the legal team and people applauded. Many must have interpreted this as a call to action, got up and left the assembly to continue with the construction of the wooden cabins.

Claudio: "And the facilitator of the discussion took the megaphone and said that there will be no minority-versus-majority voting and that maybe this means that there will be no clear decision."

Darius: "Yes, and she said in this moment that to her it became apparent that some people would stay on the square 'no matter what' – and this meant probably that they were going to resist the eviction to keep the square as the space of the community that they participated in."

Me: "I also remember people making a point on their differences, on the fact that they came from different political backgrounds."

Darius: "In what sense?"

Me: "Maybe trade unionists would not be ready to build barricades against the cops. And there were many other people who believed maybe that formal organisation means that there are hierarchies. This speaker said that it was important to be supportive of each other's actions."

Claudio: "Lots of people made concluding remarks but there was no new development in the discussion."

Me: "Then the facilitator said that she had the feeling the assembly would be supportive of those people who decided to disobey the orders of the city authorities and attempt to stay on the square overnight. Not everybody was going to join but nobody was against it."

Claudio: "There was no structured end to this assembly. At the point that you described, lots of people who were previously listening had already left the assembly space and were doing other things."

Night Shift Reflections

The site of dissent is a squatted wasteland near the business district of a middle-sized city. "There was nothing when we first arrived, just grass and some bushes. Now, look . . . " it looks like a village. Ian and I started talking with Helen after a workshop. Helen explains that the place for "the camp," as its inhabitants call it was chosen because it is urban enough, because its location offers the possibility "not only to stay amongst ourselves all the time." To bring messages to the outside world, those who camp here needed to be able to reach the centre by foot. Additionally, lots of bikes that everyone could borrow had been organised for the camp participants.

The camp had attracted lots of people who were involved in autonomous struggles for freedom of movement and against racism from all over Europe. They were wandering between the paths of little and big tents, gathering in groups, huddling in the tents for workshops. Lots of speakers were invited to give talks; lots of discussion events were planned and partly announced spontaneously as well as demonstrations and creative actions in the city. The wasteland had been fenced in. It now had two entrances where the fence got removed by the camp participants. All the rest of the fence had been hung with banners: "Papers for all or no papers at all!" "Against racism, against capitalism."

Coming in or out through the bigger entrance, one has to pass an info point. This is a table in a little pavilion where people take shifts to answer questions of visitors, participants, or journalists.

The camp is self-managed. This means that everyone participating in the camp, in its workshops, discussions, talks, its cultural programme or its actions, contributes to the reproduction of the camp: cooking, cleaning dishes, fixing the little shower cabins, doing shifts at the entrance or night shifts at one of the four corners of the camp.

Ian and I signed up for such a shift and now we were sitting on a raised hide that had been constructed from recycled planks. From 2:00 a.m. until 6:00 a.m. we now had to watch out for threatening moves by police or local right-wing hooligans who had publicly announced to come and visit us. Three other night shift posts were installed at the other corner of the squatted field as well as on the two entrances. We had something to make a sound of alarm and tools for communication with the others on the shift. "People said that it is quite likely that the cops might come to evict us," said Ian as he watched a police patrol drive by. During our first hour on the shift it had become apparent that they were driving past our camp very regularly. "I don't think so," I said. "They are just checking up on us like we are check up on them."

"Well, the organisers seem to think that we might be under threat at night. Otherwise, they would not have set up such a good security structure. It is quite hard to organise eight people being on posts all the time during the night – and still they made this effort. Someone told me that the local authorities were not very keen on having us here, although they know that it will be a temporary squatting."

"I still think it is more about the local right wing who might come to attack the camp at night. We had a special assembly about local right-wing groups because they are particularly big and dangerous here."

Ian replied: "It does not matter whether it is because of a right-wing attack or because of eviction – the fact that we spend so much energy on night security means that our site of dissent feels threatened, that it feels a strong antagonism to the outside. And I feel this too: every time I go out of here, I feel like on enemy-territory – even when we did the last demonstration. The cops where really close to us all the time."

"Doing the security shift is a special task," Ian continued. "It means guarding the borders of the autonomous zone and taking on responsibility for its conflictuality with the exterior – with guests, with police, with political enemies. You can compare it to other sites of dissent easily – even to sites of dissent that have a totally different character than this one! Just think of doing the door at a party in an autonomous social centre."

On the last day of the camp, the site of dissent transformed its shape and we had to debate the question of security again with the remaining camp participants. The showers and big tents had already been deconstructed and only a few little tents remained in the middle of the squatted wasteland. Our position was different now: with less people on the site we had to decide about how many people we wanted to have awake all night to be able to respond to eventual threats and how we were going to react if something happened.

The site of dissent dissolved the next morning. When the last camp partici-pants were packing their stuff into cars or standing already on the road next to the field, a police van arrived and parked at the entrance. The policemen took a controlling walk across the empty field whilst we stood on the street next to the wasteland, packing the last things in our backpacks. "Unimaginable to have them coming whilst this place was still a camp," Ian said and we shouldered our bags.

Candlelight Analysis

A summit of the most powerful political leaders of the world was going to be held in the metropolis. I am not going into the details of the topic of the sum-mit. Political decisions that were concerning the future of all of us were going to be bargained between those in power – possibly not to the advantage of the marginalised. The summit could have been in any of the megacities in Europe where flows of capital concentrate, their description is always the same: sparkling shop-windows, chronic dissatisfaction, fashionable clubs, houses under video surveillance, indifference in social networks, wellness centers, xenophobia. . . . Many different call-outs invited people to come to the same place as the political power holders and to articulate their dissent against the hierarchical practice of decision-making. It seemed like the summit of the power holders could turn into a convergence of different forms of political protest and people. Fedric, Eva, Gina and I arrived in excited anticipation late at night. We had some directions for our sleeping place – a big industrial building in a side street of a poorer neighbourhood on the outskirts of the city centre. Approaching from a distance, Eva spots three vans of the police near the entrance and I make a nervous call to a friend inside the building: "No worries, the cops are here since the beginning of the week. They don't do searches. You can just walk past them. I will be at the door," he tells me over the phone. Two knocks on the big metal door, my friend opens, hugs and familiar faces follow, a collective kitchen serves delicious food. The inhabit-ants of the building had opened their doors to those who came to participate in the convergence of resistance. Other such home places have secretly spread across the city, too: old hotels that had been squatted especially for hosting those who travelled to participate in the convergence, artist ateliers that had been transformed into self-managed workshops and laboratories of creative spatial practices designed to subvert daily life in the metropolis.

We are sitting on some wooden palettes in the main room of the squat. Around us people are enjoying dinner, drinking, chatting and listening to music. "We had a house search in the beginning of the week. The riot police broke the door in the early morning hours and took everyone's ID. They did not confiscate anything. Other than that, small groups have been regularly stopped and searched in the city centre because they are young or look a bit strange. I guess they are trying to target and intimidate potential protesters. There has been a big banner drop at some ministry and five people got arrested. The meeting hall of the politicians has been daubed," my friend who had opened the door for us tells me.

Fedric, Gina, Eva and I put our sleeping bags next to each other in the big collective sleeping space. We find out about a demonstration that is planned in the city centre and get invited to join a meeting.

On one of the last days of the convergence, Eva, Gina, Fedric and I are sitting in the living room of a squatted convergence space. "Isn't this magic?" Fedric asks and points in the direction of the table with shared food, some of it recycled from the bin and cleaned with lots of consciousness – it was displayed like a buffet for everyone to enjoy for free. The building had no electricity and the atmosphere was indeed somehow magically lit by many different candles. Some young people were spray-painting in the backyard where I had just met an old friend who was now playing guitar with several others on the roof. "So what is this magic all about?" asks Gina. "How do you mean?" I reply. Gina is silent for a moment and then starts telling us:

> During these two weeks I felt like hunting some invisible resistance in this incredibly posh city. We would stumble into a meeting, get told a time and a place that we'd never been to before, then spent hours wandering through the city. Somehow we would always recognise other people in the street who came to protest against the summit. I had constantly the feeling of being chased by cops and secret police in civilian clothes, always paranoid. Walking from one event to another we had to cross the entire city again and again – we would see little traces of resistance everywhere: a political graffiti, a banner, a sticker. . . . There were some actions of civil disobedience, too. Somehow the little demonstrations, pickets and public performances had contributed to turn this summit into an event that was somehow conflictual. The cops had been very alert all the time, the newspapers spoke of thousands of "violent protesters." Somehow we had managed to become a constant invisible opposition to this summit.

Eva continues this reflection about the temporarity of such events:

> Such convergences are not only a practice of articulating that one does not want to accept power structures that are reproducing oppression – they are also spaces and times for encounters; for meeting old friends, learning the names of

already familiar faces that one had met one or two years ago; they are an occasion of getting together as a network of struggle, of forming or strengthening relations to people who live in other places and whose struggles are connected to our own ones.

With the people you meet on the protests against the summit, you start talking at some point – about gentrification, about the oppression and surveillance, about your political perspective on the protest, about why you are here. Maybe it is a bit of an utopian illusion that by participating in a protest event in another city which is not yours, you are able to express some kind of dissent that is perceived in public space. The feeling that it works – this is often a short, addictive moment in time and then it is over. The question of what we leave behind once the convergence is over, once the collective kitchens have packed their stuff, and the squats have been evicted or cleaned up, is a painful one.

Recalling and Reflecting a Week of Contention

I arrived in the city where my friend Gino lives as everything seemed to have just about become quiet again. All that reminded us of the week of riot and resistance that had taken place here were the windows of banks that stopped being repaired after having been trashed several times in a row. They were now covered with wooden planks. Wherever I went these days, be it the most peripheral neighbourhood or the city centre, thousands of spray-painted tags and posters marked the walls: "Punkto32 stays!" and "Solidarity is a weapon!"

Punkto32 used to be a squatted social centre that had existed for almost twenty years in a popular neighbourhood. When the local authorities announced its planned eviction, the squatters launched a campaign together with local residents for the preservation of Punkto32. With its concerts, its gardening group, its regular collective dinners and discussion events, Punkto32 had been part of daily life in the neighbourhood. It had also been a meeting place for autonomous political working groups. After several demonstrations against the eviction of Punkto32, police arrived one early morning to break through the door of the social centre and demolish its interior as well as several bearing walls.

"Punkto32 is completely empty now? Does someone still live there?" I asked Gino. We were having a coffee on the roof of his house. He sighed: "I told you to come earlier. No, it looks like a ruin. No one will squat it ever again." Gino showed me several posters that were billposted in the streets of the city. They had been signed by different political groups. One of them was critiquing the eviction of Punkto32 in relation to a critique of gentrification which was expelling popular life and noncommercial meeting places. Another poster contained a text against capitalist social relationships and stated that the eviction of a noncommercial social centre that was self-managed was an oppressive capitalist act and should be opposed.

"What happened here in this one week was not only about Punkto32 as such. It was about all the self-organised, autonomous spaces, it was about our dissent to capitalist relations and hierarchies," Gino said. I asked him if he could write down for me what happened during this week to turn it into one of the case-study stories of sites of dissent in this research project.

"Writing isn't really my thing," he replied, "I'd rather tell it to you and you write it down."

About two weeks ago, police arrived in several vans to evict Punkto32. It was easy for them to block the narrow street where Punkto32 is. Nobody expected them to come in daytime. Only a few people managed to get out onto the street. They got pushed aside by the cops. I have not been there but those who have, told this story many times and everybody knew that Punkto32 was evicted within one hour anyway. The cops broke into the house and destroyed everything. Then they brought machines to demolish it so that it could not be used like before. The same night a big demonstration was called for in the neighbourhood. By word of mouth the invitation to the demo on the big square near the place of Punkto32 seemed to have spread well and fast: I don't know how many thousands we were in the darkness on this square. The first demonstration was the biggest one, for sure. And whilst the demonstration turned into a riot, many people standing on their balconies applauded! Barricades got erected and set on fire so the cops could not come and catch the demonstrators – and even when they tried, people would simply run into the side streets and the cops would get lost chasing after them. The demonstrators were from the neighbourhood or had visited the area of Punkto32 several times, the cops were not. Only very few people got arrested that night, and lots of banks on the main streets got trashed.

The next day when people had woken up and started to discuss the events of last night, it became apparent – again by word of mouth – that several autonomous groups were going to return to the neighbourhood of Punkto32. Some of them had started to form already into a demonstration in their own neighbourhood. Not all of them managed to cross the city and to come together at the ruin-site of Punkto32. The police blocked the way of some of these demonstrations and attempted to arrest the demonstrators.

Three days after the eviction, one of the machines that had demolished the walls of Punkto32 was burning. It was still standing near the ruin of Punkto32 which had been fenced in. The people who stood near the machine were strangely calm as it was burning. This moment turned into some kind of symbol. After this moment of silence, those who had seen the machine burning started to build barricades again. The media coverage of these events was not very sympathetic to the struggle, although all kinds of political groups, unions, associations and youth groups had tried to convey to the media that the city had wrongfully dispossessed those involved in autonomous self-organisation.

Riots continued on the fourth night as well and had an again different character. People were learning to take space on the street and to defend it. I think some of these people were really young, maybe fourteen years old. Others were maybe residents who had never engaged in a riot before and now felt the necessity to do so for the first time in their life. Nothing had been announced or communicated this night. People simply knew that they would meet in the neighbourhood of Punkto32 again.

Something beautiful happened during these days: People from other squats and social centres and from all over the city came together to get onto the demolished site of Punkto32 and started to clean and to build a new social space there. Now you can see benches and little vegetable beds there as well as photos from how it used to be before. Lots of posters were hung up on the walls in the streets and lots of people wrote comments on the walls. It looks like an exhibition or like a massive memorial plate that stretches across the whole street.

Gino and I were now standing with our back to the ruin of Punkto32 looking at the murals that had emerged next to it. "It is not only about Punkto, it is about capitalism" got tagged in red on one of these walls. Images and pictures had been glued to the wall for several metres along the street. Some of them would be on many other spots in the entire city, too. One of the messages: "If you touch Punkto32, you touch us all." Photos were documenting how people were cleaning up the ruin of Punkto32 and constructing an open-air café there. Other pictures showed a protest in front of the city hall. We also noticed a calendar announcing events that used to take place in Punkto32 next to about thirty declarations of solidarity (some of them hand-written) to those arrested in the riots after the eviction. Next to them, someone painted a comic strip that critiqued the idea of democratic parliamentary decision-making. I pointed at something that seemed to be a logo in the corner on one of the posters – it showed a burning demolition machine. "I understand much better now why you said that it became some kind of symbol." Gino smiled: "It was one of those acts, contentious spatial practices in your words, that articulated all the dissent that people felt towards a society where it is possible to simply order dispossession, eviction and destruction of what people had created from a grassroots perspective.

Punkto32 is everywhere. This was proven by the wave of solidarity for those who got arrested in the week of riots and by the fact that resistance spread all over the city. Punkto32 deterritorialised: it became more than this ruin site, more than one building. What people wanted to defend in Punkto32 even after its demolition was suddenly to be found in every street of the neighbourhood and in the entire city. Rioting then, is an act that points to the structures that make the violent eviction of a self-managed autonomous resource possible."

Gino was not the only person reflecting on the collective articulation of dissent that had taken place. He told me:

> There are volunteer working groups who deal with the legal side of the arrests, there are solidarity bar nights in other social centres to raise money for the future construction of the open-air café here at Punkto32 – yes, people do not give up on this specific location, even if it is just a memory now – and there are discussion events about police violence, eviction, self-management, repression, all the time.

We decided to spend time participating in popular assemblies, talks and discussions that were taking place in the remaining sites of dissent and in public spaces all across the city. Gino and I wanted to connect our individual reflections to the local, diverse and decentralised reflection processes that were taking place during the time of my visit. One of them took place during a free public dinner in a square. About thirty people sat in a circle on the floor and shared their experience of police violence, their critique of a hierarchical decision-making process that had been imposed upon them by the city authorities. A microphone was passed around and different people spoke, sometimes for several minutes holding small speeches. An older person told how the neighbourhood changed in the last few years, how rents were rising, how people had been kicked out of their flats. A younger person shared experiences of racist police controls and another person spoke about how social spaces were getting commercialised or shut down, how Punkto 32 had been such a space that was violently taken from the neighbourhood, ripping it out of its social tissue and leaving a hole. Their voices got carried through the streets of the district, people were even listening from balconies and from across the street. Their voices had to raise against the noise of cars filling every moment of silence. They were mourning for Punkto32 and at the same time situating this mourning in a context of struggle against gentrification and processes expulsion in the neighbourhood and in the city, escaping passivity and shaping the history of a diverse community of struggle and dissent.

SECOND CYCLE OF JOURNEYS: WALKING, WANDERING AND DRAWING BORDERS

The second cycle of journey took me to sites of dissent in urban environments, geographically located in different cities of different European countries: It took me to the large squatted cultural space of Caput, to "the hood" – a site of dissent comprising a whole neighbourhood, to the small space of a rented Infoshop, to a squatted house that has been set up as a resting space for migrating women and children. All of these sites of dissent are constituted by spatial practices which created a permanent space for articulations of dissent. Since some of the sites of dissent visited on the second cycle of journeys were places that consisted only of a few rooms and other sites were encompassing entire territories, the myriad of methods that was employed to explore the sites of dissent inevitably comprises the act of walking.

De Certeau evokes the practice of walking and wandering through urban space as a pedestrian speech act, a form of language that brings the pedestrian into dialogue with the surrounding space (de Certeau, 1988, 97–103). The wanderings through the hood allowed me to explore it as a space that accommodates difference (Higgins, 2006, 254), as a heterotopia appropriated by those whose subject positions, needs and spatial practices deviate from and rebel against the panoptic power of spatial organisation in the city (de Certeau, 1988, 95). When wandering through the hood, I dropped my usual motives for movement and action to let myself be drawn by the terrain and the possibility of encounters that the hood offered, to perform a situationist-inspired psychogeography (Plant, 1992, 58), to engage with how homeless people had transformed the playground near a square into sleeping places, with how the inhabitants created a park with a playground in a place where local authorities had other construction plans, with the communication and expressions on the walls and urban furniture of the hood.

The storytellers who travelled with me as well as myself experienced the territory of Caput and the hood as sites of dissent that were fractured into many different places, not as having a single spatial meaning. We saw it as a space traversed by a multiplicity of relations between different entities, connecting different kinds of lived space. It was a space composed of those who are involved in the self-management of a park, the space of those who use it as a shelter, the space of those who make benefit gigs in its locations, the space of those who meet in its corners. These are different rhythms and ways of appropriating and transforming space – different ways of escaping its regulatory attempts. Deleuze and Guattari use the word *plateau* for describing a space which is orientated towards a conceptual openness instead of a spatial closure, which has different readings and usages (Deleuze and Guattari, 2013), like the spaces of the hood and of the cultural centre Caput. Based on these stories the word plateau, to describe a horizontal space of multiplicities, will be picked up in the collective analysis later.

On the sites of dissent visited in the second cycle of journeys, I also encountered different ways to draw borders between the sites and the kind of spatial order that "becomes *administration* (. . .), a machinery of authority which extends through and structures territory" (Negri, 2003, 190). On the site of Caput, some borders were drawn through labyrinth-like accesses to the upper floors of some buildings, thousands of small gates, the keys to which get passed on through relations of personal trust and affinity. Whilst other parts of Caput, the courtyards, were frequently crossed by police forces, the upper floors never did. In the hood, some of the boundaries were physical: big streets with heavy traffic that are difficult to cross and push the pedestrian to move on instead of stopping, dwelling and appropriating this space. Such streets acted as delimiting landmarks.

On a smaller scale, borders were drawn in front of the Infoshop as well: the pavement was appropriated by those involved in the Infoshop, transformed into a collectively inhabited social space in summer with chairs and tables and chalk on the floor. It was not a simple place of passage anymore but a border between the self-managed Infoshop and its exterior managed by the city authorities.

In the squatted house for migrating women and children, the door was the most controlled border of the site of dissent. The person on the door had to decide whether the person knocking was allowed to enter or not: is the person (still) a child? A woman? A person on his or her autonomous move of migration across borders of nation states? Or just a supporter of such people? The person on the door was to keep the function of the site of dissent as a refuge for women and children on the move in place. One had to get initiated to "doing the door."

In this cycle of journeys, we discovered that borders and boundaries play different roles for large and small-scale urban and permanent sites of dissent. For the small-scale sites of dissent they are not only important as delimitations of their place but also constitutive of the social dynamics of inclusion and exclusion into the site of dissent. For the large-scale sites of dissent, the constitution of their boundaries and borders plays into dynamics of de- and re-territorialisation of their material spatiality in the city – with the police and urban processes of gentrification and recuperation into the administration of the urban project. On our journeys we also discovered that borders and boundaries of sites of dissent are spatial practices which are to different degrees determined by collective decision-making processes in different sites of dissent.

THIRD CYCLE OF JOURNEYS: REBELLIOUS BODIES AND CONTENTIOUS APPROPRIATIONS OF SPACE

A third cycle of journeys took me and the memories of my friends to a large-scale occupied part of a forest and its neighbouring meadow, to a squatted house on the countryside, as well as into an empty urban building that was attempted to be reopened as a shelter for homeless people.

The occupied forest and the squat on the countryside where my friend Rom lives, are both rural sites of dissent. They are located some kilometres away from the next villages and surrounded by fields outside of an urbanised area. The squatted building was, in contrast, situated within the urban environment of a city.

The occupied forest stretches across a larger geographical scale of several hectares of land and includes different localities into its territory: the meadow with kitchens, huts, clay buildings and caravans as well as a part of the forest where tree houses, walkways, secret paths and barricades have transformed the territory into a site of dissent. The squatted building and the village squat are just the size of a house – they are thus concentrated sites of dissent.

Both rural sites of dissent dispose of an infrastructure which allows its inhabitants to live there for prolonged periods of time. The village squat has been occupied for many years and is not threatened by eviction. It has seen several generations of inhabitants making it their permanent home. Although the site of the occupied forest has been attacked by the police in the past, it has equally been a permanent, yet very contentious, home for different people and activities in different periods of time.

The squatting of the building did not last long. Creating this unwillingly temporary site of dissent caused a momentary rupture in the daily life of the neighbourhood.

None of the sites of dissent encountered on the third cycle of journeys can be compared with an MSSD. Yet, comparing them with an MDSD allows us to ask questions about the similarities of contentious spatial practices, antagonistic de-territorialisations of space, and spatial appropriations made in and through the small-scale, temporary urban squatting action and the large, permanent forest occupation.

All three sites of dissent are reclaiming space for a self-determined life in rupturing with dominant modes of socio-spatial production and reproduction. Yet this rupture and its continuity have different flows and intensities. It might help to look at how spatial appropriations took place on the three sites of dissent to understand why.

"When Rebellion starts, it nearly always begins with the body," writes Richardson in a book about bodies that transgress cultural norms (Richardson, 2016, 14). With our bodies we are located within a socio-spatial order and it is with our bodies that we physically transgress its norms and rules. Transgression "is a process of continuously shuffling boundaries, the boundaries of acceptable behaviour" (Wilson, 1993, 110). These transgressions can be individual ones as well as collective ones, forming rebellious bodies in space when a body becomes a weapon in the struggle for a self-determined life within socio-spatial order. The body becomes a tool for the articulation of sociopolitical dissent. Becoming a rebellious body is a personal experience of empowerment which takes place in the context of a collective contentious spatial practice. When climbing up the lamppost to enter into the empty building that me and my friends attempted to squat, I transgressed my personal boundary of physical limitations. I was surprised that I managed to climb up to the roof. My body was moving where it was not supposed to move – high above the pavement, crawling between cables along rooftops. Urban spatial order restricts the spaces that we are supposed to occupy with our bodies in the city. In committing this transgression together (if one of us would have discovered this, it would have been the end of our squatting mission; if one of us slipped, we could all have fallen off the roof), we formed an antagonistic organism consisting of several rebellious bodies. Being part of this organism, my attention and perception transcended my own body when we were moving on our invisible trail leading into the building.

The process of this formation of an antagonistic organism can be compared to other experiences of physical co-dependencies and empowerments – for example, to the experience of participating in the rural protest camp narrated in the first cycle of journeys. Here, none of the contentious actions that happened on one of the last days of the camp would have been possible if participants had not been able to form an antagonistic organism when collectively maintaining a self-managed infrastructure for cooking, sleeping and meeting places near the contested gold mine. In contrast, for Rom the experience of being in a squatted building is entirely different: he lives his daily life without forming an antagonistic organism with others. In his everyday life, the village squat does not require him to become a rebellious body – because it exists since several years and is not under threat of eviction. Rom does not have to put the barricade in place, nor does he have to think about escape routes from his kitchen window together with his squat mates. It is interesting to note that Gina recalls how being present in the permanent forest occupation required her to learn new skills and to shuffle her boundaries as well as the boundaries of acceptable behaviour (living in a tree house in the forest). It is not the location on the temporary/permanent axis of comparison of a site of dissent that determines whether the people involved experience individual and collective transgression of boundaries or the becoming of an antagonistic organism that collectively engages in contentious spatial practices.

FOURTH CYCLE OF JOURNEYS: PLATEAUS FOR MULTIPLICITY AND TIME-SPACES OF ENCOUNTER

During the fourth cycle of journeys my companions and I will be present in a protest camp in the mountains, in a tiny urban social centre called Vagana and on the squatted grounds of an old factory referred to as BUT. The protest camp in the mountains only occupied a rather small territory – just enough to place all the facilities and the infrastructure that permitted to live in a tent for some days to about three hundred people. The objective of this camp was not to occupy as much territory as possible but to create a site where workshops could take place, where food could be cooked for a larger number of people. In contrast to Vagana, the urban social centre that hosted me on another journey, the camp was a rural site of dissent – no urban infrastructure, just a small village road in the distance leading to a tiny village with only two shops and one bus stop. The camp was set up for some specific days and then taken down again as planned by its organisers.

Vagana is located in an inner city neighbourhood. Its surroundings are marked by the urbanity of a capital metropolis. In contrast to the extended territory of BUT including various localities and buildings with a distinct character of usage each, the spaces of Vagana and the camp are small-scale. Both, BUT and Vagana are set up for a permanent existence. The territory of BUT exists since many years and various people have arranged the space according to their permanent needs. Vagana was created by a group of people who took the decision to open a queer and anarchist social centre for various activities. They see Vagana as a permanent project with a political future for which they made the effort to secure funding. BUT is equally located in a central area of the city. It is surrounded by walls and fences and stands as a separate entity in the proximity of office buildings and a main traffic road leading to the central station.

Giving an Interview to Militant Researchers

Tina and Ulla want to interview me. "About what?" I ask.

"You probably noticed that there are not really good vibes between Vagana and the people from the Red and Black Star Collective. It has been like this for a whilst now, and in our assembly we took the decision that we should stop the little fights we constantly have between the only two autonomous spaces that exist in town. We believe that we should really make an effort to understand each other, to understand where we are coming from," explains Tina, and Ulla adds:

> We want to do some self-research about our spaces and our communities and how we see ourselves to show it to the people from the Red and Black Star Collective. We need to create a base for uniting in a collective struggle against oppression in this city, against the invisibilisation of the marginalised groups that often have no other spaces to go than Vagana and the cellar of the Collective. So, we want to write about ourselves and our militant position against capitalistic oppression and alienation in the city. And we are writing this from our perspective. But there are different people participating in this space to different degrees. You have been here for a whilst now – and you know the Collective as well. So we wanted to ask you some questions about how you perceived this space when you first arrived and how you perceive it now. Would you be alright with this?

Why not? I had come as a traveller to the city where the people from Vagana and from the Collective are active doing demonstrations, people's kitchens for homeless people, creating space for women to empower themselves against street harassment and many other things. I was welcomed to stay for a week and got involved in the activities here. I am happy to get invited to participate in a collective research process and agree with giving an interview.

"What was your first impression of the space when you arrived in Vagana?" asks Tina and Ulla prepares to take notes of my answer.

> I remember that I thought the neighbourhood was a bit deprived. There are lots of really rundown houses and dark alleys. It is not one of the posh hoods. And then I saw the little shop window of Vagana. First I thought that this place is a gentrifier. You know, one of these alternative places that open up in areas where rents are first cheap and then start rising because more and more hipster cafés and bars and later art galleries are opening. I thought Vagana is one of these. It looked so tidy and so alien to this neighbourhood. All around you have places where people gamble and kebabs or internet cafes. Vagana seemed to be made

for another audience, not for the residents. I was suspicious. And when I entered, it didn't get better at first. Everything looked really clean and I wondered: Is this a place where people struggle? Later I found out more about what is going on in Vagana. I found out that it is organised like a social centre although it pays rent, I found all the interesting literature that deals with patriarchy and how to oppose it. I saw that you make many interesting events there and host discussions to inform each other. And I saw that it is a horizontally organised space – this is what I like most. There are different collectives participating and everyone comes to the assembly where people decide together what is happening in the space, how to share the resources, and so on.

Tina: "And did you think that we are too single-issue? That we focus too much on queer politics and gendered oppressions? I mean . . . the space self-identifies as a queer space. The idea is to give space to people who are oppressed by the binary categories of male and female, who feel unsafe in this city because they get aggressed. Do you think Vagana is not fighting other forms of oppression – such as economic deprivation, for example?"

"Well, first yes. Because all you see on the walls of Vagana, all the posters and all the graffiti are about fighting sexism and homophobia. The space does not say so much about your ideological position. There is not a red and black star or an anarchist A on the wall. And it is true that only a certain kind of people comes to Vagana. I perceive most of the people who participate in the space as white and middle-class queer people, most of them with university education. But it is not true that in Vagana people only work on issues that concern non-male people. It is a collectively managed space and no one has to pay for it. This could be seen as acting against economic deprivation. And there are various things happening in the space – you have had information nights about the refugee struggles while I was here. And we helped organise an anti-fascist demonstration. So I don't think it is a single-issue space. First I did not understand that the cultural climate in this place is so aggressive against those who do not fit the categories of women or man, who are perceived as queer or homosexual. Now I think, such spaces are really needed."

Tina: "Vagana is a rented space. Some university students applied for some funding from an NGO to get the money for rent. The people from the Collective have approached us saying that we are not really a combative space because inside everything is neat and clean and the people are, too. We are not fighting for space, we are renting it to create our own universe and we do events just for ourselves. Do you think Vagana is not enough of an antagonistic place to liberate people from oppression and to help them rupture with normality?"

"After a few weeks in this city I started to understand how difficult it is to occupy a place without paying rent, without entering into a business relationship. I know that squats get evicted violently by the police pretty quickly or really poor people move in and it does not work to create a social centre there any more – because there are so many people in need of a place to sleep that has a roof. Ulla was telling me that it is really impossible to create a safe space for queer people in these circumstances. So I don't think that renting a space automatically means that the place you create is not antagonist, not working to create horizontal alternatives to how social order is now. But I think there is one thing about the identity of people who come to Vagana. I don't know how to explain it. . . . There is a contrast if you compare Vagana with the cellar of the Collective: in the cellar, you have people who were homeless before and who now are involved in the self-organisation of homeless people, some of them are or have been alcoholics, some of them are on workfare – they clean toilets for one Euro an hour. This is what a woman told me who was having some drinks there. Few of them are speaking English – in Vagana most people are students with good English-speaking skills. Almost everyone has a funky urban look in Vagana. The cellar is more than just a bar. There are no fixed prices and everyone can bring their own drinks and food inside. The visitors share a lot and they are very different from each other. Well, maybe not. Maybe in a sense they have something in common: they speak a lot about their own precarity when they drink and smoke together. One man who is involved in the big public kitchen that they organise in the biggest square of the city said to me that this is a place 'where people come to share love.' But then he laughed and pointed at the poster of Bakunin and said that they are not hippies. All of them perceive themselves as being oppressed by the government. And some of them are students, too. It's just that they have more diversity in the space."

Tina: "And do you think we have a lot in common with the people from the Collective regarding our political perspectives and actions? And the second question is: why do you think we do not get on well with these people?"

"I think you have a lot in common, politically speaking. Those who are involved in the Collective as well as the people from Vagana, want a world that does not oppress people who are not male or people who do not fit into gender norms, or poor people who have to live on the street, or immigrants. And in both spaces people are trying to find a collective form of organisation to fight these mechanisms of oppression, or at least to create a space where the marginalised can come together and start something – a collective healing process. But I see that for you [those involved in Vagana], the people from the Collective have some kind of macho territory complex.

Maybe it would be interesting to explore collective forms of action with the people from the Collective? I think it would be nice if they could use this space, too though. Their cellar is quite rotten. I am sure there are lots of topics that you could work on together."

Tina, Ulla and I agree upon using this interview for our different research projects. In a few minutes a workshop on women's health will start in the main room of Vagana where we are sitting. The first visitors start to arrive and we clean up our cups and help putting up the projector.

Collective Drifts through a Protest Camp

"All protest camps are the same," says Gina and throws a bored glance at the camp with its obligatory shower spaces, the settlement of tents all next to each other, the eating area and the workshop tents. Bill stretches on a pile of straw. "I disagree with you," he says calmly. "This time it will be really interesting."

"Why do you think so?"

"Look at how many local people came from the villages. They are all here in the camp. And although we do not speak their language they seem really interested in our critique of the coal mine and our perspective on it. Yesterday night an old guy from a village where they have been organising demonstrations against the mine for years, gave a talk which was translated. And he said that for him, personally, this camp is a historical moment. And that he hopes that the local struggle could unite forces with the anti-capitalists – that is the people from all these different countries who came to the protest camp."

I am impatiently observing one of the workshop spaces from our comfy seats on the straw. A talk about the history of the local struggle of the villagers against the coal mine is supposed to have started fifteen minutes ago. I am also quite looking forward to making a move into the shadow of the workshop tent. "But look at all these white university kids from central Europe in the camp. . . . Do you think they really want to unite forces with the local struggle? We are making this camp here – a one-off event – and then maybe there will be a fight with the cops at the protest action tomorrow. And then all these kids go home and that's it! I feel what we are doing here is rather taking over the images that will be produced of this struggle against the mine. How can we unite forces with these people from the mountain villages? We don't even speak the same language!" Gina has been sceptical of the camp even before we came here.

"Well, first, let's take the opportunity to learn about the local struggle. I agree that it would be completely ignorant to do an action tomorrow without being informed about the political context. But this is why this talk has been organised. It will start in a few minutes, I think." I am trying to make my friends move and get up on my feet. Lots of other camp participants start walking in the direction of the workshop space, too. "And then what?" says Gina and crossed her arms. Bill finishes his drink and makes a proposal: "After the talk we just drift around the camp, like normally. Maybe we stop and talk to some people, have some food, go to some other workshops. And in the evening we meet again and we speak about what we have observed is happening or not happening between the locals who came to the camp and the 'kids.' We can also walk around together if you like. But the thing is we have to be attentive to certain situations."

"Like what?"

I help Bill get onto his feet from his nest in the straw. "Like all the situations when people meet in the camp because they are here to protest against the extraction of coal from the grounds of this area – because it is always multinational companies who make profit from the sell-out of land and never the local population. Because environmental destruction is horrible. And I am sure we will discover plenty of situations where local people and the camp participants somehow come together over this. Or, maybe not."

"You mean we walk around in the camp and hang out, like a drift, here and there? Basically the question would be whether and how a shared articulation of dissent is possible."

We start walking to the workshop tent.

In the evening of the same day, Bill, Gina and I have a cup of tea before going to sleep in our tent. "Let's speak about our drifts. I have witnessed some interesting situations. And being attentive to how the villagers connect with the camp participants actually changed my opinion." Gina takes out some notes that she made.

"So, I think the camp facilitates a physical proximity between people who would normally never meet – the villagers and the kids from the North. I observed several times how the local people speak about the organisation of actions with the young anti-authoritarian people from the nearest city who have put the showers and the kitchen in place for the camp. They have a common language and they co-organised the talk in one of the villages last night. And the local kids are really well connected to international activists."

"Maybe let's stop calling them 'kids,'" I suggest.

"When I was having lunch I listened several times how different people spoke about the effects of environmental destruction with the villagers, some-times with translation from local activists. And one villager who was speaking English told a whole group of campers about her village – at length."

I add to Gina's observations: "I have been to several workshops in the after-noon, because that was what interested me. And I noticed that although the workshops covered different topics, they all were somehow in relation to environmental protection, autonomy and self-management. In the discussions with participants, I noticed that villagers as well as the younger protest people who are, I think, all more or less anti-capitalist in their thoughts, related the content of the workshop to the concrete struggle against the mine here. So the workshops were like momentary spaces of encounter and exchange of politi-cal perspectives and practices."

"I went to the local villages today," says Bill and tells us about having lunch with a sixty-year-old man who told him that he wished for a big riot at the mine and that he hoped that all the young people would set a symbol of militant resistance. "He saw it more like completing each other. We received a really warm welcome in the villages where we got guided around and ate tasty food prepared in the community hall. We had lots of language barriers, but I realised that they wanted to share and explain their passion for the struggle."

"I have had a chat with some camp participants about this, too. It was when I walked from the toilet to the eating area," Gina says.

Bill, Gina and I stay up for some more hours reflecting about our observations made in the drifts through the camp and the villages. Before going to sleep we come to the conclusion that the event of the protest camp is a space and time of encounter between different dissenting subject positions united in a concrete locally rooted struggle. This is facilitated through the self-organised workshops, talks, excursions and visits for the camp participants who bring a curiosity to learn about the local context of a struggle.

"Told you: it will be really interesting," says Bill.

Inhabitant-Led Mapping

Ian and I arrive at the corner of BUT. We had stopped several times on the way because we thought we had recognised a hole in a wall covered in graffiti as the entrance to the territory. Several times we thought BUT would start in a narrow side street and then turned around saying: Maybe this isn't it? We see the banner of the Anticapitalist Front, a group that we want to visit in BUT, behind the fence. Ian and I look up and down the street and then climb over the fence. We had no idea about what BUT looks like when we did it. Even in the dark I can see that Ian opens his mouth in astonishment: "All this . . . ?" He points to the massive factory building in the distance. There are several houses on our left and right and a street seems to lead across a huge empty field. There are almost no lights. Just the windows of the house with the banner of the Anticapitalist Front shed a yellow glow. Ian and I knock on the door of the house and enter a big room with a very raspy wooden floor. A group of people is sitting in a circle around a wood burner at one end of the room. There is a long bar and posters along the walls of the room. We came just a bit too late to join the meeting and get welcomed with warm tea. Xenia, a participant of the Anticapitalist Front offers to take us on "an excursion through BUT" after the meeting.

"You should take some pen and paper to draw us a map afterwards. Or for yourselves, so you don't get lost," jokes Vagelis, another participant of the meeting.

Xenia laughs: "This is a very good idea. Let's make a map together – to understand better what this space is. We are thinking about this every day here. And we should get some of the artists who live here to come with us."

So we grab pen and paper and the three of us get out into the darkness of the huge wasteland. Xenia lits a torch.

"You need it in BUT. There is no electricity in the buildings. People work with solar panels and wind turbines. To walk from one place to another it is good to have a torch. There are many buildings and many hidden entrances. BUT has been squatted almost ten years ago. Some people live here, some just have ateliers and there are lots of meeting places like our house. Let's go and see some ateliers," proposes Xenia and we make our way across the wasteland drawing a line on our paper which starts at a square in the shape of the house we just left.

"And the house we just left – it is actually a bit like a social centre. We hold film screenings there and we have events. But where we are going now, the ateliers, it is more like lots of little hangout spaces that are not made to host bigger events. And people make their art there, also costumes and creative accessories for protests."

Lots of little rooms and garage doors are lit by candles and lights of different colours. Approaching them we can see the silhouettes of people.

"Hi," says Xenia as we enter a bigger garage stuffed with metal sculptures and in between them people with thick scarfs and jackets are having some wine. "I am showing BUT to our visitors and we are making a map of the place." We introduce ourselves and a man whose face we can barely see says: "Maps. Great! I come with you. But you know, mapping always starts with the people who live in the place that is to be mapped."

"It's his atelier," says Xenia.

"And our community here is a fragile thing. In the beginning, when this territory was squatted there were two hundred people involved. We were all very different from each other. Some just wanted an atelier to put their sculptures, some wanted to make art in a free community. Some were homeless and others wanted to create a political social centre to work on the topic of precarity," saying this the man points at Xenia.

"And then we had many fights. Again and again," she adds, "In the beginning we used to have assemblies in which we decided all together and without leaders what to do with the place. And as some groups started to establish their projects on the ground, the fighting started. I guess it was because we had different imaginations of how to take care of the place, how to make it invitational to other people. And we had very different approaches to this. Some were more into parties and some just build a massive indoor skate park in the old factory buildings that is self-organised until today. Some wanted to create a group dynamic that would turn BUT into a participant of urban politics in our city. And some were saying that BUT is a man-dominated place and that all those involved don't deal with it adequately. Now we just started to have meetings again. The first meetings where we all come together."

"And there are things to discuss. BUT is threatened by eviction. And again, we had very different ideas about what to do against it. Or not to do." Xenia and the artist take us to the big factory hall that is a skate park now.

On the way we walk along a wall and then a fence, and a wall again.

"Is the street just behind this wall?" asks Ian.

"Yes, the wall is kind of our border. But look: there is an entrance here. Small. For those who know," the artist points at a place where the wall is not straight and we see that there is a gap. Big enough to squeeze through.

"This is the path of the skaters," he says. "They are urban youth who used to hang out in the street because they have no place to go and no money. And they probably don't have much of a job perspective either. When they started getting involved in BUT they made this." We arrive at a massive entrance gate. I can see a huge hall with lots of ramps in all shapes, all painted and made of pieces of metal or wood. I can see lots of little cabins and benches in between the ramps. Kids are smoking and listening to music, there in the distance or high up above our heads.

"This is their space. They have their own entrances and ways in and out of BUT. They just build all this themselves without asking anyone. And all the back area is the space of the graffiti artists. They have their own bar there at the wall and they also do exhibitions."

We have drawn the path along the wall and the factory hall on our map. Now we draw a windy path across rotting machinery pieces all scattered across the ground behind the big factory hall. We walk along the space of the skaters which is also at the border of BUT. "The wall is quite important here," I notice. "Yes," says Xenia "behind the wall is a street and the city and normal life. And on this side it is our space and the wall has turned into a canvas, into a social gathering space and into a public space sometimes, too. Behind the wall people do what they want. And this is BUT."

"But the relationship to the wall is not so easy," tells us the artist. "There is one gate in the wall. The main gate. We call it like this. And it is controlled by the municipality. You will see."

The main gate is a white metal gate that opens and closes if a watchman presses the button. He sits in a tiny room with huge windows lit by very bright neon lamps. "It is the only gate through which cars can pass. And this dude has the control over it. The ramp and his job have been created by the municipality which owns the grounds of BUT."

Looking at the man who seems to be sitting in a transparent neon cage, I say: "This is quite horrible. You can't move bigger things or cars in and out of BUT without his permission."

"Yes," Xenia sighs. "But we get on well with them. It is a very shitty job and they are poor people who need something to live off. They don't want to get involved in any kind of politics, but we speak with them about the exploitation of workers. Maybe, when the eviction comes, they will be on our side. The municipality just tries to get control over what is happening on the grounds of BUT. But there is no way they can control it actually. Because people do what they want and we have meetings again now." "And because BUT means different things to us. For some, it is a living space. For others, it is a place of autonomous political content. Hopefully, it will be difficult for them to label us as squatters who just make drug parties and hit each other with scrap producing more scrap," the artist adds.

We are walking back along the wall with its many secret entrances and exits past a bar that appeared on the squatted land between the factory hall and the gate.

"This is our part again then." Xenia points at the house where we just had the meeting with the Anticapitalist Front. "You want to come in?" she asks the artist.

"This is the part where they have a weekly event calendar. And I live on the other side, where there is no rhythm of waking up in the morning when the sun rises. People just potter about all night. And when some go to sleep others wake up. It is quite a different rhythm," he tells Ian and me.

He was just about to start working on something and will return to his atelier, he announces and says goodbye. We part ways and I take a look at the piece of paper which is our map now. It consists of many bubbles and twisted lines which represent the paths we were shown.

"I think the bubbles of the different space might represent the different groups of people that are creating BUT. But there are some groups missing. The homeless people are invisibilised. They sleep everywhere in the dark." Xenia takes the pen and draws several little bubbles around the factory buildings and near the bar. The map looks like an abstract painting.

FIFTH CYCLE OF JOURNEYS: TRANSGRESSIONS
AND (TRANS)FORMATIONS

On the last cycle of journeys, I travelled through sites of dissent created between bus stops, shopping centres, tourist destinations, office blocks, corner shops . . . and spatially concentrated into buildings in urban environments. All sites of dissent that I have encountered here are thus spatially concentrated rather than large-scale. However, on the permanent-temporary continuum, there were considerable differences between them: In one of the journeys, I was sharing my research diary with those friends with whom I was inhabiting a squatted house since one month. We were collectively reflecting on how the previously empty building is transforming through our spatial practices of gathering furniture, securing the door, dwelling in the space. Another journey took me to a squat that has just opened its doors to the neighbourhood, right into the moment when the public was invited to come and help to re-inhabit the house whilst the police could come any time. The last journey even took me to a bench instead of a site of dissent. Here, Gina and I were evoking an imaginary of the empty building in front of us as our site of dissent. In making the first plans and taking the first precautions, in observing the rhythm of the neighbourhood and getting to know its movements, we started the process of formation of a new site of dissent. This difference of the three sites of dissent is seemingly linked to their location on the permanent-temporary axis of comparison: in the case of the new squat and of my imaginary of a squat formed with Gina on the bench, it was unclear for how long it was going to exist, whether it will turn into a permanent site of dissent or remain a temporary articulation of dissent. The difference between these sites of dissent cannot be explained through a variation of classification on this continuum. We thus needed to add a fourth axis of comparison: the continuum of forming and transforming sites of dissent. One of the journeys took place on a site of dissent that already exist and is evolving and transforming into something else through spatial practices – into a lived place, a squatted home instead of an empty building. This is different in the case of the last two stories. On the journeys, I encountered them as spaces that are just about to form as a site of dissent. They either had no material reality yet, like the house opposite of our bench, or are just about to announce their existence, like the squat opening its doors to the neighbourhood. Their concrete shape, form of organisation, material appearance, functioning and daily rhythm has yet to crystallise. The spatial practices that will make these spaces *take place* are already forming the ground for their existence. It can be said that the three sites of dissent are in different stages of their development.

In forming sites of dissent, a classification as a rather permanent or rather temporary site of dissent cannot be made. Yet, applying this new axis of comparison to the other sites of dissent can help to learn more about contentious spatial practices that are forming sites of dissent and about the process of their becoming.

In the case of the sites of dissent presented in this cycle, comparing the forming sites of dissent with an MSSD after having compared them to the squat where me and my friends lived with an MDSD, would point at questions about the formation of social relationships that bring the necessary spatial agency to perform the transgressive act of squatting. It will also allow to ask questions about how sites of dissent form a relationship with their exterior and immediate surroundings.

My research diary in the first story of this cycle of journey contained the lived experience of a collective transformation – from an empty building into an inhabited site of dissent. The creation of a bricollage of our livelihood in the squat, made of recycled objects from the street, was what attracted my attention to the process of transformation. My squatmate Felippa added another layer of meaning to it: Gathering objects at night from the street to turn them into furniture is part of a transformation within us. It partially frees us from reproduction of daily life in capitalist society. "Under capitalism, daily life consists of related activities which reproduce and expand the capitalist form of social activity. The sale of labor-time for a price (a wage), the embodiment of labour-time in commodities (saleable goods, both tangible and intangible), the consumption of tangible and intangible commodities (such as consumer goods and spectacles)," writes Freddy Perlman (Perlman, 2008, 2) about paid labour; the alienation of living activity to be able to consume within the set framework of behaviours, roles and commodities to sustain daily life in capitalism.

All this requires us to sell our time within the reproduction of capitalist social relationships to reproduce ourselves and the system within it. Within capitalist social relations "Labour is *indifferent* activity: indifferent to the particular task performed and indifferent to the particular subject to which the task is directed" (ibid., 3). Collecting our trash-furniture from the street was labour, too. A different labour performing a task which actually directly mattered to us, to our daily life and its reproduction.

We did not go into a furniture chain shop to buy what we needed to create a space for living – we did not have the money to do so. Instead, we have the time to roam the streets at night and sleep in late the next day. Our self-made trash-furniture is a little crack within the alienation of living activity. Creating a crack in our reproduction of daily life in capitalism is a collective form of political action, it is a collective transgression of the pattern of working – having little time left after work-consuming ready-made products to have more free time – working to be able to consume these products.

This transgression resulted in a different everyday life. Our rhythm of daily life had its own stubborn hours of waking and sleeping. Creating this everyday life together is a transformative process of horizontal learning about multiple transgressions, acquiring skills *for* these transgressions. The relationships that facilitate this horizontal learning, for example in the case of working with electricity or learning to reflect on our spatial practices, create another way of being in the world which projects horizontal social relationships into the present practices within our house. It becomes the site of dissent in our everyday life which had been in constant transformation since I had started to write my research diary about it.

In the squat that had just opened when I was sitting on its doorstep with Ian and Malu, relationships with the exterior had just started forming through spatial practices: the squatters were walking up to neighbours in the street and forming relationships with them whilst waiting for the police to arrive. In contrast, in the first story of this cycle of journeys, when I was sharing my research diary with my squat mates, we had already survived a visit of the police, spoken to neighbours, dwelt in our new home.

Comparing the freshly squatted building with our squatted home full of recycled furniture, the moments of their formation appear as contentious spatial practices in both stories. On different sites of dissent, moments of formation will take different shapes.

Permanent as well as temporary sites of dissent can be in the process of formation and/or transformation. However, the process of formation of a site of dissent does not include only material reality. It is a social, relational process. This is what Gina told me on the bench in one of my last journeys: learning, establishing a network of supportive relationships and a radical imagination is a necessary precondition for transgressive and contentious spatial practices creating sites of dissent.

The new axis of comparison between forming and transforming sites of dissent lays out and visibilises that sites of dissent not only consist of material things, like painted gates, barricades or tents, but also of the social relationships and the horizontal learning process about becoming a site of dissent. All sites of dissent go through a process of formation; some of them enter into a process of transformation afterwards. The formation and transformation of sites of dissent can be conceived as a continuum of different stages of unfolding contentious spatial practices.

THE SETTLING OF THE NOMAD

These reflections on an additional axis of comparison are a movement towards royal science. Returning to royal science after these journeys is helpful because it allows to structure and to comprehensively summarise the impressions, experiences and adventures collected sometimes in a rush when creating knowledge with nomad science on the journeys through sites of dissent.

Whilst nomad science could now proceed to discuss the stories with others, to collect different opinions, to find a consensus for analysis in a conversation, royal science stops and takes a deep breath. It strives to hold together what we have already gathered, it sticks to the precious data, not to lose a single bit of it (nomad science would be more indifferent – what counts is the process). Royal science would start to systematise the experiences to be able to look at them from a distance: was our comparison exhaustive, was it extensive enough to analyse contentious spatial practices on *different* sites of dissent? It takes time to answer these more general questions about comparative analysis which can help to keep an eye on the details during the interactive and messy process of analysis with nomad science. The expanded epistemology of border-thinking thus entails a permanent movement between ways of thinking about "empirical material" in royal science and ways of creating knowledge from collective experiences in nomad science. A movement towards royal science thus provides the nomad coming back from the journeys with a place for dwelling and reflection. It offers its perspective on what the nomad has collected, to put the backpack down for a moment and to go through its contents.

In the perspective of royal science, the content of the backpack of stories from the journeys through sites of dissent is a structured overview of the positioning of the stories from the five cycles of journeys on the three axes of comparison visualised in table 4.1. A fourth axis, the one of formation/transformation of a site of dissent has been added on the right side.

Table 4.1   Overview of the Case Studies

Narrated as Story in the	Case Study							
	Three Axes of Distinction						Additional Axis	
	Urban / Rural		Permanent / Temporary		Large-Scale / Concentrated		Forming / Transforming	
	Urban	Rural	Permanent	Temporary	Large-Scale	Concentrated	Forming	Transforming
1st Cycle of Journeys								
1st	X			X		X		X
2nd		X		X		X		X
3rd		X		X	X			X
4th		X		X	X			X
5th		X		X	X			X
2nd Cycle of Journeys								
1st		X		X	X			X
2nd		X		X		X		X
3rd		X		X		X		X
4th		X		X	X			X
3rd Cycle of Journeys								
1st		X		X		X	X	
2nd	X		X			X		X
3rd	X		X		X			X
4th Cycle of Journeys								
1st		X	X			X		X
2nd	X			X		X		X
3rd		X	X			X		X
5th Cycle of Journeys								
1st		X	X			X		X
2nd		X		X		X	X	
3rd		X	X			X	X	

Source: Author's own.

What does the perspective of royal science on the collected material uncover? It allows to see gaps in the comparison – it helped to add a new axis of comparison along which sites of dissent can be analysed and visualises that a rural/temporary/large-scale site of dissent is not included in the comparison. It can then speak back to nomad science in asking whether the nomad might have missed out on rural/temporary/large-scale sites of dissent during her chaotic journeys. It can raise the question of whether rural/temporary/large-scale sites of dissent would simply be too hard to maintain – after all, it would be a giant effort to create a temporary yet large-scale zone in a rural location. In doing so, royal science can point at possible tracks for an analysis of the material that the nomad has brought to the border zone.

Yet, for the nomad the act of sitting down and unpacking the material collected from sites of dissent has another additional dimension which is not visible in royal science. She is required to settle for a moment, to stop being on the road, to interrupt the nomadic movements between places that attract her, to resist the seductive attraction of being unseizable and to make herself available for reflection and critique.

Coming back from journeys directed by the logic of nomad science and accepting to settle in the border zone of royal science and nomad science is a moment when the travelling storyteller can seize a possibility of self-critique offered by royal science in return – after having exposed its rigidness, epistemological privileges and mechanisms of domination in the process of research.

Having been on the road for several years, cultivating a lifestyle of travel and flexibility, I am confronted with the question of my own contribution to sites of dissent whilst piecing the field notes together, transforming experiences into chapters of a manuscript. I have not become sedentary only to write, I was writing in trains and in the back of cars whilst hitchhiking long distances already, I was writing in guest rooms of friends and squatted gardens almost forgetting my laptop and papers outside in the rain. I have become sedentary in recognising that the movement of a nomad has no ethical guiding principle – it could depart in any direction: because of getting bored, failing to create meaningful tasks for oneself in a place, romanticised and individualised desires for adventures, or imaginaries of being particularly useful somewhere – in a specific place for a specific task.

Nevertheless, the lifestyle of the nomad performs a resistance to capture in changing one's position in space: resistance to being captured in a job, in recurring patterns, in dependencies of all kinds, resistance to being captured in a position or by administrative apparatuses. But is the movement of eluding capture necessarily a constant physical movement which leaves the travelling storyteller as individualised as the expert researcher?

On the journeys I have thus also discovered that the travelling storyteller can be sedentary and rooted in a place, can take on responsibilities for sustaining and maintaining these places if she discovers the power to resist capture, rigidity and fixation all in travelling between royal science and nomad science, in continuing to learn, travel and to be flexible, spontaneous, in giving space to self-critique and self-transformation.

I start to chop and store wood for the winters to come in several years, to give it enough time to dry. I put all my books on a shelf in one place, I start to project myself into the future collectively and to make plans with others, I accept that co-dependencies are not capture, are not stagnancy. A site of dissent turns into home, a home where I am still dwelling in the border zone when doing research, still travelling, still involved in struggles and collective theorisations. Settling thus does not mean to sit down and to write to become a researcher but to continue dwelling in the border zone whilst getting rid of the romanticised and individualistic aspects of picturing the figure of the travelling storyteller as a nomad. It is a further step towards ceasing to portray one's perspective as distinct from other perspectives, stopping to think that it has something *more* to say because it gained a special overview; it is a further step towards situating it in a place that one consciously chooses to belong.

It is from this place of belonging that I proceed to move towards nomad science with a collective analysis of the stories collected on the sites of dissent. This collective analysis creates another participatory space in which different types of knowing and knowledge are interwoven, put into relation to each other, each as a legitimate but different ways of knowing. Nevertheless, the collective analysis does not have to vacate its position in the field of royal science. Everything still takes place in the "right" order of a "proper" research project: I have presented my epistemological positioning, my concepts and theoretical frameworks. I have outlined my research focus, my methodological approach and presented my process of fieldwork. I am proceeding to a critical assessment of its outcomes. Yet, this critical assessment, the collective analysis, will be a patchwork of different ways of speaking and thinking again, will include the voices of co-researchers and participants and at the same time create a structured account of this process of analysis. It is situated in the border zone of royal science and nomad science, travelling back and forth between them, expanding their epistemological scope.

Chapter 5

Collective Analysis

INVITATION AND TRANSLATION

I am guilty of the nomadism that some authors accuse academic activists of (cf. Hoofd, 2010). In the moment of collective analysis, I could not bring all co-researchers and participants back together. Only some of them were present. Although I brought together stories from places where I was also rooted in a community of resistance, I have also been absent from these communities. Absence is the inevitable and uncomfortable consequence of engaging in nomad science as a travelling storyteller. It leads to my constant separation from different participants and co-researchers involved in different sites of dissent that are part of this research.

I am never in the company of all co-researchers and participants of this PAR at once. I could not take a collective decision with all of them on when to start a collective analysis. This choice was spontaneously taken with a few co-researchers instead. At that time, we were involved in the processes of self-organisation in an autonomous cultural centre. We were participating in the weekly assembly of the cultural centre, cleaning its kitchen and concert room, dealing with threatening letters from diverse institutions, organising events. Moments of collective knowledge creation regularly occurred during these activities. Different people would reflect in small groups about formal and informal hierarchies within the cultural centre, have debates about social inclusion over a cup of coffee, keep chatting together after a meeting and explore techniques of self-critique, analyse group conflicts and share experiences from other sites of dissent with a visiting band after their concert. "I would like to invite everybody to make a collective analysis of the stories collected in my field work in different sites of dissent," I told Ian.

"Sure. Let's do it. If your field work is completed, this week could be a good moment because we have some free time and I feel lots of people are up for discussions and reflections anyway," he said and added: "Why not? We could hang out in the garden and clean it a bit. There are no other events this week." I am thus inviting the reader to follow me into the garden of an autonomous cultural centre where the collective analysis took place.

During the collective analysis, the group of participants created dialogical, horizontal relationships between individual thought processes and gained insights which were worked out with our own rules and patterns. This process led to a collective discovery of the texture and refrain, of the differences and commonalities of different sites of dissent. This spontaneous, uncontrollable process of knowledge creation with nomad science was building on the comparative setting of case studies prepared by royal science.

It lasted over five hours and ended at night due to our mental exhaustion and tiredness. Those who participated described the session as enriching but also extremely wearying.

> When you create some kind of output together with other people, you first have a moment when your thoughts cross the thoughts of others. You have to explain your perspective and understand the perspective of the other person to decide together about whether you can form a collective representation of reality. (. . .) It is slow, too slow, it requires a lot of time and it requires focus and concentration. For me the discussion is enough. I do not need to participate in the writing of a text. I will remember the things that seem important to me. Maybe I do not follow the protocol of scientific knowledge all the way through, but I participate in making knowledge,

Ian said on the next day when I asked him if he could imagine writing down the results of the collective analysis with me.

About fifteen people gathered to analyse and contribute stories of spatial practices on sites of dissent.

I started with the narration of one of the stories from my fieldwork and other participants picked it up and added other stories, tracing the commonalities in the social dynamics that I had described. A conversation emerged between the people involved; some were speaking more than others. While the stories were being discussed and questions asked to the storytellers, I took notes of most parts of the conversation.

I would like to illustrate the difficulty of "translating" horizontal collective knowledge creation with nomad science into the language of royal science.

To do so, I will briefly return to my notes and memories of this moment of collective analysis:

Sina stutters slightly when she starts speaking. She picks up some aspects of the story about urban riots after the eviction of a social centre. These are the aspects she wants to focus on, she says.

"Mmh," she starts and makes a long pause. "Shared thoughts. I believe this is very important. How else can you hold a bigger space with many people? When people share the same thoughts, they can share a space and create a space. There, these thoughts are expressed." She makes another pause. "I mean . . . I think, shared thoughts are something like this: this social centre cannot be destroyed. It would be pure oppression to destroy community-made resources. And we are not going to watch this happen. (. . .) I don't know. . . . You know what I mean though? Mmh . . . it is about a resistance against something. It is a shared holistic perspective; it includes more, much more, than just the question of liberated space. And this is what I want to say: that the people who share it actualise their relationships in space, while struggling for greater social justice – or call it whatever – *together*."

Now, several people lifted their hands to show that they would like to speak. We negotiate who is speaking next with body language; many participants are happy to defer their turn of speaking to someone else so that they could take more time for reflection.

In this session, we are building on the way of speaking in horizontal culture established in the assembly in the cultural centre where decisions are taken in consensus. There is a shared, implicit understanding of the discussion rules: everyone has the right to speak and to finish speaking without being interrupted, everyone's opinion is worth the same and is a valid contribution.

After Sina has finished, the next participant takes a turn speaking and adding thoughts to the collective analysis. Sometimes other aspects of the story are developed further, sometimes oral contributions draw connections between previous contributions or weigh them against each other. The result is a collective development of a story, told by myself or another participant. Connections between different stories covering similar aspects of sites of dissent emerged in the course of the evening. The collective analysis is a patchwork of stories and enunciations that form a rhizomatic structure of knowledges containing various nodes and connections. It is held together in an oral presentational form that emerged temporarily – as a collectively created meaning in a specific social space and time.

How can Sina's oral contribution be translated into the language of research? Neither can this form of knowledge creation be isolated from the context in which it takes place, nor is Sina's way of speaking reproducible in a paper that counts as research in the sense of royal science.

In translating the knowledge of participants from nomad science into a form of knowledge which is closer to royal science, I had to structure, cut, recollect and recompose the statements, assertions and utterances of participants into this textual presentational form which retraces a rhizomatic process of analysis. Yet, the discussion itself was not a linear process; loose ends of the conversation were lost and picked up much later or not picked up at all; parallel trains of thought were started at the same time and intermingled chaotically. People got lost in their own thoughts and did not finish sentences; spontaneous insights were given space and concluding remarks were missing.

Keeping in mind that my translation is also a distortion, I will now present the collective analysis of the outcomes of this PAR in two rounds. To face this problem of translation, I have chosen a writing style that includes both – the ways participants are speaking (to make their form of knowledge visible) as well as paragraphs in which I have made a summary of contributions (to keep an acceptable length of this text) and retrace the structure of the session (to shape it along the lines of royal science and to bring it into a presentational form that is able to speak back to research). No doubt, there are other presentational forms that succeed in overcoming the problems of translation between royal science and nomad science. This is the form that I found suitable in the specific context of this process of collective knowledge creation.

Back in the garden of the autonomous cultural centre, on that evening, the process of collective analysis consisted of several steps. In the first step, I took the role of the storyteller in re-narrating the stories presented in the previous chapter. In the second step, questions were raised (by myself or by other participants) and discussed collectively. In the course of the evening, after the first few stories, the questions quickly started to be based on several stories (also on stories contributed by other participants). In the third step, at a later point during the discussion, we started to notice and highlight several recurring issues around which the questions revolved. I will thus present and structure our discussions of these issues: *Becoming Organism(s)*, *Appropriation of Space*, *Borders*, *Time-Spaces*, *DIY and Dwelling*, *Contention*, *Plateaus* and *Transgression and Transformation*. For us, these are the social formations that shape the texture of sites of dissent.

A texture is a pattern in the consistency of a social phenomenon made of social relationships and dynamics within a political context. On sites of dissent, these patterns are not regular; they consist of several social formations which are variously interwoven.

In the first round of our collective analysis of the fieldwork, questions concerning *Horizontal Social Relationships* occurred as a refrain in the analysis. A refrain draws a continuation between different social formations (Anderson, 1980, 67). What is between the refrains, the pattern of the texture might change, cover and connect different social formations in different ways – depending on the social relationships, dynamics and their situatedness in different contexts. The refrain connects these variations and turns them into one song, one choreography, one articulation (McCormac, 2013). In relation to the social formations which it connects, a refrain can be captured in terms of ideology, social values, morals or ethical codes of conduct as well as political positionings. It is something which gives a common ground to the practices which are shaping the social formations in the texture of a social phenomenon – here: a site of dissent.

OPEN/FOCUS GROUP DISCUSSION

Becoming Organism(s)[1] – this issue emerged in our discussions in relation to the build-up of collective energies and affinities between people in the story about the rural action camp where I was present with Brian and Angelo. It also emerged in relation to my story of an experience of squatting an empty building.

In our discussion, the term *becoming organism(s)* is an interpersonal relational process which designates the possibility of a collective experience of empowerment. The social formation of *becoming organism(s)* is something that takes place between people in and through a site of dissent.

The questions we formed in relation to the process of becoming organisms were: What creates social cohesion on a site of dissent? What kind of shared desire or social vision is forming communities?

The topic of horizontal social relationships as a politics of prefiguration that is attempted on sites of dissent is intertwined with the process of becoming organism(s). Using the words "becoming organism(s)" in relation to spatial practices on sites of dissent means to suggest that a special relationship has formed between people present on the site. This relationship enables them to exist as antagonistic organisms capable of defending themselves and actualising their political desires. *Becoming organism(s)* thus designates an intensity of collective experience on sites of dissent. This experience includes a feeling of organic unity with others in full consciousness of one's individuality, of what this feeling means for oneself, individually. It is a self-made way of relating to each other, one that does not accept any pre-set social rules or norms of relationships, and one that does not fit into any group category of the sociopolitical order.

Penny: "That's it! A site of dissent has to reward people somehow. Otherwise, maybe it is not worth its existence? And then I think it is exactly this feeling of collectivity, but not of an enforced collective with shared characteristics or an identity, no way! . . . it is exactly this organism-thing that people want. Because it gives them some new freedom of relating to each other. Here, for example, we are not a group of students and we do not relate as students. We are not an association and we do not relate as members of an association. We relate in a way that is unimaginable for the system."

Vini: "I don't think that becoming an organism solely means that people are in resistance together. This is important, but this should not be everything. Not everything is about resistance. A big and important part is. On a site of dissent, people are not only united by what they are against – they are united by how they are against it. Some kind of holistic ideal, or maybe, yes – a political vision of the world."

Our reflections on the issue of *appropriation of space*

Were triggered by the stories about the occupation of an urban square, about the riots after the eviction of Punkto32, about the situation of just opening a squat in a neighbourhood, as well as the story about my reflection with Gina on a future site of dissent while sitting on a bench in the fifth cycle of journeys.

In the discussion, we asked ourselves whether a site of dissent is restricted to its physical space; when and how does it expand? How is space appropriated, transformed?

For us, appropriation of space is a praxis of social transformation which includes personal transformational processes (the construction of autonomous identities, interpersonal processes leading to a collective intensity of experience [cf. Peterson, 2001]) as well as transgressive and transformative spatial practices (creating a materiality of sites of dissent, a physical space for dwelling, encounters, political articulation). This praxis of social transformation is directed at a fostering of horizontal social relationships. These are neither given in the space outside of sites of dissent nor within sites of dissent. Yet, sites of dissent are the fertile ground on which horizontal social relationships can blossom.

Appropriation of space means that an *other* kind of space is created, a space which has not existed before in its physical location. Appropriated space cannot be managed by administration. It is a crack in socio-spatial order and therefore offers to its inhabitants, users and creators an escape route from gentrification, from numeration, from institutional control. It is a way of creating space that is brought about by contentious and escapist spatial practices: to not register, to not sign in, not enroll, to not apply for something – a contract or a grant, to hide from view, to do it at night, to circumvent the usual flows of spatial organisation, to disobey regulations. Although appropriation of space can include the opposites of several of the itemised spatial practices, it will always also include some contentious and/ or escapist spatial practices, too – be they the smallest "hidden transcript" (Scott, 1990) of resistance.

Penny: "We are constantly being alienated from the physical spaces around us. What I mean, is what some – including you – call gentrification. Signs say: You can't do this here. This is private. And, more and more, the urban space turns into a commodity; an investment – to build new buildings to make money. There are very few spaces where people can create something entirely different. (. . .) What is the space that you can really design yourself? It is not even your own flat, because it belongs to your landlord. Autonomous means: I want to have a stage here and I am going to build it with my friends now."

Felippa: "When and how is space appropriated for a site of dissent? Mmh, I think this depends on two things: whether there is a collective vision of resistance – something like a shared feeling of 'the world is not right and we should do something against this' – and collective praxis of dwelling and DIY. I think that if these two things are given, it is possible to take space for a site of dissent or to expand an existing one."

For the appropriation of space, we have elaborated a comparative perspective of the notion and importance of (1) a praxis of dwelling and DIY and (2) a shared vision of sociopolitical dissent in relation to different forms of sites of dissent. Comparing temporary and forming sites of dissent to permanent and transforming ones, we found that on temporary and forming sites a "collective vision of resistance" is a driving force for the appropriation of space.

On permanent and transforming sites of dissent, the appropriated space is maintained through the spatial practices of DIY and dwelling.

Our reflections about the practices of *DIY and dwelling*

on sites of dissent were stimulated by the part of the story about my arrival at the action camp with Angelo and Brian which resembled a self-build village, by the story about the construction of wooden cabins and huts on the occupied square in the city centre as well as the self-build infrastructure at the camp on the wasteland, together with my account of how I was collecting furniture for the interior of the house that I was living in with my four friends. In all these stories practices of DIY and dwelling emerged as a constitutive element of sites of dissent. But what does DIY mean in this context? Is it simply about the skills that one needs in order to build a wooden cabin with a hammer and some nails? Is dwelling purely about having the time to hang out in the physical space of a site of dissent, having a drink and a chat?

DIY is an autonomous approach to spatial appropriation. It "is the idea that you can do for yourself the activities normally reserved for the realm of capitalist production" (Holtzman, Hughes and Van Meter, 2007, 44). DIY is therefore a possible escape route out of capitalist production. It includes thereby a diverse range of activities: starting from cultural production of music, magazines, independent media, it includes the provision of alternative and self-managed infrastructures (such as field kitchens for food distribution, sleeping places, hospitals) and the learning of vital skills such as setting up electric circuits in buildings, repairing old cars, growing vegetables. DIY is thus a spatial practice of autogestion and self-management. It fosters and facilitates appropriation of space and horizontal learning processes:

Vallerie: "Whether I am here cooking for the collective cantine, taking on a task or just hanging out and doing nothing at all – it is all the same: there is no capitalist purpose of producing some market value. (. . .) Here, as on many other sites of dissent, you have the space to withdraw from all this. And it is in this moment of withdrawal that other things emerge between people. These are the moments when those who dwell on a site of dissent are becoming one organism, when we exist together – not for the purpose of capitalist production but for our own purpose. It is also about a kind of dissent that is a bit special . . . the kind of dissent against the pressure to perform, against the pressure to perform productive subjects and successful lifestyles. . . . It is saying: I am refusing to do things that feed this system. Isn't it surprising, all the things that are contained in the meaning of dwelling?"

Contention with the status quo – this is another issue

Which appeared in our discussions about the relationship between sites of dissent and their exterior. Many different stories triggered these discussions several times. What is *the exterior* in relation to the riots that occurred after the eviction of Punkto32? In the cases of inhabited squatted buildings, the contention with the exterior is the constant threat of eviction. The queer social centre Vagana is in contention with dominant social (gender) norms.

We asked ourselves: What forces play into the contention between a site of dissent and its exterior? In our discussion, we elaborated if and how sites of dissent facilitate a liberated everyday life which is at the heart of their contentious relationship with the sociopolitical status quo.

Fedric: "I think the main argument against sites of dissent is that people keep saying: it is not possible to live outside of capitalism, it is not possible to be free. Well, here we see that it *is* possible – at least for a moment, at least for some moments, as long as we are here and as long as we keep and defend this space. Why do sites of dissent constantly need to be defended? Because the ruling order is against these possibilities."

Ian: "I like the notion of nomad warriors. . . . Sites of dissent are also created and maintained by nomad-warriors. Warriors can be very different: unemployed, students, young punks, people who are fed up with their jobs, refugees, ecologists, people who had their life turned upside down, people who have all kind of problems with the world. . . . I think it is true that on sites of dissent we don't want war with the state. But a site of dissent is always threatened by the state in one way or another. Because the life that is being led here – it simply does not comply to laws and regulations.

For example, if you build a skate park yourself, it does not comply to the government's health and safety regulations and it will be closed down; if you open a free canteen giving away recycled food, it will be closed down for the same reasons; if you take an empty building, you get evicted. The nomad warriors simply don't do what the state expects them to do. Therefore, there will always be problems, there will always be 'war,' if you want to call it like that. (. . .) This is something that is not supposed to happen in capitalism: to have time for each other and develop collective desires. Outside of capitalist production and reproduction. Sorry for speaking that long . . . I have finished."

What about *borders*?

Does a site of dissent have to draw borders? If we are against borders, isolation and restrictions, why not build bridges instead?

These questions came up during the narration of the story about the camp on the wasteland which was fenced off from the outside and disposed of a night-watch that kept its borders safe; they also came up during the discussion about the invisible social border of the Infoshop on the pavement which was said to exist even if the door was open.

In our discussion, we established that the borders surrounding a site of dissent can consist of very different dynamics. Yet, every site of dissent disposes of borders – be they made of physical obstacles or of social dynamics. Borders are lines of power crossing space. They have a great influence on the dynamics of contention between a site of dissent and its exteriority.

Felippa: "Sites of dissent need social borders, too. Sometimes . . . especially when they are supposed to be a safe space for some people. Automatically some other people will be excluded. This requires constant communication between the people who are involved in the space. Here, I have the desire to make some social borders, too. I am neither a waitress nor a social worker. There are some people I don't want to have constantly inside of the space. And this is the reason for exclusive behaviour – which is a problem! I know."

Vallerie: "In a site of dissent, my personal borders are respected. For me, personally, this means: no discrimination. Making such borders together means to have confidence in the group process. But I think there is a difference if a collective on a site of dissent reacts against a threat and makes borders to protect itself, or if it is actively building these borders to exclude other people. (. . .) The problem is about the borders between people. Can someone be my partner in a struggle although we are completely different? Of course! Of course they can be . . . but the borders that we make between us prevent us from thinking that. Often we say: oh, they are just hippies! Or: they are just students, they are not political. And then people feel unwelcome . . . because we put their identities in a box. And this is the problematic border."

"Of course, we need to overcome borders between us and our fellows that are forced upon us, that create a hierarchy between us. They are artificial borders. Stripped off artificial borders we can start to form new social spaces – outside of categories and classifications. But in this world, we need to create borders ourselves, too. To keep existing. Unfortunately," said Ian.

In our discussion, we compared different sites of dissent and came to the conclusion that on rural, urban, permanent, temporary, forming, transforming and on large-scale as well as on concentrated sites of dissent physical borders (material obstacles in space delimiting the site of dissent, such as walls or fences) are used as self-defense mechanisms. On all these types of sites, social borders (for example, giving new people weird looks or other kinds of exclusive behaviour) can equally function as a self-defense mechanism where physical borders were not erected. At the same time, borders can be drawn between people on the inside of the site of dissent, too. They are then often based on framings of prescribed identities which open the possibility for the discursive construction of Otherness – that kind of different Other who cannot be included in a common decision-making process because he or she is supposed to have different interests.

On some occasions, we used the word *plateau*

To refer to sites which provide a diversity of places for different cohabiting subject positions as well as time-spaces of encounter between those.

We took the questions about borders with us into the comparative analysis of some large-scale sites of dissent (Caput, the hood and BUT). They also re-emerged when we were discussing the stories about the dissonance between the spaces of Vagana and the cellar of the Collective. We asked ourselves how sites of dissent can accommodate the differences between those who inhabit and use them and how they can provide time-spaces of encounter for different subject positions which empower themselves collectively in finding and acting upon a shared vision of sociopolitical dissent.

Plateaus are the opposite of borders. They designate a space which is not wilfully cut up into snippets of a forced upon shape, a space in which different identities do not need to erect a fence between each other to coexist. A plateau is a horizontal plane on which different identities and pockets of meaning exist in relation to each other. This part of the meaning of *plateau* is to be found in the theoretical, Deleuzian plateaus as well. For us, however, plateaus are also a form of spatial self-organisation which escapes the social organisation of space and create sociability with self-made rules instead – in including the social formations of becoming organism(s), appropriation of space, (transgression) of borders.

Vini: "Then we know: places where different groups of people coexist can emerge even inside a single, small squatted house. It is not the space that counts. What this means is that it is okay if not everybody has exactly the same political vision, looks the same, thinks the same, comes from the same or similar social background . . . under certain circumstances all this does not matter. That is when there is the possibility to find and share a political expression. This can be: we are all against this coal mine . . . because . . . and the *because* can look very different. A space like this emerges if all those who are against the coal mine find time and space to chat to each other about *why*. In your story, this happened in the workshops in the camp. But okay, hey, this can happen everywhere. Maybe in BUT this happens during their assemblies, maybe on walks through BUT . . . not sure. But it is not only and not simply about encounters between different people. One of the things that are necessary is that people have time for each other. Time for talking and an interest in getting to know each other."

Penny: "A site of dissent should be a place where the margins meet. I mean the social margins, the marginalised of this society. A site of dissent has its margins, too: these are the people who feel they do not really belong to the site of dissent – for different reasons. Some might think: I am just a single mother, not a political activist. Others might think: I am against Nazis, but I am not sure if we really should get rid of all cops. This is just an example. . . . To form a horizontal space, everyone who is present in the centre of the site of dissent has also to be present on the margins; there should be no margins – or at least as little as possible."

Time-spaces of encounter are social formations

In which different subject positions meet and connect on an affective level whilst exploring the possibilities of a shared articulation of sociopolitical dissent. In the preceding part of the discussion, we had already established that these are necessary for a site of dissent to live out a (spatial) articulation of sociopolitical dissent and to create horizontal social relationships.

Vallerie: "Mmh . . . what I am going to say now is especially about the more permanent sites of dissent: I think when a site of dissent is forming, other things are important than later on, when it already exists since a good while. In the beginning, the direction is more clear: we have to unite our energies to make something new happen, a new space, a new event. It is something additional, something that has not been there before, something that clearly makes the world a little bit better because it adds our political expression and makes everything a bit more colourful, a bit more intense. Later on, it is about finding our commonalities again, because . . . we have a site of dissent, so what now? I don't think that it is absolutely necessary to organise everything together as long as everyone is sure about what we have in common: a collective radical vision, the certainty that we need to keep this space with all our forces united. Just as long as everyone has their space to contribute to this. Once this certainty is less certain, other things are necessary: socialising, parties . . . "

Fedric: "Socialising can be the same as a party. It can give you the same feeling of letting go. Time does not matter, what you do tomorrow does not matter. You are here, talking, spending time with these people because you feel you are sharing something. It is this process of getting to know each other, what we called becoming organism a few hours ago. You don't need loud music and blinking lights for this. You just need to be aware of what is happening. (. . .) It is about keeping a radical space and caring for the people you are doing it with. It is about taking time for each other. If you take time for each other, to listen to each other, to hear other political opinions, if you show that you care for the people, it means you care about what they think. You will learn about *why* they are doing what they are doing. Being on a site of dissent together is not enough. You can build a barricade together and not care for each other. Your barricade is worth nothing then."

Through our comparative analysis of the emergence of time-spaces of encounter on sites of dissent, we noticed that these are "particularly important to keep transforming sites of dissent alive," as one participant has phrased it.

The issue of *transgression and transformation*

Dominated our discussion towards the end of the session. It was already past midnight and we have been focusing on the discussion since more than four or five hours at this point. Some of the participants had stated that they were tired but refused to interrupt the discussion and to postpone it because they felt that this question was of particular importance to them.

Sina: "Sites of dissent have a cycle of life. When they are forming, it is a completely different kind of effort that we need to make to articulate our dissent and our practical utopian visions through them . . . when a site already exists – this is more difficult. Of course . . . if we do nothing and just use it and hang out: who guarantees that the space that formed will stay a radical space? A space that questions authority and domination? Let's finish this."

Ann: "I have a suspicion: I think, if I would ask people who live on sites of dissent that already exist since quite a while . . . if I would ask them: what keeps you up? What makes you believe that resistance is not futile, that you can live in constant opposition and work on alternatives? I think they would mention things that keep them antagonistic – breaking rules, doing direct actions, being open to new people. It is about a constant transgression of one's situation, about not accepting the confines, the social confines."

We concluded the discussion about transgression and transformation in agreeing that a site of dissent is a space where norms are constantly challenged in one way or another. Transgressions are also acts which usually get punished or repressed. If a site of dissent offers the possibility for its users to oppose these repressions collectively in fostering mutual aid and solidarity, it will be in a constant process of transformation in which the conditions for this solidarity are negotiated. These conditions are based on the collective desire for horizontal social relationships – the recurring refrain in the texture of sites of dissent.

In this discussion, we concluded that the *desire* for horizontal social relations is what brings people to participate in sites of dissent; it is a political leitmotiv which brings people to enter them and to spend time there. The desire for horizontal social relationships develops from discontent with the world how it is. It is a desire that stretches out beyond one's personal living conditions – it is thus a desire for more profound and radical transformations that one cannot achieve alone in one's personal life.

Sites of dissent are then the physical places where this desire is given the opportunity to be lived out, where it is no longer suppressed. Sites of dissent are the locations of *power to* transform the social world: There are no other spaces for horizontal social relationships without oppression, no other spaces than the ones we create for ourselves through the desire for a world that has not yet come into being but shines through in the cracks of the world that is now. Sites of dissent are thus spatial prefigurations of social utopias.

The darkness of the night has swallowed the garden of the autonomous social centre completely since a long time. Our faces are slightly lit by a few candles which I had placed around myself to be able to take notes. Ann sighs: "This is intense . . . I am exhausted. But it was very good. We should do this more often: sharing our politics like this."

"I cannot focus any longer," I say and put the pen down. "I would like to contribute to what you say and take more notes, but it is impossible. We have been here too long."

"Let's do this again – another time!" Penny says and we start cleaning up the tables.

ANALYSING IN THE KITCHEN

"What did you think about this discussion?" I ask Penny whilst cleaning up.

"This discussion? . . . you mean, what I think about the outcomes – well, that is if there *are* any clear outcomes at all . . . what do *you* think?"

We carry some cups back into the house. Outside everyone is saying goodbye to each other. I am trying to think about the clarity of the outcomes. Penny picks up the conversation in the kitchen: "I think we have traced some lines of escape, of flight; out of the world how it is and towards change. But they are just lines, just some directions. Nothing substantive."

"Lines of flight?" I know them as a concept, as a sociological or philosophical one. And Penny seems to see them in our analysis. Maybe she sees something different in the "lines of flight" than me? Ian joins us in the kitchen while we speak about lines of flight and wash the cups. "Lines of flight? We are talking about multiple way of breaking out of control? This is what you see as the results . . . ? Interesting! This is what I see as lines of flight: energy that breaks through the cracks in a system of control, that shoot off. And as they do so, they show the space in which it is still possible to flee and to disappear, despite the system of control."

Penny asks me: "You said lines of flight are a sociological concept, though . . . ?"

"Well, it is a term. It was developed by Gilles Deleuze and Félix Guattari in their book *A Thousand Plateaus* which I like a lot. It means that there are infinite possibilities of escape from reality in reality. From the reality that you want to see change. The moment when you cross a line, a threshold. *Line of flight* is how Brian Massumi translated *ligne de fuite* from the French original of the book. I think in French *ligne de fuite* could mean a lot of other things, too: winding-away, fleeing, escaping. Deleuze and Guattari represent power relations in terms of lines. Lines of power. The power of the state against the people, the state apparatus against the nomad warriors and such power relations. Through lines of flight people become *other* and empower themselves in escaping that which has power over them. It is used in therapy and conflict resolution, in gender studies and in lots of other contexts (cf. Winslade, 2009)."

Penny says then: "Okay, another example for a line of flight would be in this book *Anarchy in Athens* – a guy speaks about the protests in Thessaloniki; how a radically transgressive act can produce solidarity and connect people . . . because it is a radical act which cracks the system of control (Apoifis, 2016, 143). Is this moment in the protest a line of flight then?"

"I would say so," replies Ian hesitantly. "How does Deleuze and Guattari sound when they define the lines of flight?"

> Multiplicities are defined by the outside: by the abstract line, the line of flight or de-territorialization according to which they change in nature and connect with other multiplicities. The plane of consistency (grid) is the outside of all multiplicities. The line of flight marks: the reality of a finite number of dimensions that the multiplicity effectively fills; the impossibility of a supplementary dimension, unless the multiplicity is transformed by the line of flight; the possibility and necessity of flattening all of the multiplicities on a single plane of consistency or exteriority, regardless of their number of dimensions. (Deleuze and Guattari, 2013, 8)

Deleuze and Guattari evoke a triad of conceptual lines: molar lines, molecular lines and lines of flight – which are co-implicated although they "express different compositional processes" (Windsor, 2015, 158). This means that lines of flight can be found in other compositional processes, such as molar lines or molecular lines, and the other way around, there can be molar lines and/or molecular lines in lines of flight. "Molar lines subject bodies to essentialising principles" (ibid., 158), such as, for example, the social policing of gender norms. Reading Deleuze and Guattari's concepts, it could be said that "Molar lines territorialise, organize and stratify, relaying dispersive flows of desire into administrable regimes and patterns" (ibid., 158), such as, for example, the commercialised promotion of heteronormative sexuality. Molecular lines are the forces of *shift* within molar lines. They have rather processual powers over the bodies and organisms, they shift them into directions and into forms of becoming (cf. ibid., 159), such as, for example, a course of life that can be represented in a CV in order to get a specific internship to become a better flexible, neoliberal working subject in Western capitalist societies. Here, lines of flight or "desire lines" break away from prescribed pathways: "Where molecular lines may loosen molar segmentaries, lines of flight are a decisive escape" (ibid., 164). Lines of flight decenter centers and disrupt hierarchies. They can be understood as a metaphor for everyday resistance, they are bridges to a new social formation within the everyday (Usher, 2010, 71). In the everyday, lines of flight are moments of escape which connect different points and people, in different social formations. The decentering of power flows is felt as a collective experience of flight, of connectedness in this movement of transgression. The discussion of the G8 protests in Scotland by *The Free Association* is another example for lines of flight applied to (political) practice as a sociological concept:

> Meetings are normally painful exercises in frustration, but here it was different. There was such an intense concentration of effort, such focus, that creativity, wit, imagination, flexibility and good sense seemed to come naturally. You could stagger out of a meeting drunk on the sense of connection with other people. Vibrating with it. It was that visceral. (. . .) When we heard about the successful blockade of the M9, we felt as if we had been there too. . . . When we heard that the Gleneagles fence had been breached, we felt it was us who'd torn it down. (The Free Association, 2005, 18–22)

"Well, in our analysis people actually constantly kept tracing lines of flight," remarks Penny. "For example Fedric, when he was talking about how you, in the house with your friends, kept collecting furniture and breaking the law or just transgressing standard ways of behaviour; he was saying how this was a line of flight – to do it again and again; and how it helps to emotionally survive in capitalism. Remember? I have the feeling people constantly kept doing that: retracing lines of flight within the different topics that we discussed, the different social formations, becoming organism and so on."

"This was in our discussion, wasn't it?" says Ian. "Finding out where we trace lines of flight and jumping from one line of flight to the next. Lines of flight are also part of the texture of sites of dissent, so it was natural to speak about them so much."

We sit down in the kitchen, make another tea and start thinking a bit more about the lines of flight that suddenly appear to us as the key concepts of our collective analysis of the stories.

"We have focused so much on the distinct topics – appropriation of space, DIY – we asked ourselves: What is it? Why is it important to us? How can it liberate us? What else does it mean? This is the conceptual path to the line of flight," Penny says.

"Let's retrace it bit by bit," I suggest and Ian starts talking about "the moment when we spoke about appropriation of space":

> I remember only bits of what we said about appropriation of space. But one thing we said clearly shows that we were retracing lines of flight: we said that appropriation of space means that another kind of space is created. This is because the line of flight shoots off into unknown territory. It explores the space beyond administration, the space that is born out of revolt – not registering, we said, not signing on, not applying for something. A movement of escape, of flowing or fleeing, as you said in French. And we also have noticed that appropriation of space and the line of flight that is traced is never purely a line of flight. It can be co-implicated with molar lines.

"Yes, Vini and Vallerie have been speaking about DIY like about a line of flight, too," Penny says. "An escape route from capitalist production – a line of creativity and speed as you say Deleuze would say. To build something up here, to create something new there. Vallerie said that DIY makes you free. That with DIY you can trace a line of escape. She said that if you do things yourself, you can suddenly get up and say: Now, I go dumpster diving. It is time to get food. You do not obey to fixed working hours. You are following the line of flight. With your body and with your time you invent another way of being in the world. One that was not foreseen, one that does not fit into a box."

"And you have said something else that was clever, too," I laugh. "It was in relation to the social formation of borders. Everyone was talking about how we need borders on sites of dissent. Well, that was kind of the proof that lines of flight and molar lines are co-implicated. Because for sure we want to over-come borders between people, overcome the lines and fences that divide us. You have said that borders create hierarchies between us – and forced upon distinctions, too. Lines of flight are then those wild moments when chains break and something is unleashed, when it shoots across social borders and explores the spaces on the other side. (. . .) In this sense, being anti-racist is kind of a line of flight."

"After all, another way of tracing lines of flight is to be in motion," adds Penny yawning. "I need to go to bed," she says. Our conversation was not going to continue much longer. We had become aware of all possible lines of flight that we had traced in the collective analysis.

"So what did we learn now?" asks Ian. "That sites of dissent consist of a texture. This texture is made of social formations like borders, time-spaces for encounter and so on. And these social formations open up lines of flight on the sites of dissent."

"Then, actually, all the social formations that we were talking about, you see them as progressions, *processes of becoming*? As in becoming what we desire to be; that *free* desire that is autonomous from molar lines and molecular lines?"

"This is getting very abstract," says Penny, "I am really going to bed now." She gets up and stretches.

Through this interruption I become fully aware of what had just happened between Penny, Ian and me. My participatory quality of attention is activated as it shifts away from the content of our discussion and towards the key interactional moment that we had just shared as co-researchers. *This was a moment of reflection during the participatory action research. It is part of the collective analysis of research outcomes.* Says a voice in my head. It is the voice of the researcher who does not speak to Penny and Ian any more. Are they aware of the research process? Just as I form this question in my head, Ian jokes: "Well, we have now secretly analysed the analysis again. In the inner circle. This is not very horizontal."

"Why not?" says Penny. "Horizontality does not mean that everyone does everything together all the time. Of course, there can be a participatory process of analysis which runs in concentric circles. Good night!"

"Concentric circles?" I look at Ian and he shrugs his shoulders.

"I guess she means that you start analysing in a group and then you make a second circle of analysis in a smaller group and then in the end maybe you can have a go at the outcomes yourself. But our voices would still be present because your circle of analysis emerges from and is inspired by our discussion – just like our discussion was inspired by the group discussion just before and the voices of the others were still present in our reflections – it is like a spiral." I like Ian's suggestion.

I will take time for writing down what Ian and Penny have contributed; I will attempt to bring all loose ends of the theoretical concepts that we touched upon together into a web of theorisations; I will weave the body of a text. In the following chapter, I will pursue the question of the relevance of lines of flight for articulations of sociopolitical dissent. How do they translate into political practice?

Chapter 6

Lines of Flight towards Horizontality

LINES OF FLIGHT TOWARDS HORIZONTAL
SOCIAL RELATIONSHIPS

Desire is the driving force of lines of flight (Windsor, 2015). But there are different ways of conceptualising desire in a political context. The psychoanalyst Jacques Lacan states that desire is always the desire of the Other (Lacan, 1998, 235). It is the desire for recognition from this "Other," and secondly also desire for the thing that we suppose the Other desires, the thing that she lacks. To put it in different words, desire pushes for recognition by something essentially Other than ourselves. It is this dependence on the Other for recognition which is, according to Lacan, responsible for structuring our desires. For Deleuze, who adapts Lacan's account of the oedipal structure in desire to analyse the workings of capitalist societies, desire cannot exist without lacking something, it is subjected to law, so that it desires what is forbidden (Deleuze, 1988). "Desire is defined negatively as the limit structuring consciousness, while itself escaping reality and consciousness," explains Philip Goodchild about the Deleuzian vision on desire (1996, 125). As for Deleuze, desire is not something pre-existent and repressed but something which invests social relations.

"The spectacle transforms each of our desires into something it can cope with," observes Ravage (1999) just as there is the desire to break away from repression and to transcend the limitations that are set for desires. In the article *Desire is Speaking* in the magazine *Do or Die: Voices from the Ecological Resistance* a squatter is quoted:

I feel at home in the squatters' movement because I can live and work there and be politically active, together with people who generally have no illusions, without getting stuck in a "no-future" attitude. People who have no illusions about the welfare state regarding housing, work, culture, love and whatever else is for sale. No illusions about parliamentary politics. People who resist nonetheless, not against the establishment, nor randomly, but because they have their own ideas about how they want to live and who want to fight for a space to realise that. In short: people who do not want the patterns and perspectives of their lives being dominated by what society has to "offer," but by their own insights and desires. (Ibid.)

Here, desire is a line of flight from the capitalist system of production and reproduction, from capitalist temporalities in the everyday. It spills over into contentious spatial practices of autonomous social movements, as the quote shows, "live and work [there] and be politically active, together with people who (. . .) resist nonetheless, not against the establishment, nor randomly, but because they have their own ideas about how they want to live and who want to fight for a space to realise that." This is what is desired here: to live and to be able to actualise one's desires together with others. It is the desire to be able to shape one's life autonomously, together with others who are enabled to do so, too. A desire for horizontal social relationships between oneself and the Other, that which is exterior to oneself. The desire for horizontal social relationships thus pushes towards drawing lines of flight. Turned into concrete spatial practices it could manifest in squatting, creating contentious spatial events in riots and protests, in temporary sites of dissent, in square occupations, land occupations and in permanent social centres in neighbourhoods, but also in many other spatial practices.

Horizontal social relationships are the political leitmotiv of autonomous social movements. They are something which lacks, something which will never be achieved completely because domination and discrimination are integral parts of the current social order, the current capitalist system of production and reproduction, with parts of the state apparatuses enforcing it on a global level and within the everyday lives of its subjects.

Prefiguring horizontal social relationships into one's present practice – this is something which can be forbidden by law in those instances where it decenters relations of power. For example, in most countries it is forbidden by law to squat and to live according to the desires of the squatter quoted in *Do or Die*. Such a lifestyle escapes the control of the state and disobeys to some of its rules.

Yet, lines of flight directed by desire for horizontal social relationships can be found and traced in diverse places within the everyday. They are not exclusively in autonomous social movements spatial practices.

The mundane practice of hitchhiking can be a line of flight, for example. Hitchhiking is a way of travelling that escapes commodified forms of movement. There is no customer-service relation when buying a train ticket, there are no fixed schedules and no passenger registration; no bureaucracy such as the one of buying or lending a car from a company; no contract, no fees; no subjection of one's personal movement from A to B to anything other than the spontaneity on the road and the unplanned encounters with other travelers. The hitchhiker can leave spontaneously, knowledge of the roads, of the lay of the land, will direct the hitchhiker to a petrol station on the motorway near a big city, or to a large road with enough space on the sides for cars to stop. Who will pick him or her up?

It is a coincidence, an unplanned encounter with someone who travels into the same direction and voluntarily stops to pick up a co-passenger out of curiosity, for a good story or just for a conversation in the car so as not to fall asleep. Anyone could decide to pick up a hitchhiker, maybe even to one's surprise. The hitchhiker turns into a fellow traveller, one that is about to make the road just like oneself. It is a spontaneous and horizontal way of relating while travelling. Hitchhiking decentres the power relations that control travelling as a commodity (an all-inclusive holiday trip, a travel-company ticket sales auction, or becoming a car owner); it crosses the boundary of what counts as a legal and acceptable way of traveling, it horizontalises means of transportation: everyone could ask another person if there is still space in their car and if they are up for giving a lift (Purkis, 2012).

Hitchhiking follows the same logic as the lines of flight in spatial practices of autonomous social movements: it escapes control, decenters the centres of power, shoots off across boundaries and explores new territories; it follows its own rules and actualises desire; it is directed at transformation and therefore runs in a contentious relationship to molar lines: the rules of the state, the systems of representation, social norms and commodification, (institutional) processes of administration.

Yet, the line of flight in hitchhiking never breaks completely free from molar lines. In some places, hitchhiking is made illegal and hitchhikers get harassed by motorway police. Sometimes the luck of a hitchhiker leaves him or her in the lurch: no one is at the petrol station or all drivers refuse to give a lift. The hitchhiker too can feel subjected to the decision of others, of those who have the resources that he or she lacks. He or she is subjected to the pressure on making a good impression when asking others for a lift, to present oneself according to social norms. The line of flight is also not completely inclusive: not everyone can hitchhike; it is only an option for those who are healthy enough to live through a possibly long and exhausting journey, for those who are self-confident enough to travel with strangers and so on. Also the hitchhiker never completely ceases to depend on the commodities of travelling: the toilets in the petrol station, the cars of others.

A line of flight creates moments of rupture, of breaking out of set forms and practices, but they are never completely separate from molar lines. To stick to our example of hitchhiking: the commodification of travel will keep on restricting travelling to fixed categories (passenger, customer, train connection, airline manager, customer services, ticket fee). Hitchhiking as a line of flight will break out of this commodification, yet it can always be taken back by molar lines of commodification, too. The same is true for the lines of flight in autonomous social movement's spatial practices, and for other lines of flight directed by the desire for horizontal social relationships.

How does such an escape through a line of flight take place, how does one leave the old ways of thinking behind and starts weaving social relationships anew? Actually, here it is less fruitful to look at specific examples such as hitchhiking or squatting. They all have their specificities; they all have their situated how-tos. It is instead more interesting to look at what unites each example of a line of flight. Hitchhiking and squatting are of course not the only lines of flight, not the only practices that escape into something new. If we want to escape the old ways of thinking and weave social relationships anew, we need to learn to do it ourselves, by hand, in many different situations. What are the learnings on which we can draw here? How is a line of flight traced? From here, we can start moving towards the learnings of this research project in learning about the lines of flight in the creation and maintenance of sites of dissent; we have learned to recognise and to name them, we have created the terms to debate them. We can now learn to trace them.

These learnings can never be turned into a set of rules or fixed lessons. We can attempt to trace the lines of flight to their origins (like Penny, Ian and I did in the kitchen). We can try to reproduce them but they are unique to their environment.

In the following part of the chapter, I will first return to the analysis of the group discussion that Penny, Ian and I did in the kitchen. I will then attempt to trace the origins of the lines of flight that we have identified in the political practices discussed in the collective analysis of the stories. The aim is to summarise and make visible articulations of sociopolitical dissent driven by desire for horizontal social relationships as a political practice and an organising principle which can be placed and retraced in everyday life to draw lines of flight.

LINES OF FLIGHT AS AN ARTICULATION
OF SOCIOPOLITICAL DISSENT

In retracing these lines of flight, I will narrate how the actualisation of desire for horizontal social relationships became possible and hopefully contribute to movement-relevant knowledge on the creation and maintenance of spaces where this is a possibility. To do so, I will pick up material from the PAR process. I will return to the stories of sites of dissent, add insights from our collective analysis of them and insights that Ian, Penny and I gained in our late discussion in the kitchen. I will recount all of the three concentric circles of analysis.

How to draw a line of flight?

A first practical approach lies in *critical self-education towards horizontality.*

Late at night in the kitchen, Penny, Ian and I had established that lines of flight can be drawn in *becoming organisms.* Becoming organisms. In the collective analysis, this almost mystical term often used in Deleuzian writings (Deleuze and Guattari, 2013, 271–75) meant a creation of affective and empowering bonds between groups practicing autonomous politics. Becoming is an experience within a horizontal assemblage of pieces where one piece is drawn into the territory of another piece changing its constitution as a piece and bringing about a new unity, a new form of collective being (ibid., 298). For Deleuze and Guattari *becoming* is not about imitation or assimilation, it is generative of a new way of being and relating to each other which does not force different pieces into resemblance, which does not impose a function but brings about new ones. In the collective analysis of the stories and in the discussion with Penny and Ian, we have found examples for this process of becoming in the self-transformation of people on sites of dissent. Being present there together requires a self-education to learn the techniques of consensus decision-making in assemblies or educating each other to horizontal social relationships (through anti-discrimination workshops, awareness teams,[1] self-reflection on group behaviour in assemblies). This self-education to horizontal social relationships takes place through practices of taking time to reflect on dynamics of exclusion and oppression in ones' own practices, in ones' own social environment. Taking time to critically reflect on oppression and structural domination, as well as on possibilities of (self-)empowerment is a practice of horizontal approaches to learning and education (Freire, 1973). The line of flight consists of self-reflection, of actively fostering a critical consciousness for one's own social relations and actively inviting each other to join the reflection process, collective action on how to create less oppressive and hierarchical social relations. It is a line of flight from dominating and oppressive constructions of social relationships.

There are other tools to draw lines of flight, too. They can be found in the time-spaces consciously created for self-reflection processes within a social assemblage, any group running for example an autonomous social centre. Techniques helping to foster self-empowerment and conflict resolution within groups of autonomous social movements, dealing with social prejudice, and equal access to power have started to be developed many decades ago by social movements (cf. Butler and Rothstein, 1987). Other tools can be found in anarchist and horizontal pedagogies, where learning, self-education and creating knowledge is decoupled from formal and hierarchised distribution of competence (cf. Haworth, 2012).

Appropriation and transformation of space is another line of flight. In transforming the spatiality of social order, it shoots off into uncontrollable new territories. In the collective analysis and in the discussion with Penny and Ian in the kitchen, we have been speaking about the possibilities that squatting can offer as a line of flight: Amongst other things, squatting as a spatial practice opens up new spaces for creating another, horizontal and self-determined, kind of social relationships (cf. Ravage, 1999).

Horizontal social relationships need *places* to be put into practice. Without these they remain a theoretical idea and not a (real political) *practice* (taking place in material space). How to trace this line of flight? Occupations of squares for protest camps, squatting empty houses to create a new life within them, doing guerrilla gardening on an urban piece of wasteland – all these transformations and appropriations of space are examples of the line of flight accounts of which can be found in various books and zines (cf. Squatting Europe Kollective, 2013). In transforming spaces and recycling empty space, autonomous social movement participants also create places to meet and to come together – time-spaces of encounter, as they were referred to in the collective analysis. The creation of these requires a constant transformation process within existing sites of dissent, too. The spaces of sites of dissent constantly need to be re-appropriated to create collectivity within social relationships that are always in the process of becoming horizontal. An example of this can be found in the story about the recommencing assemblies in BUT. Collectivity is not simply something that is created through a singular action – it requires constant re-creation and renewal. Appropriation and transformation of space is a line of flight which also stretches beyond autonomous social movements spatial practices. It can be traced by anybody in public space, too.

I want to give an example through sharing an experience of taking the underground in a European city:

The train arrives and the doors open. Passengers stream out of the doors while I hear music coming from inside. On the ground, just to my feet in the middle of the compartments, a group of young people plays music with an old guitar, singing and offering chocolate to everybody, inviting them to come down from their seats and sit with them on the floor. Some other passengers have followed the invitation – amongst them an old man with a dog. The group of people sitting on the floor and getting to know each other for the time of a few underground stops is getting bigger and more diverse. I join, too. The entire compartment of the underground has suddenly transformed into something else. It is not any more a simple container to get transported from one place to another for the price of a ticket; it has turned into a social event, a time-space of encounter. New passengers enter the compartment in astonishment. It is not what they expected to see when taking the underground; it is not the place that it used to be. The young people and everybody who joined them are behaving out of place in the sense that they transgress and thus transform social norms and expectations of this behaviour in the space of the underground (Cresswell, 1996).

Here appropriation and transformation of space as a line of flight reveals a spatial practice which can be used, copied, studied, applied and performed in everyday life.

Method in research means tracing a learning process and making it possible to apply it elsewhere, in a different context. This is how these lines of flight should be taken. They are not simply lessons learned from personal and collective experience which has been analysed and reflected upon – they are guiding patterns which can be changed and adapted to different contexts, on different sites of dissent and outside of them. Notably, they can be used to study our own research questions, too. It is possible to trace lines of flight in the sphere of academic research, too.

LINES OF FLIGHT TOWARDS A PRACTICE
OF HORIZONTAL RESEARCH

This PAR project has been a learning process for how to draw lines of flight in research. To trace a line of flight through one's approach to research means to expand the epistemology of research, to move towards working with nomad science and to rupture with the confines of royal science, to deconstruct epistemological privileges in research in order to horizontalize it and to admit the voices of different people (from a *diversity* of backgrounds, not solely from an academic background of knowing) into a knowledge creation process about the world.

There are numerous academic accounts and introspections on the ways in which universities have become more entrepreneurial, more business-like, targeting at marketable subjects with their product of higher education on an increasingly globalised market (Considine and Marginson, 2000; Slaughter and Leslie, 1997). While this product is designed to make marketable subjects even more marketable, access to it is exclusionary for subject positions from poorer countries and for socioeconomically less privileged and less marketable subjects in wealthier economies (Appadurai, 2007, 168). This exclusion also runs along gendered, raced and classed lines of power (cf. Hoofd, 2010, 8). The distribution of access to research reproduces these sociopolitical lines of power and oppression. It also reinforces them in turning *research* into "the epitome of a context-free, cosmopolitan, abstract activity" (Appadurai, 2007, 169). This activity produces a truth about the world which keeps it a world of sociopolitical oppression at the advantage of marketable subjects – who are the only ones capable of doing research and are thus stabilising their position of power through the production of "truth" (Foucault, 1991, 79; 194).

Tracing lines of flight in research is thus a political struggle against these lines of power.

This PAR project has paved some paths along which a line of flight towards the horizontalisation of research can be traced.

The first path towards a horizontalisation of research that this project has traced runs along the lines of the *subversion of scientific method.*

In the logic of scientific research, we are confronted with one "reliable" type of knowledge production that is *methodically* discovering one objective "truth" about social reality. The power figure of the researcher is the protagonist of this type of knowledge production. This figure is constructed as the expert of scientific research which is setting and carrying out the fixed methodological guidelines borrowed from the natural sciences which elevate the knower (as in the researcher) above the known (as in the researched) (Herising, 2005; Heshusius, 1994; Moosa-Mitha, 2005) through his mastery of scientific method.

Scientific method is a set of rules produced under the condition of a research program following a certain theoretical commitment that is based on a predefined set of assumptions about reality. It is a tool of power transforming experience into "data" to be used and defined by the researcher who, through his mastery of this tool, reproduces an epistemic culture which provides the dominant answers for when it is possible to claim to know something about the world (cf. Brown, 2009; Fraassen, 2000).

Rigorous scientific methodological guidelines stand in the way of a horizontalisation of research where the ability to do research is a generalised capacity which knows no single, dominant way of speaking, writing, citing, or authority to define how research is to be done but is accessible to all those who need to know something they do not know yet (cf. Appadurai, 2007; Feyerabend, 1975).

In the first chapter on nomad science as a logic of knowing from within a horizontal plane, I have outlined how the notion of valid research methods excludes ways of knowing which differ from the academic way of knowing and stating truth about the world. As long as one is capable of reproducing the methods of royal science within its epistemological confines, one is legitimate to state how the world is and what should be done about the world. As soon as one refuses this fixed framework of knowledge production, one is made an outsider of valid knowledge production about the world and ones' voice is devalued, one is not capable of doing research, not a legitimate part of the superior scientific system of signification (Barthes, 1967, 9). One has become a heretic.

Conscious methodological heresy is a way of doing research "in, against, and beyond" itself (Holloway, 2016) which has been explored in this project with the aim of ceasing to reproduce its system of epistemological domination and turn *research* into a truly generalised ability. The subversion of research methods is a pivotal point for this line of flight.

Subversion is a technique also used by the Situationists. It has been consigned to the status of strategy – of a political disruption of the existing order of things driven by the situationist "ultra-radical desire to commence a new society" in the here and now, in the shell of the old (Bonnett, 2006, 23). Subversion is thus a means of displacing the habitual contexts, rules and meanings of social systems of signification. In destabilising the power relations within these systems of signification, subversion became a technique with wide political application (Plant, 1992, 60). When subversion creates space for horizontal relations in decentering and dispersing relations of power, it can also turn into a prefigurative practice. Subversion "is plagiaristic, because its materials are those which already appear within the spectacle and subversive, since its tactics are those of the 'reversal of perspective'" (ibid., 86).

Applied to academic research and its methods, subversion means to use the material of an existing method or methodological approach to achieve a reversal of perspective from within. Working with scientific methods this reversal of perspective means that the researched become the researchers; that what previously counted as unacceptable suddenly can turn into a new legitimate element of knowledge production.

Not all research methods are equally easy to subvert, although it must be admitted that all kinds of subversions are probably possible – even within positivist research. Necessary for subversion is some kind of hook, some point of entry, which can be used as an axial point of leverage to subvert a scientific method. Some methods have more or easier hooks than others. In PAR, this hook is its participatory approach to those who would normally be outside of academia which can be expanded into a horizontal way of doing research with many different people having a free choice of concrete methods. Numerous other research methods dispose of such axial points if one is to scrutinise them with an eye for their subversion.

Subverting a method allows one to appear as working within the frame of scientific research. One needs to expand on one's personal approach to the specific method which is an acceptable modus operandi within academic research; one needs to expand on the history of the method, to give an overview and to prove that it perfectly fits within the framework of royal science or is at least acceptable within this framework; one needs to pick up its vocabulary and to start working with it giving it new meaning – "phases of research," "observation," "collection of data," "analysis" – all these words can host parallel worlds where "observation" takes place in a situation of direct action, of struggle and antagonism and not in the orderly setting of a research experiment in the ivory tower of university lecture halls; "analysis" is not an isolated individual act of tearing one's hair bent over the text of an academic journal – it can suddenly turn into an animated discussion with drinks and uncertain outcomes, a collective energy of knowledge creation – something which has long transgressed the border of acceptable academic behaviour.

Hereby, the subversion of method does not mean that any methodological approach is completely repudiated. Method remains a way to structure the process of knowledge creation – it simply subverts some of its rules "to import a system from outside science" (Feyerabend, 1975, 53), nonacademic ways of knowing which have previously been excluded (for example, mythology, "the ramblings of the madmen" (ibid., 53), stories (Lewis, 2011) theatre (Motta, 2013a) or drawing (Cox and Flesher Fominaya, 2009).

The *narrative inclusion of* those who would remain *voiceless* in academic writing is another line of flight towards horizontal research. Academic writing follows a more or less fixed style which marks the presented knowledge as scientific and therefore true. It thus actively excludes nonacademic ways of speaking and enforces a specific form of knowing through disciplining the language of the writer in enforcing rules and restrictions. Some examples can be found in various university tutorials:

"The passive voice is often used in academic writing as it is seen as more impersonal and therefore more objective." "Use formal language"; "If you are writing about established knowledge then use the present tense. For example,

'Diabetes is a condition where the amount of glucose in the blood is too high because the body cannot use it properly'" (University of Leeds, n.d.).

De Certeau examines ways through which storytelling helps people to escape the disciplinary control over language in knowledge production. Stories preserve the memory of successful tactics to escape control. They are gimmicks that can be used in everyday life. Their status as "naive" and asymmetric discourses allows them to perform this service because they flourish beyond or beneath the regulatory mechanisms of science. Stories are a less serious and therefore less regulated spaces. Nevertheless, they pour out of this space into official discourse and academic writing in various forms: interviews, group discussions, research diaries (de Certeau, 1988). Stories are also not only conveying knowledge through words, but also through the development of the story, through its twist, the way it is told and developed, the context in which it is told.

Academic writing knows no space for the coups, twists and tricks of storytelling, no space for narrative interaction and lively dialogues which mirror the lived experience of the storytellers.

To include such presentational forms of knowing which deviate greatly from academic writing styles, one needs to invent new forms of academic writing – in, beyond, and against academic writing. This invention can take on experimental forms which make space for another use of language in academic texts. In this research, I have combined my transcriptions of dialogues with co-researchers and participants in colloquial style with academic theorisation. In tracing lines of flight through storytelling and the inclusion of narratives, there is plenty of space left to keep experimenting with the insertion of different voices into academic discourses which narrate instead of state truth about the world and thus open a dialogue with other voices.

There is another line of flight towards horizontal research which *dislocates the researcher* (cf. Herising, 2005, 133).

Moving towards a horizontal research which does not need a power figure to legitimise knowledge but in which different subject positions are capable of doing research, the dislocation of the researcher as the producer of knowledge and its unlearning of itself as the power figure that he or she represents in the production and legitimation of knowledge, is another line of flight which transgresses the established roles of royal science. In chapter 4, I have given an account of my personal process of unlearning which can hopefully enable future research to retrace this line of flight.

It has shown that dislocating oneself from one's epistemologically privileged position made space for others in a horizontal and collective learning process within the research (cf. Motta, 2013b). These "others," my mostly nonacademic co-researchers and participants, co-shaped the research process in becoming the protagonists of the stories in chapter four. They collectively provided the analysis of the fieldwork and assessed its outcomes in chapter five which is shaped by their discussions and reflections. This line of flight constitutes a rupture with the roles and rules of royal science which leads on to another, last line of flight to be mentioned on the prefigurative journey towards horizontal research.

The last line of flight which I am going to excavate from the research project is the *expansion of the epistemological scope* of research.

To expand one's epistemology means to be open to diverse forms of knowing and to cede participation in the research process to them, although they might be different from the forms of knowing that one habitually encounters in research. Expanding ones' epistemology means to critically question what forms of knowing are legitimate, visible and why. It includes being attentive to other forms of knowing which we encounter in everyday life – those forms of knowing which do not have an entire apparatus of institutions, academic literature, famous intellectuals, grants and employment opportunities in their back.

Expanding ones' epistemology is thus a de-hierarchisation of knowledge production. It is not the question of whether one has "reached" an expanded epistemology but rather whether we can let go of the dominant norm of knowledge (cf. Heshusius, 1994, 18). This line of flight takes us to forms of knowledge where the accepted alterity of the Others' knowledge might include dance, drawing, debates, singing, telling stories, or making maps instead of writing academic articles or presenting research outcomes at a conference. It is a prefigurative movement towards horizontal research because it practices research as if it already *is* a horizontal process of knowledge creation. It is also a *political* practice because it enters into a sociopolitical contention over knowledge as something of the public sphere; it challenges ownership and social relations of power and authority of those who claim to know how to define knowledge and thus strive to "own" it. *Moving towards horizontal research* is thus a political aim and practice with wide consequences. If one is to believe that *doing research* is a generalised capacity that is to be distributed equally in working against epistemological privileges, putting this into practice includes a radical transformation of sociopolitical inequalities and relations of power on which the scientific production of knowledge is based.

These four lines of flight – the *subversion of scientific method*, the *narrative inclusion of* those who would remain *voiceless*, the *dislocation of the researcher*, and the *expansion of epistemology* – are the prefigurative and emancipatory movements towards horizontal research which I have traced in my research. Just like the lines of flight in the spatial practices of autonomous social movements, they are to be seen as hints and suggestions for where to start searching if one aims at developing own lines of flight. They are the pivotal points from which one can start to develop multiple critical, radical, transgressive and prefigurative perspectives of research. The other lines of flight are for confronting the world that is and for transforming it into something more horizontal.

Figure 6.1   Artwork by Kata. *Source*: Author's own.

Conclusions

PREFIGURATION AS A YARDSTICK OF EVALUATION

In prefigurative politics, "there is a clear and strong link between means and ends and this is why organizational forms, decision-making processes and forms of action are not just means to an end, but ends in themselves" (Flesher Fominaya, 2007, 339).

It is an inherent part of prefigurative practices to critically assess the distance between prefigurative practices and their desired outcomes. As Azzellini and Sitrin put it, "The concept of walking and questioning, or making the road as one walks, has been used throughout history. Most recently, it was popularised by the Zapatistas through (. . .) the 'Story of Questions'" (2014, 38). Prefiguration is thus a movement towards the utopian outcomes of a radical imagination that includes the constant critical questioning of this movement – "walking we ask questions" (preguntando caminamos) (Sitrin, 2005). Prefiguration is thus a movement towards the desired aim of horizontal co-creation of knowledge, decisions, practices in which all means are mobilised to achieve the utopian end result – not the declaration of an achieved end result itself. In prefigurative practices, there is always a distance between its aim and its present prefiguration. It is vital for prefiguration to acknowledge this distance in order to keep moving towards the desired transformation.

Horizontal knowledge creation was pictured as the creation of a horizontal dialogue between heterogeneous entities requiring the recognition of different types of knowledges, the recognition of differences between research participants and the creation of space to live out these differences in the research process – whilst at the same time challenging power relations within scientific research.

In what way did this research process move towards a lived practice of horizontal knowledge creation? What challenges and pitfalls were on the way of this movement? What was achieved and how can future research keep progressing towards horizontal research processes? What is in the gap between the practice of participatory and horizontal research and its goal?

To answer this, I will turn to the pitfalls of prefiguring horizontal knowledge creation.

PAR researchers noted that PAR is "frequently a solitary process of systematic self-reflection" (Kemmis and McTaggart, 2007, 277). What they mean is that when presenting PAR *as research*, in the process of writing it up in a way that fits the form of academic research, the writer of the text is frequently left alone in this endeavour. It is thus important to distinguish at which point in the text the writer acts as a narrating co-researcher, and at which point he or she is presenting the research process or methodology to engage in meta-theoretical academic discourses as an individual researcher. Here we see how the process of unlearning oneself as a researcher (and thus unlearning one's epistemological privilege [Motta, 2013b]) is not a constant progression but rather a corrugated movement of ups and downs during the research process (when facing diverse challenges). It is important then to distinguish between individual and collective desires, demands and expectations towards the research process. These desires flow together differently in different parts of the project. While it is normal that within any group of co-researchers individual desires, demands and expectations towards the research are varied, in *horizontal* PAR, varying forms and degrees of participation in the research process and in the shaping of its presentational form are admitted: In a horizontal PAR, participants and co-researchers in the research process do not necessarily have to take part in the writing up of the project to be participants or co-researchers. However, those who present the research process as a *text* have a different degree of control over this presentational form, in comparison to those who participated in other forms of contributions. In the textual presentational form of the research, individual desires and expectations of the writers will thus attain more visibility than the ones of other participants. This is mediated through the process of unlearning oneself as a researcher. But the process of unlearning is a self-reflexive learning process, never a perfected outcome. A critical self-reflexivity needs to be employed to visibilise where the writing process was shaped by collective desires and where it was shaped by the individual desire of the researcher.

It is my individual desire to engage in academic discourses about science. To do so, I needed to establish a ground for "speaking back [to research] through research" (Webster, 2014). The collective desire that I share with the other co-researchers was to learn about political articulations of sites of dissent. In the research process these two desires flow together most of the time, but there are also spaces that are solely dedicated to my individual desires, requirements and expectations towards the research. To proclaim that the entire research was a horizontal and collective process of knowledge creation would mean to stumble into a pitfall: it would be a denial and an embellishment of the reality of the research.

This research process is not solely and not purely a collective, horizontal knowledge creation; it is also my academic work; it is my personal contribution to epistemological and methodological debates. As a pure collective knowledge creation, the project would possibly have taken another shape. It could have been a storytelling series or simply something completely different to an academic text. Horizontal and collective knowledge creation nevertheless occurred during the research. It is therefore important to acknowledge that horizontal and collective knowledge creation takes shape within something else – and not to take academic research about horizontal and collective knowledge creation *for* horizontal and collective knowledge creation. Doing so would erase all the moments and points at which my co-researchers were critical of the research process and the negotiations that took place between us.

Although both my academic contributions and moments of horizontal knowledge creation appear as one same topic or under the same sections, as texts belonging to and movement in different directions, they pursue different objectives. Shifting back and forwards between them manifests in a rupture or a transformation of my narrative tone. Moments of collective and horizontal knowledge creation crack the epistemological privilege and hegemony of institutionalised scientific knowledge production. When fixing these moments in a written text, my narrative tone bursts out of the academic framework of scientific conventions in which it is frequently captured. I chose to highlight these moments and processes instead of obscuring them as scientific weaknesses. The latter tendency is the result of an academic pressure to homogenise the body of the text, presenting it as something unitary, rupture-less and made of a single perspective. I tried to stand up against this pressure and buckled several times.

Horizontal and collective knowledge creation about autonomous social movements spatial practices and sites of dissent took place long before this project even existed as an idea. It took place in mundane moments that I now am able to conceptualise as moments of horizontal knowledge creation. Back then, it just seemed like what we were doing at the time, doing the things that we were doing, and doing the things that seemed meaningful. In a sense, this research is also an act of valorising everyday knowledge creation, knowledge creation that could be done by anybody not only academic researchers. This could be seen as an act to "democratise" the realm of knowledge creation (Muller and Cloete, 1986, 14) which usually only takes place in "trusted" institutions reproducing hierarchical binary opposites between "scientific" knowledge and the insurgent "naive," "popular," "disqualified," "local" knowledges outside of these institutions (cf. ibid., 13). Within these insurgent knowledges, everyone could produce knowledge at any moment; we just need to learn to see its multiple aspects and to value it in its diversity. To do so, it is necessary to intervene into the academic practice of knowledge production and to start inventing own recipes.

(IM)POSSIBILITIES OF HORIZONTAL KNOWLEDGE CREATION

> Participation is performative, and it sells. Shops, restaurants, bars, petrol stations, hospitals and whole cities are "themed," with the aim of providing consumers with a memorable experience that will lure them to spend money, writes Helen Nicholson in "Problems of Participation." (Nicholson, 2013, 113)

Participation in itself is neither good and empowering, nor bad and oppressive. As Nicholson put it nicely, "There is, then, nothing inherently good about participation, if notions of 'goodness' are defined in terms of equality and social justice" (ibid., 114). Participatory approaches do not always claim to be first and foremost interested in empowerment. And even when this is the case (for example, in participatory approaches to development), they do not necessarily contribute to empowerment (Cooke and Kothari, 2001b).

"'Do group dynamics lead to participatory decisions that reinforce the interests of the already powerful?'" ask the critical participatory action researchers Bill Cooke and Uma Kothari (ibid., 8). This is a question that relates as much to the privileges of particularity vocal participants and co-researchers that exist independently of a specific research project, as it relates to the group dynamics between participants and co-researchers within this specific process of research. Since prefiguring horizontal social relationships is one of the key elements of participation in autonomous social movements' spatial practices, the question of deconstructing power dynamics within the group is a collective responsibility which is also taken outside of the research process.

This does not mean that informal hierarchies between research participants do not need to be addressed. Quite the opposite, it requires a constant attentiveness to the needs and desires of other people, of a critical self-reflexivity (on an individual and collective level), of the collective visualization, articulation and transformation of different lines of exclusion and oppression (for example, racism, sexism . . .), and of a conscious modelling of horizontal and inclusive decision-making processes (for example, consensus decision-making).

> Is there self-deception in the scheme whereby the researcher participates in a double role: as a fellow human sharing the interests of the people he or she works with, but also as a researcher or a development worker employed for the purpose? Addelson (1994, 60) calls this "double participation." (Swantz, 1996, 134)

Although in the case of this project, I am not "employed for the purpose" (ibid., 134) or funded by an agency to take care of the "underdog" (cf. David, 2002, 12), I nevertheless agree with Swantz on the issue of my own "double participation." Unlike my co-researchers, I am writing this book as a student with a scholarship and I am *also* a participant in the project. These circumstances give me more time than others to dedicate to the project. I am using this time to do the work that is necessary to *present* it as a research – to outline its methodology and its analytical framework, to put it in relation to an already existing body of academic literature, to write it down in the shape of an academic contribution to research. The time and dedication that I have available, as well as my position as a PhD student, is precisely what creates my double participation and a research process which is not horizontal in every work step. As Cornwall and Jewkes notes, "in practice there is a considerable degree of fluctuation between [conventional and participatory] poles [of research] which suggests that the difference between modes of research might be more of a degree than of kind in some instances. Frequently the relationship between the two approaches takes the form of a zig-zag pathway with greater or less participation at various stages, rather than vertically following either one" (1995, 1668).

It is not only the temporal barriers to participation that are accountable for this. Bresnihan and Dawney outline that participation "is understood to be a formal activity separated from daily life – perhaps attending a community stakeholder meeting or taking part in a protest or signing a petition. Participation is stripped from the fabric of everyday life and turned into a specific exercise for those who decide they want to 'make a difference'" (Bresnihan and Dawney, 2013, 129). At the same time they state that the problem is not only about what is defined as participation. It is also about the capitalist pressures on our time:

As we have seen there is little time for our activities when one works a 40 hour week, and maintains a home and family at the same time. When this amount of time spent working is necessary both for having a job to begin with (the "normal working week") commitments to caring for family members, or for self-improvement preclude the time and the will for active participation: when one is expected to maintain one's appearance, to cook and eat healthy and fresh meals, and to conform to the many expectations that saturate our time. These pressures on time are by and large the effects of the market, and need to be considered as such, rather than as a lack of engagement by individuals. (. . .) These pressures on our time mean that there is very little left to do anything "more," including getting involved in our communities, in decision-making, in trying to make a change. (Ibid., 133–34)

This means that the people who take part in the horizontal PAR process are able to reject these pressures or privileged enough to escape them – their composition of subject positions is similar to the one of autonomous social movements in general: mostly young, mostly able-bodied, mostly non-raced subjects who are frequently from a socioeconomically rather privileged background (cf. Giannaki, 2016; Milkman, Luce, and Lewis, 2015, 34). Within autonomous social movements, there are numerous attempts to address inequalities in the possibilities of participation. They include addressing these inequalities through political work against oppression: in forming support groups and groups for self-empowerment, creating discrimination-poor spaces (safe spaces), or practices of horizontal decision-making. Of course, these attempts are not enough to erase inequalities between participants and never enough to subvert the structural barriers to participation.

Yet, there are still possibilities for horizontal knowledge creation in research. *Scientific* practices have not accomplished fabricating an answer to the question of what way, type, or form of knowing should constitute *research*. There is still space for negotiation, debates and confrontations to fight for an inclusive version of this answer. This is the epistemological battleground over the conception of knowledge gained through horizontal PAR. It is a horizontal and collective research process that includes various ways, types and forms of knowing, not exclusively scientific ones, and thereby still remains *research*.

As a result, the presentational form of knowledges that flow into the horizontal and collective knowledge-creation process might look clumsy. Forms of knowledge are diverse and only few of them would easily be transformed into a coherent text. From the perspective of academic research, most of them look bare and raw because they do not appear coated in scientific terms or garnished with academic concepts. Its articulation might seem insecure because the epistemological privilege of academic knowing subjects created a loss of self-confidence (since nonacademic knowers are deemed incapable of developing a conscious relationship between methodological artefacts and representations of reality [cf. Cerf, 2011]). Horizontal PAR helps to valorise such knowledges, to pick them up and grant them equal epistemological privileges in recurring to nomad science. It makes these knowledges visible in royal science in arranging these knowledges into a research process – or something that can be read as such in the logic of royal science.

When people take time to create knowledge together, it is often a painful process of listening to each other stammering – a process that takes ages and has nothing to do with the efficiency that is required for the production of academic texts. In this process, something also happens between the people who participate: creating valuable knowledge is a collective act of empowerment which forms relationships of affinity: We learn about the other participants, about what is important in their lives, we learn about their perspectives and ways of thinking, we learn to create valuable knowledge collectively and develop trust and familiarity with each other. While academic knowledge has rarely been seen crafting affinity between people and having an empowering effect, moments of horizontal and collective knowledge creation require a lot of patience and attention for each other to achieve this.

TWO QUESTIONS, TWO INVITATIONS

It is time to return to the questions that I brought forward in this research. In reinventing the rules of academic research methods and in transforming its linguistic expression into the language of everyday discourses accessible to as many as possible, does one succeed in doing horizontal and collective research with diverse forms of knowing? In other words: Did I break out of my isolation as an individual expert in the field? Did I manage to disperse the power/knowledge nexus of academic knowledge production? Did I let it out of my hands; did I loosen the grip of the knowledge production process? Did I make it more horizontal in distributing parts of it into many hands?

This research project has given shape to different techniques of horizontal and collective knowledge creation within scientific research. In the last chapter, I have summarised them as three lines of flight.

In the stories assembled into cycles of journeys we, the co-researchers and I, have been altering and jumping between research methods. We were picking and choosing the methods suitable for our situation and our endeavour. We refused to follow the pre-set methodological guidelines of sticking to one and the same method throughout the project and created our own, dynamic approach instead. No way of knowing or sharing information was superior to another. We have thus made an exploratory step towards the aim of horizontalising research.

Learning how to transform, adapt and collectivise research steps and phases is a process as challenging as the resulting task of overcoming barriers of social privilege in the distribution of possibilities and capacities for (political) participation. At the same time, it can be said that a horizontalisation of research practices created space for collective knowledge creation in some phases of the research project.

Flows of exchange and cross-fertilisation between royal science and nomad science allowed to broaden the epistemological scope of this research project. The format of a structured comparative analysis was mixed with the formats of storytelling, conversations and narrations of situations. The logic of royal science and the logic of nomad science are not mutually exclusive. It is possible to break out of one logic of knowledge production and complement it by another. This helps to value academic, structured discourses in the same way as collective knowledge creation that makes its own rules on the spot, all in acknowledging their different functions and advantages. The flows of exchange and cross-fertilisation between royal science and nomad science conceived the process of knowledge creation not as a linear process (as it is the case in royal science) but as a patchwork of different logics of knowledge creation, including those that take effect in everyday life. Such a patchwork offers more points of interconnection with everyday life where it is easier to put knowledge at the service of praxis.

The second question – What is the common leitmotiv of autonomous social movements' spatial practices of dissent – if there is any? – is answered in our collective analysis of the stories, the "field work." Contentious spatial practices of autonomous social movements

> no matter whether they take place on the countryside as rural occupations against the exploitation of environmental resources, whether they take the form of squatting in the urban context, whether they are temporary events such as riots and demonstrations or permanent dwelling environments, whether these practices stretch out over a larger geographical area such as a neighbourhood or a several hectares large rural territory and include hundreds of people, or whether they are small and experimental alternatives to the socio-political status quo such as a social centre consisting of two rented rooms.

are driven by a shared political desire to create horizontal social relationships.

What does this imply? A riot and a community garden are not the same. Their levels of confrontation, their level of militancy to articulate sociopolitical dissent are different – one could say so. But is this really the case if both practices strive towards a utopian social vision of horizontal social relations on every level? Aren't all of these practices then a radical articulation of dissent towards the world that *is* and at the same time attempts of empowerment to create something else – another world, another kind of social relationships? Autonomous social movements' contentious spatial practices are judged in very different ways: some are framed as criminal, destructive, aggressive, as an attack on social order. Others are framed as admirable social commitment or democratic practice. Seen from outside of a horizontal plane of encounter with autonomous social movements, the utopian vision directing their confrontational practices is more difficult to comprehend: The attention of the distant observer is used to focus on the broken glass and the painted facades left after a riot. It is less used to contextualise the riot and to listen to the voices of the voiceless: What happened? – A shelter for homeless people was evicted, a community centre was attacked by the police; the marginalised experienced violence, marginalisation and despotism once again. This will not go unanswered, this should not happen again. What happened? Did the voiceless stop to believe that the world that *is* and its apparatuses of stabilisation will listen to their voices? Militancy and confrontation is a question of strategy, not a moral question because domination, oppression and exploitation will not simply pack their bags and leave in saying: "Ah okay, you want a horizontal society – then I go away and you can start building it." Autonomous social movements create and destroy. A lot of things need to be created anew for a horizontal society to come into being – just as a lot of things need to be confronted. Confrontation is necessary and it is perturbing. A community garden or the meeting of a self-empowerment group is less perturbing, although it can be confrontational.

Autonomous social movements' contentious spatial practices are aiming at the creation of all-encompassing horizontal social relationships. This leads to the question of what is in the way of creating horizontal social relationships. It sheds another light on the confrontational position of autonomous social movements, makes us able to raise questions about dissent, militancy and struggle in view of a horizontal form of social organisation and structure. The answer to this second research question about the leitmotiv of autonomous social movements' spatial practices is thus an invitation to struggles creating cracks in the world that *is*, all in becoming minoritarian, disquieters of social order and an invitation to becoming antagonists together.

Deleuze and Guattari have insisted to "make thought a war machine," to place it in an immediate relation to practice (Culp, 2016, 21). The answer to the first research question can be read as an invitation, too: becoming a methodological heretic means to enter in a contentious relationship to lines of force and oppression, means resistance to dominant discourses and thus means becoming minoritarian and marginalised. In research, this resistance entails a radical transformation of research practices; As "all modes of research have political consequences" (Dadusc, 2014, 48), horizontal research is a *political* practice.

It will always be in a contentious relationship to institutionalised science. It will break its rules and I will get told that the writing is not *research*, that it lacks academic rigour, that the loose ends of its reflections are not coherent.

The answers to the two research questions, and the resulting two invitations, could really be one; they could be part of one and the same practice of *making thought a war machine*. Along with social movements that see "the social order as contested and malleable rather than as natural and given," horizontal research focuses on research practices as the locus of its societal intervention and transformative practice (Buechler, 2000, 5). Research practices, the way knowledge is produced, is a nexus of power/knowledge. If it is possible to horizontalise the production of knowledge, it is also possible to horizontalise a distribution of power and to work against oppressive power relations. This book is an invitation to take part in these struggles.

Appendix A

Angelo is a student in his early thirties who had a passion for environmental protection since a very young age. Roughly ten years ago, he went to his first environmentalist protest actions where he experienced police brutality. He lives somewhere near a bigger city in Europe. In this PAR project, he is a co-researcher.

Bill finished school, moved out of his parents' place and never wanted to become a student. He became good at climbing and learned how to facilitate consensus decision-making in big groups. Sometimes he feels tired and burned out, as if it was impossible to change something. As a participant, he contributes to research on several sites of dissent.

Brian dropped out of university because he is much more interested in autonomous education projects than in formal research training. He is now living in a shared flat in a big city. He is a co-researcher in this PAR.

Claudio is a squatter who lives in a small town. He likes learning from books and from other people. He sometimes participates in urban struggles and has many friends who are squatting in other cities whom he visits often. As a participant, he was part of this PAR project.

Darius spends a lot of his time on the streets where he is spray-painting and putting up posters or hanging out with friends. He used to be involved in a Right to the City reading group. In this PAR, he contributes as a participant.

Fedric dislikes schools and similar institutions for their authoritarian practices and tried to avoid to live from paid labour as long as possible. He survives on recycled or stolen food in a squatted social centre where he often does the bar. Towards the end of this PAR project, he became one of my co-researchers. He first started to contribute as a participant.

Felippa – when Felippa started to study in the city where she grew up with her family, it was clear for her that she wanted to move out and live autonomously. Her part-time job is poorly paid and squatting is for her, both politically and financially, the only alternative. She is a co-researcher.

Gina makes music since she is eighteen years old. This is also when she started to get involved in anarchist self-organisation. In the last ten years, she has participated in self-managed groups. She is one of my co-researchers.

Gino deserted from a well-paid job at young age and kept squatting, fighting, and traveling all over Europe ever since. He is involved in anti-racist self-organisation and in participatory action research. He is also one of the co-researchers in this project.

Helen is a self-taught moviemaker. In this project, she was a participant who contributed to one story.

Ian used to travel a lot and to live in the South of Europe, far away from where he was born a long time ago. Anti-fascism is very important to him. He is one of my co-researchers and participated in many journeys.

Janinka – Eight years ago, she was working for a film production company, renting a flat with her daughter and paying her university fees. When her daughter moved out, she travelled to another country to visit her friends. One day she decided that she does not want to work anymore and squatted a house with people who were a lot younger than her. She learned how to do many things with her own hands: electricity, repairing furniture and bicycles, replacing a broken window. She is one of my co-researchers.

Malu feels that he is extremely privileged to have grown up in Western Europe. He feels that he lives in an unjust world that systematically oppresses people from the Global South and is driven to act against these oppressions. He writes short essays and articles about this, too. He is a participant.

Sina struggles with her health a lot. This has often inhibited her from doing the things she wanted to do. A few years ago, she joined an autonomous medical collective that would come along to demonstrations to take care of people's injuries. She participated in this PAR on one site of dissent.

Tina identifies as a woman of colour with university education. She chose gender studies as an academic subject to learn more about oppressive power relations in the world. Together with Ulla and I, she co-created the research process on one site of dissent.

Ulla got politicised in university when she was studying gender studies. She started to get active in Vagana because she felt something more hands-on than writing essays should be done for the equality of all genders. She participated in this PAR project in shaping the research process that took place in Vagana, one of the sites of dissent.

Xenia is a single mother. Being a mother takes up a lot of her energy and time, but she has a lot of it. She helped to squat the territory of BUT and is involved in several anarchist groups in her city. She also has a part-time job and spends a lot of time with her kids. As a participant, she co-shaped the research on BUT, the site of dissent where Ian and I met her.

Appendix B

PROTAGONISTS OF THE COLLECTIVE ANALYSIS
IN CHAPTER FIVE (IN ALPHABETICAL ORDER)

Ann always had the feeling that she wants to break out of her normal life. Since she was a child she was thinking about how to do things differently – in a way that she feels more free. She started to read about anarchism and for a long time was wondering how it looks like in practice. She still does not have answers, but through her involvement in a site of dissent she feels that she is getting closer to finding some.

Fedric dislikes schools and similar institutions for their authoritarian practices and tried to avoid to live from paid labour as long as possible. He survives on recycled or stolen food in a squatted social centre where he often does the bar. Towards the end of this PAR project, he became one of my co-researchers. He first started to contribute as a participant.

Ian used to travel a lot and to live in the South of Europe, far away from where he was born a long time ago. Anti-fascism is very important to him. He is one of my co-researchers and participated in many journeys.

Michel grew up in a tiny village on the countryside. He moved to a bigger city to start his studies. A year later he got involved in a site of dissent and developed the desire to learn about how people can live collectively.

Penny used to be involved in an animal-rights group. She moved to another city and met people who are involved in different struggles against oppression and social movements. These people became her friends. She now works only ten hours a week and has a lot of free time for martial arts and for her political involvement with different groups.

Sina – since she started studying she participates regularly in the assemblies of a social centre in her city. She is interested in learning more about the topic of mental health and how helping people with mental health problems can be organised horizontally and collectively within communities.

Vallerie is a young person who likes having time for herself, for music and drawing. She is involved in a self-organised cantine taking place regularly on the site of dissent where she often hangs out.

Vini lives without paying rent. This is important for her. It liberates time for doing other things: organising protest camps, festivals, demonstrations – and especially: time for other people. She likes working with wood and building things.

Appendix C

Postscript

Am Mi., 26. Mai 2021 um 02:36 Uhr schrieb Choi, Shine:

Hi Alissa,

I had a quick look at the MS you sent against the commented MS I sent through – much of the substantial editing suggestions on how you use quotes and adding clarity to the text have not been done? Could you include your rationale for this and/or an explanation of what you've done, so I can better understand what is going on here?

Thanks,

Shine

Am, 28. Mai 2021 um 12:35 Uhr schrieb Alissa Starodub:

Dear Shine,

Yes, of course: In many places, I have changed the way I use quotes – for example, in places where the quotes are saying generic things that I could say "myself," too. Or in the places where I am not at all introducing those people I quoted in length. What I tried to do is to soften my style of quoting. But I also wanted to keep some of this style – specifically in places where the quotes also work as a collage in the text. What I am trying to underline with this way of quoting is: what I am proposing is a recomposition – of what others have said, views and perspectives that already exist as utterances, and what I am seeing, touching, experiencing. So when quotes suddenly appear in the text, I want to show that a text-flow can nevertheless exist, that what I am saying is embedded somewhere. And that it does not matter so much if it is "mine" or somebody else's. . . . And I would like the readers to get used to a style of writing that flows as a composition, to gradually get less attentive to quotation marks (this is really what I hope will happen).

I tried to react to all the places where the use of quotes was awkward – and yet, some of this awkwardness will stay. I could even imagine to write in a way that only uses quotes (and my own contribution would be the composition then), but with this kind of text it was impossible. Also I thought that changing the style in a way that it treats quotes properly as quotes would really change the style of expression a lot. The way I have been taught to use quotes is to remove myself always a bit from the quote. Here, I am trying to do the opposite: to appropriate the quotes.

Do you think this works?

All the best,

Alissa

Am Fr., 28. Mai 2021 um 01:04 Uhr schrieb Choi, Shine:

Hi Alissa,

Thank you for this explanation. I suspected that there is something else going on there along these lines . . . but to help the text/readers along, would you consider adding this explanation (or even this email exchange) as a postscript in the MS? This way, you don't pre-emptively overexplain (which is probably why you left this unexplained) but you still include a key for readers who need it at the end. As the final reviewer said, they were left unsettled and confused as to whether or not they understood the text (which is great!) but also, I think it would also be productive to say – yes, I know this is unsettling/confusing, here is something for that, a little key/gesture to say, stay with that feeling, continue the good work, reader! A short explanation of this can also be included in how you talk about nomad/royal science as a mixture (a moving back and forth), but I don't think just inserting this explanation there would be enough (some would miss it because it is too deep in the middle of the text). Up to you though, hope you would consider adding an explanation somewhere. I know you are short on time. Let me and Rebecca know either way so we know what to do with the MS.

Thank you,

Shine

Am Fr., 04. Juin 2021 um 04:05 Uhr schrieb Choi, Shine:

Dear Shine,

Sorry, I am not replying very fast now – I will try to have a look in my emails in the next week again.

Ok, I like your suggestion of including this email exchange (our last four emails including this one) as an Appendix C into the manuscript.

Because you have the feeling that it helps, and I trust your feeling. I am also completely fine with not including anything more and leaving everything as it is.

So if you feel like this is useful information for readers, maybe you could copy our last emails and make an Appendix C?

I would be totally fine with this.

Thank you for thinking this,

Alissa

Notes

INTRODUCTION

1. Angelo and Brian are invented names for anonymisation.
2. It would also be appropriate to use the more common terms "to democratise knowledge production," if "democratising" means to put power in the hands of people (as in everyone concerned by knowledge production which would literally mean everyone – inside and outside of academia).

CHAPTER 1

1. I do not like the term "activism" and I usually refuse to label myself or other people as "activists." Here I am using this word as a shortcut to speak about people who are involved in struggles against oppression.
2. Name changed for anonymisation.

CHAPTER 2

1. "Self-legislation" or "self-government" is the etymological meaning of the word "autonomous" (Greek: auto-nomos).
2. A person who does not subscribe to conventional gender distinctions but identifies with neither, both, or a combination of male and female genders.
3. An organisation representing the interests of lesbian, gay and bisexual people.

CHAPTER 3

1. PAR in Spanish.

CHAPTER 5

1. In the collective analysis we have been speaking about "becoming organism(s)" to include the idea that autonomous social movements are not one single organism but consist of many different organisms.

CHAPTER 6

1.   The awareness team consists of people who help to organise an event, a party or another gathering in volunteering to be approachable all the time when participants feel discriminated or threatened by words or by actions of others. Often members of the awareness team wear a specific colour or sign that makes them recognisable. Their role is to deal with instances of discrimination, domination, and oppression during the event and to offer help to the affected to act against these. In empowering the marginalised, the awareness team thus helps to horizontalise social relationships.

References

Abramsky, K. 2001. *Restructuring and Resistance: Diverse Voices of Struggle in Western Europe*. London: Resresrev.

ACME Collective. 2001. "Black Bloc Communiqué." In *Do or Die 9*, 125. Accessed December 21, 2013. http://www.eco-action.org/dod/no9/seattle_black_bloc.html.

Albrecht-Crane, C. 2011. "Style, Stutter." In *Gilles Deleuze: Key Concepts*, edited by C. J. Stivale, 121–130. Durham: McGill-Queen's University Press.

Anckar, C. 2008. "On the Applicability of the Most Similar Systems Design and the Most Different Systems Design in Comparative Research." *International Journal of Social Research Methodology*, 11 (5): 389–401.

Anderson, P. 1980. *Arguments with English Marxism*. London: Verso.

Apoifis, N. 2016. *Anarchy in Athens: An Ethnography of Militancy, Emotions and Violence*. Manchester: Manchester University Press.

Appadurai, A. 2007. "The Right to Research." *Globalisation, Societies and Education*, 4 (2): 167–177.

autonome a.f.r.i.k.a. gruppe, Blissett, L. and Brünzels, S. 2001. *Handbuch der Kommunikationsguerilla*. Berlin, Hamburg, Göttingen: Assoziation A.

Azzellini, D. and Sitrin, M. 2014. *They Can't Represent Us! Reinventing Democracy from Greece to Occupy*. London: Verso.

Bargal, D. 2006. "Personal and Intellectual Influences Leading to Lewin's Paradigm of Action Research." *Action Research*, 4 (4): 367–388.

Barthes, R. 1967. *Elements of Semiology*. London: Jonathan Cape.

Bey, H. 2008. *The Temporary Autonomous Zone, Ontological Anarchy, Poetic Terrorism*. Forgotten Books.

Blumler, H. 1951. "The Field of Collective Behaviour." In *Principles of Sociology*, edited by A. Lee, 167–222. New York: Barnes and Noble.

Boggs, C. 1977. "Marxism, Prefigurative Communism, and the Problem of Workers' Control." *Radical America*, 6 Winter: 99–122.

Böhm, S., Dinerstein, A. and Spicer, A. 2010. "Impossibilities of Autonomy: Social Movements in and Beyond Capital, the State and Development." *Social Movement Studies*, 9 (1): 17–32.

Bonnett, A. 2006. "The Nostalgias of Situationist Subversion." *Theory, Culture and Society*, 23 (5): 23–48.

Bondi, L. and Domosh, M. 1992. "Other Figures in Other Places: On Feminism, Postmodernism and Geography." *Environment and Planning D: Society and Space*, *10*, 199–213.

Bourdieu, P. 2010. "Teilnehmende Objektivierung." In *Algerische Skizzen*, edited by T. Yacine, 417–442. Berlin: Suhrkamp.

Bradbury, H., Mirvis, P., Neilsen, E. and Pasmore, W. 2008. "Action Research at Work: Creating the Future Following the Path from Lewin." In *Handbook of Action Research*, edited by P. Reason and H. Bradbury, 2nd edition, 59–73. London, Thousand Oaks, New Delhi: Sage Publications.

Breda, K. L. 2015. "Participatory Action Research." In *Nursing Research Using Participatory Action Research: Qualitative Designs and Methods in Nursing*, edited by M. de Chesnay, 1–12. New York: Springer.

Brown, L. and Strega, S. 2005. "Introduction: Transgressive Possibilities." In *Research as Resistance: Critical, Indigenous and Anti-Oppressive Approaches*, edited by L. Brown and S. Strega, 1–18. Toronto: Canadian Scholar's Press/ Women's Press.

Brown, T. 2009. *Imperfect Oracle: The Epistemic and Moral Authority of Science*. Philadelphia: Pennsylvania State University Press.

Brydon-Miller, M., Greenwood, D. and Maguire, P. 2003. "Why Action Research?" *Action Research*, 1 (1): 9–27.

Buber, M. 2008. *Ich und Du*. Stuttgart: Reclam.

Buechler, S. 1995. "New Social Movement Theories." *The Sociological Quarterly*, 36: 441–464.

Buechler, S. 2000. *Social Movements in Advanced Capitalism*. Oxford: Oxford University Press.

Butler, C. T. and Rothstein, A. 1987. *On Conflict and Consensus: A Handbook on Formal Consensus Decisionmaking*. Portland: Food Not Bombs Publishing.

Butler, J., Laclau, E. and Zizek, S. 2000. *Contingency, Hegemony, Universality: Contemporary Dialogues on the Left*. London, New York: Verso.

Cadman, L. 2009. "Non-representational Theory/Non-representational Geographies." In *International Encyclopaedia of Human Geography*, edited by R. Kitchin and N. Thrift, 456–463. Amsterdam: Elsevier.

Cahill, C. 2010. "Participatory Data Analysis." In *Participatory Action Research Approaches and Methods: Connecting People, Participation and Place*, edited by S. Kindon, R. Pain and M. Kesby, 181–187. Oxon, New York: Routledge.

Cameron, J. and Gibson, K. 2005. "Participatory Action Research in a Poststructuralist Vein." *Geoforum*, 36: 315–331.

Canel, E. 1992. "New Social Movement Theory and Resource Mobilisation: The Need for Integration." In *Organizing Dissent*, edited by W. Carroll, 22–51. Toronto: Garamond.

Casas-Cortés, M. and Cobarrubias, S. 2007. "Drifting Through the Knowledge Machine." In *Constituent Imagination: Militant Investigations, Collective Theorisation*, edited by S. Shukaitis, D. Graeber, and E. Biddle, 112–126. Oakland, Edinburgh, West Virginia: AK Press.

Cerf, M. 2011. "Is Participatory Research a Scientific Practice?" *Journal of Rural Studies Rural Studies*, 27: 414–418.

Chan-Tiberghien, J. 2004. "Towards a 'Global Educational Justice' Research Paradigm: Cognitive Justice, Decolonizing Methodologies and Critical Pedagogy." *Globalisation, Societies and Education*, 2 (2): 191–213.

Chatterton, P. 2005. "Making Autonomous Geographies: Argentina's Popular Uprising and the 'Movimiento de Trabajadores Desocupados.'" *Geoforum*, 36: 545–556.

Chevalier, J. M. and Buckles, D. J. 2013. *Handbook for Participatory Action Research, Planning and Evaluation*. Ottawa.

Chisholm, R. 1966. *Theory of Knowledge*. Englewood Cliffs, NJ: Prentice-Hall.

Colectivo Situaciones. 2007. "Something More on Research Militancy: Footnotes on Procedures and in Decisions." In *Constituent Imagination*, edited by S. Shukaitis, D. Graeber and E. Biddle, 73–93. Oakland, Edinburgh, West Virginia: AK Press.

Comte, A. 2009. *The Positive Philosophy of Auguste Comte*. Cambridge: Cambridge University Press.

Considine, M. and Marginson, S. 2000. *The Enterprise University: Power, Governance and Reinvention in Australia*. Cambridge: Cambridge University Press.

Cooke, B. and Kothari, U. 2001a. *Participation: The New Tyranny?* London: Zed Books.

Cooke, B. and Kothari, U. 2001b. "The Case for Participation as Tyranny." In *Participation: The New Tyranny?*, edited by B. Cooke and U. Kothari, 1–15. London: Zed Books.

Cornwall, A. and Jewkes, R. 1995. "What Is Participatory Research?" *Social Science and Medicine*, 41 (12): 1667–1676.

Cox, L. and Flesher Fominaya, C. 2009. "Interface: Movement Knowledge." *Interface*, 1 (1): 1–232. Accessed February 13, 2014. papers2://publication/uuid/CF8FD919-B26F-427C-8368-29BAE3072168.

Cresswell, T. 1996. *In Place/Out of Place: Geography, Ideology and Transgression*. Minneapolis, London: University of Minnesota Press.

Dalton, R., Kuechler, M. and Bürklin, W. 1990. "The Challenge of New Movements." In *Challenging the Political Order: New Social Movements and Political Movements in Western Democracies*, edited by R. Dalton and M. Kuechler, 3–22. Oxford, Cambridge: Polity Press.

Danaher, K. and Burbach, R. 2000. *Globalize This! The Battle against the World Trade Organization and Corporate Rule*. Monroe: Common Courage Press.

Danley, K., and Ellison, M. L. 1999. *A Handbook for Participatory Action Researchers*. Boston: Center for Psychiatric Rehabilitation.

David, M. 2002. "Problems of Participation: The Limits of Action Research." *International Journal of Social Research Methodology*, 5 (1): 11–17.

Davies, J. 1962. "Toward a Theory of Revolution." *American Sociological Review*, 27: 5–19.

Day, R. J. F. 2001. "Ethics, Affinity and the Coming Communities." *Philosophy and Social Criticism*, 27 (1): 21–38.

Day, R. J. F. 2004. "From Hegemony to Affinity: The Political Logic of the Newest Social Movements." *Cultural Studies*, 18 (5): 716–748. https://doi.org/10.1080/0 950238042000260360.

Day, R. J. F. 2005. *Gramsci is Dead: Anarchist Currents in the Newest Social Movements*. Toronto: ON Between the Lines.

de Carteret, P. 2008. "Storytelling as Research Praxis, and Conversations that Enabled it to Emerge." *International Journal of Qualitative Studies in Education*, 21 (3): 235–249.

de Certeau, M. 1984. *The Practice of Everyday Life*. Berkeley: University of California Press.

de Certeau, M. 1988. *The Practice of Everyday Life*, 2nd edition. Berkeley, Los Angeles, London: University of California Press.

Deleuze, G. 1988. *Foucault*. Minneapolis: Minnesota University Press.

Deleuze, G. 1990. *The Logic of Sense*. London: Athlone.

Deleuze, G. 1994. *Difference and Repetition*. New York: Columbia University Press.

Deleuze, G. 2003. *Francis Bacon—The Logic of Sensation*. London, New York: Continuum.

Deleuze, G. and Guattari, F. 1994. *What Is Philosophy?* New York: Columbia University Press. https://doi.org/10.2307/3121994.

Deleuze, G. and Guattari, F. 2010. *Nomadology: The War Machine*. Seattle: Wormwood Distribution. https://doi.org/10.1111/an.1991.32.4.3.2.

Deleuze, G. and Guattari, F. 2013. *A Thousand Plateaus*. London: Bloomsbury.

Deleuze, G. and Parnet, C. 1987. *Dialogues*. New York: Columbia University Press.

della Porta, D. 2005. "Deliberation in Movement: Why and How to Study Deliberative Democracy and Social Movements." *Acta Politica*, 40: 336–350.

della Porta, D. 2008. *Consensus in Movements* convegno internazionale: il governo delle societa nel xxi secolo. Rome. 17–20 November. Accessed November 5, 2017. http://www.accademiaaldomoro.org/attivita/trentennale/ConvegnoVarie/Relazioni /dellaporta%20.pdf.

Denzin, N. K. 1989. *Interpretative Interactionism*. Newbury Park: Sage Publications.

Diani, M. 1995. *Green Networks*. Edinburgh: Edinburgh University Press.

Diani, M. 2003. "Networks and Social Movements: A Research Programme." In *Social Movements and Networks: Relational Approaches to Collective Action*, edited by M. Diani and D. McAdam, 299–319. Oxford: Oxford University Press.

Diani, M. and McAdam, D. 2003. *Social Movements and Networks: Relational Approaches to Collective Action*. Oxford: Oxford University Press.

Durkheim, E. 1982. "Sociology and the Social Sciences." In *The Rules of Sociological Method*, edited by S. Lukes, 175–208. New York, London, Toronto, Sydney: The Free Press. https://doi.org/10.2307/2072658.

Elden, S. 2004. *Understanding Henri Lefebvre: Theory and the Possible*. London, New York: Continuum.

Evans, S. 1979. *Personal Politics: The Roots of Women's Liberation in the Civil Rights Movement and the New Left*. New York: Alfred Knopf.

Fals Borda, O. 1979. "Investigating Reality in Order to Transform It: The Colombian Experience." *Dialectical Anthropology*, 4: 33–55.

Fals Borda, O. 1985. *Conocimiento y poder popular*. Bogota: Siglo XXI.

Fals Borda, O. 1987. "The Application of Participatory Research in Latin America." *International Sociology*, 2 (4): 329–347.

Fals Borda, O. 2006. "Participatory Action Research in Social Theory: Origins and Challenges." In *Handbook of Action Research*, 1st edition, edited by P. Reason and H. Bradbury, 27–37. London: Sage Publications.

Fals Borda, O. 2013. "Action Research in the Convergence of Disciplines." *International Journal of Action Research*, 9 (2): 155–167.

Faure, M. A. 1994. "Some Methodological Problems in Comparative Politics." *Journal of Theoretical Politics*, 6 (3): 307–322.

Federici, S. 2004. *Caliban and the Witch: Women, the Body and Primitive Accumulation*. New York: Autonomedia.

Feyerabend, P. 1975. *Against Method*. London: Verso.

Fine, M. and Torre, E. M. 2008. "Theorizing Audience, Products and Provocation." In *Handbook of Action Research*, 2nd edition, edited by P. Reason and H. Bradbury, 328–339. London, Thousand Oaks, New Delhi: Sage Publications.

Flam, H. 2007. "Emotions' Map: A Research Agenda." In *Emotions and Social Movements*, edited by H. Flam and D. King, 19–37. London: Routledge.

Flesher Fominaya, C. 2007. "Autonomous Movements and the Institutional Left: Two Approaches in Tension in Madrid's Anti-globalisation Network." *South European Society and Politics*, 12 (3): 335–358.

Flesher Fominaya, C. 2010. "Collective Identity in Social Movements: Central Concepts and Debates." *Sociology Compass*, 4 (6): 393–404.

Foucault, M. 1991. *Discipline and Punish: The Birth of the Prison*. Harmondsworth: Penguin Books.

Foucault, M. 1997. "Of Other Spaces: Utopias and Heterotopias." In *Rethinking Architecture: A Reader in Cultural Theory*, edited by N. Leach, 330–336. New York: Routledge. Accessed September 9, 2017. http://scholar.google.com/scholar?hl=enandbtnG=Searchandq=intitle:Of+other+spaces+:+utopias+and+heterotopias#1.

Fournier, M. 2014. "Lines of Flight." *Transgender Studies Quarterly*, 1 (1–2): 121–122.

Fraassen, B. C. 2000. "Sola Experientia? Feyerabend's Refutation of Classical Empiricism." In *The Worst Enemy of Science? Essays in memory of Paul Feyerabend*, edited by J. Preston, G. Munévar, and D. Lamb, 28–37. Oxon, New York: Oxford University Press.

Freire, P. 1964. *La educación como práctica de libertad*. Mexico: Siglo XXI.

Freire, P. 1972. *Pedagogy of the Oppressed*. Hammondsworth: Penguin Books.

Freire, P. 1973. *Education for Critical Consciousness*. London, New York: Continuum.

Friday June 18th, 1999. "1999." In *Do or Die 8*, 1–12. Accessed February 2, 2015 http://www.eco-action.org/dod/no8/j18.html.

Fuchs, C. 2006. "The Self-Organization of Social Movements." *Systemic Practice and Action Research*, 19 (1): 101–137.

Gayatri Chakravorty Spivak. 1988. "Can the Subaltern Speak?" In *Marxism and the Interpretation of Culture*, edited by C. Nelson and L. Grossberg, 271–313. Basingstoke: Macmillan Education. Accessed October 1, 2014. https://doi.org/10 .4135/9781446212233.n7.

Gelderloos, P. 2006. *Consensus: A New Handbook for Grassroots Social, Political, and Environmental Groups*. Tucson: See Sharp Press.

Gelderloos, P. 2011. "Crackdown In Spain: Wave of Arrests Sweeps Barcelona." *Counterpunch*. Accessed February 2, 2014 http://www.counterpunch.org/2011/10 /10/crackdown-in-spain/.

Genat, B. 2009. "Building Emergent Situated Knowledges in Participatory Action Research." *Action Research*, 7 (1): 101–115.

Geschwender, J. 1968. "Explorations in Theory of Social Movements and Revolutions." *Social Forces*, 47: 127–135.

Giannaki, A.-F. 2016. "The Role of 'Privileged' Allies in the Struggle for Social Justice." Accessed May 9, 2017. http://www.humanityinaction.org/knowledgebase /724-the-role-of-privileged-allies-in-the-struggle-for-social-justice.

Giddens, A. 1987. *Social Theory and Modern Sociology*. Stanford, CA: Stanford University Press.

Goodchild, P. 1996. *Deleuze and Guattari: An Introduction to the Politics of Desire*. London, Thousand Oaks, New Delhi: Sage Publications.

Goodwin, J. and Jasper, J. M. 1999. "Caught in a Winding, Snarling Vine: The Structural Bias of Political Process Theory." *Sociological Forum*, 14 (1): 27–54.

Gordon, U. 2008. *Anarchy Alive!: Anti-Authoritarian Politics from Practice to Theory*. London: Pluto Press.

Graeber, D. 2002. "The New Anarchists." *New Left Review*, 13: 61–73.

Graeber, D. 2004. *Fragments of an Anarchist Anthropology*. Chicago: Prickly Paradigm Press.

Graeber, D. 2009. *Direct Action: An Ethnography*. Edinburgh: AK Press.

Gray, R., Fitch, M. and Davis, C. 2000. "Challenges of Participatory Research: Reflections on a Study with Breast Cancer Self-help Groups." *Health Expectations*, 3 (4): 243–252.

Gruber, T. R. 1993. "A Translation Approach to Portable Ontology Specifications." *Knowledge Acquisition*, 5 (2): 199–220. https://doi.org/10.1.1.101.7493.

Gurr, T. 1969. *Why Men Rebel*. Princeton, NJ: Princeton University Press.

Hacking, I. 1981. *Scientific Revolutions*. Oxford: Oxford University Press.

Haiven, M. and Khasnabish, A. 2014. *The Radical Imagination*. Halifax, Winnipeg, London: Fernwood Publishing and Zed Books.

Halbwachs, M. 1992. *On Collective Memory*. Chicago: University of Chicago Press.

Hall, B. and Kidd, R. 1978. *Adult Learning: A Design for Action*. Oxford: Pergamon.

Hambacher Forst Buchprojekt. 2015. *Mit Baumhäusern gegen Bagger: Geschichten vom Widerstand im rheinischen Braunkohlerevier*. Osnabrück: Packpapierverlag.

Haraway, D. 1988. "Situated Knowledges: The Science Question in Feminism and the Privilege of Partial Perspective." *Feminist Studies*, 14 (3): 575–599.

Haraway, D. 1991. "A Cyborg Manifesto." In *Simians, Cyborgs and Women: The Reinvention of Nature*, edited by D. Haraway, 149–181. London: Routledge.

Harvey, D. 1993. *Social Justice and the City*, 2nd edition. Oxford: Blackwell.

Harvey, D. 2001. *Spaces of Capital: Towards a Critical Geography*. Edinburgh: Edinburgh University Press.

Harvey, D. 2012. *Rebel Cities*. London, New York: Verso.

Harvey, J. 1999. *Civilised Oppression*. Lanham, MD: Rowman & Littlefield.

Haworth, R. H. 2012. *Anarchist Pedagogies: Collective Actions, Theories, and Critical Reflections on Education*. Oakland: PM Press.

Heberle, R. 1995. "Social Movements and Social Order." In *Social Movements: Critiques, Concepts, Case-Studies*, edited by S. Lyman, 49–59. New York: New York University Press.

Heidegger, M. 1971. "Building, Dwelling, Thinking." In *Poetry, Language, Thought* by M. Heidegger, 143–157. New York: Harper Colophon Books.

Herising, F. 2005. "Interrupting Positions: Critical Thresholds and Queer Pro/ Positions." In *Research as Resistance: Critical, Indigenous and Anti-Oppressive Approaches*, edited by L. Brown and S. Strega, 127–152. Toronto: Canadian Scholar's Press/Women's Press.

Heshusius, L. 1994. "Freeing Ourselves from Objectivity: Managing Subjectivity or Turning toward a Participatory Mode of Consciousness?" *Educational Researcher*, 23 (3): 15–22.

Hetherington, K. 1998. *Expressions of Identity: Space, Performance, Politics*. London, Thousand Oaks: Sage Publications.

Hetherington, S. n.d. "Knowledge." In *Internet Encyclopedia of Philosophy*. Accessed April 28, 2014. http://www.iep.utm.edu/knowledg/.

Higgins, L. 2006. "Guy Debord and the Situationist International: Texts and Documents Review." *South Central Review* 23. Accessed January 16, 2016. https://doi.org/10.1353/scr.2006.0032.

Hobson, R. 2011. "The Untold Story of Squats: Gentrification and Regeneration." Accessed March 13, 2017. http://www.londonlovesbusiness.com/property/reside ntial-property/the-untold-story-of-squats-gentrification-and-regeneration/899.article.

Hodkinson, S. and Chatterton, P. 2006. "Autonomy in the City?" *City*, 10 (3): 305–315. https://doi.org/10.1080/13604810600982222.

Holloway, J. 2016. *In, Against, and Beyond Capitalism*. Oakland: PM Press.

Holton, G. 1993. *Science and Anti-Science*. Cambridge, MA: Harvard University Press.

Holtzman, B., Hughes, C. and Van Meter, K. 2007. "Do It Yourself . . . and the Moment Beyond Capitalism." In *Constituent Imagination: Militant Investigations, Collective Theorisation*, edited by S. Shukaitis, D. Graeber and E. Biddle, 44–61. Oakland, Edinburgh, West Virginia: AK Press.

Hoofd, I. M. 2010. "The Accelerated University: Activist-academic Alliances and the Simulation of Thought." *Ephemera*, 10 (1): 7–23.

Hughes, I., and Seymour-Rolls, K. 2000. "Participatory Action Research: Getting the Job Done" Action Research E-Reports No. 4. Accessed February 3, 2016. http://www.fhs.usyd.edu.au/arow/arer/004.htm.

Ingelhart, R. 1990. "Values, Ideology and Cognitive Mobilisation in New Social Movements." In *Challenging the Political Order: New Social Movements and Political Movements in Western Democracies*, edited by R. Dalton and M. Kuechler, 43–66. Oxford, New York: Oxford University Press.

Iseke, J. 2013. "Indigenous Storytelling as Research." *International Review of Qualitative Research*, 6 (4): 559–577.

Jasanoff, S. (2004). *States of Knowledge: The Co-production of Science and Social Order*. New York: Routledge.

Jeppesen, S. 2010. "Queer Anarchist Autonomous Zones and Publics: Direct Action Vomiting against Homonormative Consumerism." *Sexualities*, 13 (4): 463–478. https://doi.org/10.1177/1363460710370652.

Johnston, H. and Klandermans, B. 1995. "The Cultural Analysis of Social Movements." In *Social Movements and Culture*, 3–24. Minneapolis: University of Minnesota Press.

Juris, J. S. 2005a. "Social Forums and Their Margins: Networking Logics and the Cultural Politics of Autonomous Space." *Ephemera*, 5 (2): 253–272.

Juris, J. S. 2005b. "The New Digital Media and Activist Networking within Anti-Corporate Globalization Movements." *The Annals of the Academy of Political and Social Science: Cultural Politics in a Digital Age, Special Edition*, 189–209.

Juris, J. S. 2009. "Anarchism, or the Cultural Logic of Networking." In *Contemporary Anarchist Studies: An Introductory Anthology of Anarchy in the Academy*, edited by R. Amster, A. DeLeon, L. Fernandez, A. Nocella, and D. Shannon, 213–223. London: Routledge.

Kallet, R. H. 2004. "How to Write the Methods Section of a Research Paper." *Respiratory Care*, 49 (10): 1229–1232.

Karatzogianni, A. and Robinson, A. 2010. *Power, Resistance and Conflict in the Contemporary World*. Oxon, New York: Routledge.

Katsiaficas, G. 2006. *The Subversion of Politics: European Autonomous Social Movements and the Decolonialisation of Everyday Life*. New York: Humanity Books.

Keller, M., Kögler, L., Krawinkel, M. and Schlemermeyer, J. 2013. *Antifa*. Stuttgart: Schmetterling Verlag.

Kemmis, S., and McTaggart, R. 2007. "Participatory Action Research: Communicative Action and the Public Sphere." In *Strategies of Qualitative Inquiry*, 3rd edition, edited by N. K. Denzin and Y. Lincoln, 271–330. Thousand Oaks, CA: Sage Publications. https://doi.org/10.1080/09650790600975593.

Kimpson, S. A. 2005. "Stepping of the Road: A Narrative of Inquiry." In *Research as Resistance: Critical, Indigenous and Anti-Oppressive Approaches*, edited by L. Brown and S. Strega, 73–96. Toronto: Canadian Scholar's Press/Women's Press.

Kindon, S., Pain, R. and Kesby, M. 2007. "Participatory Action Research: Origins, Approaches, Methods." In *Participatory Action Research Approaches and Methods: Connecting People, Participation and Place*, edited by S. Kindon, R. Pain and M. Kesby, 9–17. London, New York: Routledge.

Klandermans, B., Kriesi, H., and Tarrow, S. 1988. *From Structure to Action: Comparing Social Movement Research across Cultures*, Vol. 1. Greenwich: JAI Press.

Koopmans, R. 2005. "The Missing Link between Structure and Agency: Outline of an Evolutionary Approach to Social Movements." *Mobilization: An International Journal*, 10: 19–36.

Kurki, M. and Wight, C. 2007. "International Relations and Social Science." In *International Relations Theories: Discipline and Diversity*, edited by T. Dunne, M. Kurki and S. Smith, 13–33. Oxford: Oxford University Press.

Lacan, J. 1998. *The Seminar of Jacques Lacan: The Four Fundamental Concepts of Psychoanalysis XI*. Edited by J.-A. Miller. New York: Norton and Company.

Laclau, E. 2005. *On Populist Reason*. London: Verso.

Landstreicher, W. 2004. *Autonomous Self-Organization and Anarchist Intervention: A Tension in Practice*. Portland: Venomous Butterfly Publications.

Larana, E., Johnston, H. and Gusfield, J. 1994. *New Social Movements*. Philadelphia: Temple University Press.

Law, J. and Hetherington, K. 1998. *Allegory and Interference: Representation in Sociology. Department of Sociology Lancaster University*. Lancaster. Accessed November 26, 2016. http://scholar.google.com/scholar?hl=enandbtnG=Searchan dq=intitle:Allegory+and+Interference+:+Representation+in+Sociology#0.

Lefebvre, H. 1965. *Métaphilosophie*. Paris: Editions de Minuit.

Lefebvre, H. and Levich, C. 2007. "The Everyday and Everydayness." *Yale French Studies*, 73: 7–11. https://doi.org/10.2307/2930193.

Leitner, H., Sheppard, E. and Sziarto, K. M. 2008. "The Spatialities of Contentious Politics." *Transactions of the Institute of British Geographers*, 33 (2): 157–172. https://doi.org/10.1111/j.1475-5661.2008.00293.x.

Lewin, K. 1946. "Action Research and Minority Problems." *Journal of Social Issues*, 2 (4): 34–46. https://doi.org/10.1111/j.1540-4560.1946.tb02295.x.

Lewis, P. J. 2011. "Storytelling as Research/Research as Storytelling." *Qualitative Inquiry*, 17 (6): 505–510.

López, M. 2013. "The Squatters' Movement in Europe: A Durable Struggle for Social Autonomy in Urban Politics." *Antipode*, 45 (4): 866–887. https://doi.org/10.1111/j .1467-8330.2012.01060.x.

Lugones, M. 1992. "On Borderlands/La Frontera: An Interpretive Essay." *Hypathia*, 7 (4): 31–37.

MacLay, G. R. 1990. *The Social Organism: A Short History of the Idea That a Human Society May Be Regarded as a Gigantic Living Creature*. Great Barrington: North River Press.

Maeckelbergh, M. 2011. "Doing Is Believing: Prefiguration as Strategic Practice in the Alterglobalization Movement." *Social Movement Studies*, 10 (1): 1–20.

Massey, D. 1994. "A Global Sense of Place." In *Space, Place and Gender*, 146–156. Minneapolis: University of Minnesota Press. https://doi.org/10.1016/j.pecs.2007 .10.001.

McAdam, D. 1982. *The Political Process and the Development of Black Insurgency*. Chicago: Chicago University Press.

McCarthy, J. D., and Zald, M. N. 1977. "Resource Mobilization and Social Movements: A Partial Theory." *American Journal of Sociology*, 82 (6): 1212–1241.

McCormac, D. P. 2013. *Refrains for Moving Bodies*. Durham, London: Duke University Press.

McIntyre, A. 2008. *Participatory Action Research*. London, New Delhi, Los Angeles, Singapore: Sage Publications.

Melucci, A. 1988. "Getting Involved: Indentity and Mobilisation in Social Movements." In *International Social Movements Research: From Structure to Action*, edited by B. Klandermans, H. Kriesi and S. Tarrow, 329–348. Greenwich: JAI Press.

Melucci, A. 1996a. *Challenging Codes: Collective Action in the Information Age*. Cambridge: Cambridge University Press.

Melucci, A. 1996b. *The Playing Self*. Cambridge: Cambridge University Press.

Menzies, H. and Newson, J. 2007. "No Time to Think: Academics' Life in the Globally Wired University." *Time and Society*, 16 (1): 83–98.

Mies, M., and Bennholdt-Thomsen, V. 1999. *The Subsistence Perspective: Beyond the Globalised Economy*. London: Zed Books.

Miettunen, J. V. M. 2015. *Prefigurative Politics: Perils and Promise*. University of Kent. https://doi.org/10.1080/00369220601100075.

Milkman, R., Luce, S. and Lewis, P. 2015. "Occupy Wall Street." In *The Social Movements Reader: Cases and Concepts*, 3rd edition, edited by J. Goodwin and J. M. Jasper, 30–44. Chichester, Oxford, Malden: Wiley Blackwell.

Miller, B. 2000. *Geography and Social Movements*. Minneapolis, London: University of Minnesota Press.

Montero, M. 2000. "Participation in Participatory Action Research." *Annual Review of Critical Psychology*, 2: 131–143.

Moosa-Mitha, M. 2005. "Situating Anti-Oppressive Theories within Critical and Difference-Centered Perspectives." In *Research as Resistance: Critical, Indigenous and Anti-Oppressive Approaches*, edited by L. Brown and S. Strega, 37–72. Toronto: Canadian Scholar's Press/Women's Press.

Morris, A., and Herring, C. 1984. "Theory and Research in Social Movements: A Critical Review." In *Political Behaviour Annual*, edited by S. Long. Michigan: Westerview Press. Accessed October 4, 2017. http://deepblue.lib.umich.edu/handl e/2027.42/51075.

Moser, H. 1978. "Einige Aspekte der Aktionsforschung im internationalen Vergleich." In *Internationale Aspekte der Aktionsforschung*, edited by H. Moser and H. Ornauer, 173–189. München: Kösel.

Motta, S. 2009. "Old Tools and New Movements in Latin America: Political Science as Gatekeeper or Intellectual Illuminator?" *Latin American Politics and Society*, 51 (1): 31–56.

Motta, S. 2011. "Notes Towards Prefigurative Epistemologies." In *Social Movements in the Global South: Disposession, Development and Resistance*, edited by S. Motta and A. G. Nilsen, 178–199. Hampshire: Palgrave Macmillan.

Motta, S. 2013a. "On the Pedagogical Turn in Latin American Social Movements." In *Education and Social Change in Latin America*, edited by M. Sara and M. Cole, 53–68. New York: Palgrave Macmillan.

Motta, S. 2013b. *The Storytellers of Critique: Becoming Otherwise in Practice and in Theory*. Counter Conducts Workshop, November 2013. University of Sussex.

Motta, S. 2014. "Reinventing Revolutions in Latin America: An 'Other' Politics in Practice and Theory." In *Rethinking Latin American Social Movements: Radical Action from Below*, edited by H. E. Vanden and M. Becker, 21–45. Lanham, Boulder, New York, Oxford: Rowman & Littlefield.

Motta, S. 2016. "Decolonising Critique: From Prophetic Negation to Prefigurative Affirmation." In *Social Sciences for an Other Politics: Women Theorizing Without Parachutes*, edited by A. C. Dinerstein, 33–48. Cham: Palgrave Macmillan.

Mucina, D. D. 2011. "Story as Research Methodology." *AlterNative*, 7 (1): 1–14.

Mueller, C. 1992. "Building Social Movement Theory." In *Frontiers in Social movement Theory*, edited by C. Mueller and A. Morris, 3–25. New Haven, CT: Yale University Press.

Muller, J. and Cloete, N. 1986. "The White Hands: Academic Social Scientists and Forms of Popular Knowledge Production." *Critical Arts*, 4 (2): 1–19.

Mullett, J. 2008. "Presentational Knowing: Bridging Experience and Expression with Art, Poetry and Song." In *Handbook of Action Research*, 2nd edition, edited by P. Reason and H. Bradbury, 365–379. London, Thousand Oaks, New Delhi: Sage Publications.

N.A. 2015. "Live in Common is Stronger than Metropolis." *Guccio*, 18–21.

Negri, A. 2003. "The Crisis of Political Space." In *Revolutionary Writing: Common Sense, Essays in Post-Political Politics*, edited by W. Bonefeld, 189–197. New York: Autonomedia.

Newman, S. 2010. *The Politics of Postanarchism*. Edinburgh: Edinburgh University Press.

Newman, S. 2011. "Postanarchism and Space: Revolutionary Fantasies and Autonomous Zones." *Planning Theory*, 10 (4): 344–365. https://doi.org/10.1177/1473095211413753.

Nicholls, W. 2009. "Place, Networks, Space: Theorising the Geographies of Social Movements." *Transactions of the Institute of British Geographers*, 34 (1): 78–93. https://doi.org/10.1111/j.1475-5661.2009.00331.x.

Nicholson, H. 2013. "Participation as Performance Sells." In *Problems of Participation: Reflections on Authority, Democracy, and the Struggle for Common Life*, edited by T. Noorani, C. Blencowe and J. Brigstocke, 113–117. Lewes: ARN Press.

Notes from Nowhere. 2003. *We Are Everywhere: The irresistible Rise of Global Anticapitalism*. London: Verso.

O'Sullivan, S. and Zepke, S. 2008. *Deleuze, Guattari and the Production of the New*. London, New York: continuum.

Offe, C. 1985. "New Social Movements: Challenging the Boundaries of Institutional Politics." *Social Research*, 52 (4): 817–867.

Olkowski, D. 1999. *Gilles Deleuze and the Ruin of Representation*. Berkeley, Los Angeles, Oxford: University of California Press.

Penshkin, A. 1988. "In Search of Subjectivity—One's Own." *Educational Researcher*, 17 (7): 7–21.

Perlman, F. 2008. "The Reproduction of Daily Life." *Untorelli Press Zine*, n.d.

Peterson, A. 2001. *Contemporary Political Protest: Essays on Political Militancy*. Aldershot, Burlington, Singapore, Sydney: Ashgate.

Pickerill, J. and Chatterton, P. 2006. "Notes towards Autonomous Geographies: Creation, Resistance and Self-management as Survival Tactics." *Progress in Human Geography*, 30 (6): 730–746.

Pile, S. 1997. "Opposition, Political Identities and Spaces of Resistance." In *Geographies of Resistance*, edited by S. Pile and M. Keith, 1–32. London: Routledge.

Plant, S. 1992. *The Most Radical Gesture. The Situationist International in a Postmodern Age.* London, New York: Routledge.

Plotke, D. 1990. "What's So New about the New Social Movements." *Socialist Review*, 90 (1): 81–102.

Polletta, F. 1998. "Contending Stories: Narrative in Social Movements." *Qualitative Sociology*, 21 (4): 419–446. https://doi.org/10.1023/A:1023332410633.

Popper, K. 1979. *Objective Knowledge: An Evolutionary Approach.* Oxford: Claredon Press.

Potts, K. and Brown, L. 2005. "Becoming an Anti-Oppressive Researcher." In *Research as Resistance: Critical, Indigenous and Anti-Oppressive Approaches*, edited by L. Brown and S. Strega, 255–286. Toronto: Canadian Scholar's Press/Women's Press.

Precarias a la Deriva. 2003. "First Stutterings of Precarias a la Deriva." Accessed March 2, 2016. http://web.archive.org/web/20061013073945/www.sindominio.net/karakola/precarias/balbuceos-english.htm.

Pruijt, H. 2014. "Autonomous and/or Institutionalized Social Movements? Conceptual Clarifications and Illustrative Cases." *International Journal of Comparative Sociology*, 55 (2): 144–165.

Purkis, J. 2012. "The Hitchhiker as Theorist: Rethinking Sociology and Anthropology from an Anarchist Perspective." In *The Continuum Companion to Anarchism*, edited by R. Kinna, 140–160. London, New York: Continuum.

Rahman, A. M. 2008. "Some Trends in the Praxis of participatory Action Research." In *Handbook of Action Research*, 2nd edition, edited by P. Reason and H. Bradbury, 37–47. London, Thousand Oaks, New Delhi: Sage Publications.

Ravage. 1999. "Desire Is Speaking." *Do or Die 8*, 137–140. Accessed December 16, 2016. http://www.eco-action.org/dod/no8/desire.html.

Rayner, T. 2013. "Lines of Flight: Deleuze and Nomadic Creativity." *Philosophy for Change: Ideas That Make a Difference*, June 18, 2013. https://philosophyforchange.wordpress.com/2013/06/18/lines-of-flight-deleuze-and-nomadic-creativity/.

Razack, S. 1998. *Looking White People in the Eye: Gender, Race, and Culture in Courtrooms and Classrooms.* Toronto: University of Toronto Press.

Reason, P. 2004. "Action Research and the Single Case: A Response to Bjorn Gustavsen." *Concepts and Transformation*, 8 (3): 281–294.

Reason, P. and Bradbury, H. 2008a. "Concluding Reflections: Whither Action Research?" In *Handbook of Action Research*, 2nd edition, edited by P. Reason and H. Bradbury, 583–595. London, Thousand Oaks, New Delhi: Sage Publications.

Richardson, N. 2016. *Transgressive Bodies: Representations in Film and Popular Culture.* London: Routledge.

los Ricos. 1993. "Traveling Autonomous Zone." *Anarchy: A Journal of Desire Armed*, 36. Accessed March 5, 2016. https://theanarchistlibrary.org/library/rob-los-ricos-traveling-autonomous-zone.

Robinson, A. 2010. "Autonomism: The Future of Activism?" *Ceasefire*. Accessed November 7, 2016. http://ceasefiremagazine.co.uk/in-theory-5-autonomism/.

Robinson, A. 2018. "Life is Magical: Affect and Empowerment in Autonomous Social Movements." In *Riots and Militant Occupations: Smashing a System, Building a World – A Critical Introduction*, edited by A. Starodub and A. Robinson, 33–55. London, New York: Rowman & Littlefield.

Ryle, G. 1971. "Knowing How and Knowing That." In *Gilbert Ryle—Collected Papers Vol. II*, edited by G. Ryle, 212–225. London: Hutchinson.

Sargisson, L. and Tower Sargent, L. 2004. *Living in Utopia: New Zealand's Intentional Communities*. Aldershot: Ashgate.

Sassen, S. 2006. *Territory, Authority, Rights: From Medieval to Global Assemblages*. Princeton, NJ: Princeton University Press.

Schneider, B. 2012. "Participatory Action Research, Mental Health Service User Research, and the Hearing Our Voices Projects." *International Journal of Qualitative Methods*, 11 (2): 152–165.

Schwartz, M. 1976. *Radical Protest and Social Structure*. New York: Academic Press.

Scott, A. 1990. *Ideology and the New Social Movements*. London: Unwin Hyman.

Scott, C. J. 1990. *Domination and the Arts of Resistance: Hidden Transcripts*. New Haven, CT: Yale University Press.

Selbin, E. 2010. *Revolution, Rebellion, Resistance: The Power of Story*. London: Zed Books.

Sewell, W. H. 2001. "Space in Contentious Politics." In *Silence and Voice in the Study of Contentious Politics*, edited by R. R. Aminzade, J. A. Goldstone, D. McAdam, E. J. Perry, W. H. Sewell, S. Tarrow and C. Tilly, 51–88. Cambridge: Cambridge University Press.

Shea, M. 2013. "Berliners Are Fighting a War Against Hipster-Led Gentrification." *Vice*, April 5, 2013. from https://www.vice.com/en_se/article/berlins-war-against-gentrification.

Simiti, M. 2014. "Rage and Protest: The Case of the Greek Indignant Movement." *GreeSe Paper No. 82*. London School of Economics. February 2014.

Singh, R. 2001. *Social Movements, Old and New: A Post-modernist Critique*. New Delhi, London, Thousand Oaks: Sage Publications.

Sitrin, M. 2006. *Horizontalism: Voices of Popular Power in Argentina*. Oakland, Edinburgh: AK Press.

Sitrin, M. 2011. "Fueling the Flames of Dignity: From Rupture to Revolution in Argentina." In *Social Movements in the Global South: Disposession, Development and Resistance*, edited by A. Nielsen and S. Motta, 250–274. London, New York: Zed Books.

Sitrin, M. 2012. *Everyday Revolutions: Horizontalism and Autonomy in Argentina*. London, New York: Zed Books.

Slaughter, S. and Leslie, L. 1997. *Academic Capitalism: Politics, Policies, and the Entrepreneurial University*. Baltimore: John Hopkins University Press.

Smelser, N. 1962. *Theory of Collective Behaviour.* New York: Free Press.

Smith, S. 1999. "The Cultural Politics of Difference." In *Human Geography Today*, edited by D. Massey, J. Allen and P. Sarre. Cambridge: Polity Press.

Snow, D. and Soule, S. 2010. *A Primer on Social Movements.* New York, London: Norton.

Soja, E. W. 2009. "The City and Spatial Justice." *Justice Spatiale Spatial Justice*, 1: 1–5.

Sparrow, R. 1997. *Anarchist Politics and Direct Action.* Accessed November 22, 2017. http://theanarchistlibrary.org/library/rob-sparrow-anarchist-politics-direct-action.pdf.

Squatting Europe Kollective. 2013. *Squatting in Europe: Radical Spaces, Urban Struggles.* Wivenhoe, New York, Port Watson: Minor Compositions.

Squatting Europe Kollective. 2014. *The Squatters' Movement in Europe: Commons and Autonomy as Alternatives to Capitalism.* London: Pluto Press.

Staggenborg, S. 2011. *Social Movements.* Oxford, New York: Oxford University Press.

Strega, S. 2005. "The View from the Poststructural Margins: Epistemology and Methodology Reconsidered." In *Research as Resistance: Critical, Indigenous and Anti-Oppressive Approaches*, edited by L. Brown and S. Strega, 199–236. Toronto: Canadian Scholar's Press/Women's Press.

Sullivan, S. 2004. "'We are Are Heartbroken and Furious!' Engaging with Violence in the Anti-globalisation Movements." *CSGR Working Papers No. 133/04.* Coventry. Accessed April 5, 2015. http://wrap.warwick.ac.uk/1998/.

Swantz, M. L. 1996. "A Personal Position Paper on Participatory Research: Personal Quest for Living Knowledge." *Qualitative Inquiry*, 2 (1): 120–136.

Swantz, M. L. 2008. "Participatory Action Research as Practice." In *Handbook of Action Research*, 2nd edition, edited by P. Reason and H. Bradbury, 31–49. London, Thousand Oaks, New Delhi: Sage Publications.

The Free Association. 2005. "On the Road." In *Shut Them Down! The G8, Gleneagles 2005 and the Movement of Movements*, edited by D. Harvie, K. Milburn, B. Trott and D. Watts, 17–26. Leeds, New York: Autonomedia.

Tilly, C. 1978. *From Mobilisation to Revolution.* Reading: Addison-Wesley.

Tilly, C. 2000. "Spaces of Contention." *Mobilization: An International Journal*, 5 (2): 135–159.

Toret, J. 2006. "Cartography and War Machines: Challenges and Experiences around Militant Research in Southern Europe." *Eipcp.* Accessed March 06, 2017. http://eipcp.net/transversal/0406/tsg/en.

Tormey, S. 2012. "Occupy Wall Street: From Representation to Post-Representation." *Critical Globalisation*, 5 (5): 132–142.

Touraine, A. 1981. *The Voice and the Eye.* Cambridge: Cambridge University Press.

Touraine, A. 1988. *Return of the Actor: Social Theory in Postindustrial Society.* Minneapolis: University of Minnesota Press.

Tuan, Y.-F. 1974. *Topophilia.* Englewood Cliffs, NJ: Prentice-Hall.

Turner, R. and Kilian, L. 1987. *Collective Behaviour*, 3rd edition. Upper Saddle River, NJ: Prentice-Hall.

University of Leeds. n.d. "Academic Writing: Language and Style." Accessed October 27, 2017. https://library.leeds.ac.uk/info/485/academic_skills/331/acad emic_writing/5.

Usher, P. 1997. "Challenging the Power of Rationality." In *Understanding Social Research: Perspectives on Methodology and Practice*, edited by G. McKenzie, J. Powell and R. Usher, 42–55. London: The Falmer Press.

Usher, R. 2010. "Riding the Lines of Flight." *European Journal of Research on the Education and Learning of Adults*, 1 (1–2): 67–78.

van Stekelenburg, J. and Klandermans, B. 2009. "Social Movement Theory: Past, Present and Prospect." *Movers and Shakers: Social Movements in Africa*, 8: 17–43.

Vaneigem, R. 2006. "Basic Banalities Part 2." In *Situationist International Anthology*, edited by K. Knabb, 269–299. Berkeley, CA: Bureau of Public Secrets.

Webster, R. 2014. "Speaking Back through Research." In *Proceedings of the Australian Association for Research in Education and the New Zealand Association for Research in Education Conference*, pp. 1–12. Brisbane: AARE.

Wilkins, P. 2000. "Storytelling as Research." In *Research in Social Care and Social Welfare: Issues and Debates for Practice*, edited by B. Humphries, 144–153. London, Philadelphia: Jessica Kingsley Publishers.

Willful Disobedience. 2001. "The Responsibility for Repression." *Willful Disobedience* 2 (8).

Wilson, E. 1993. "Is Transgression Transgressive?" In *Activating Theory: Lesbian, Gay, Bisexual Politics*, edited by J. Bristow and A. R. Wilson, 107–117. London: Lawrence and Wishart.

Windsor, J. 2015. "Desire Lines: Deleuze and Guattari on Molar Lines, Molecular Lines, and Lines of Flight." *New Zealand Sociology*, 30 (1): 156–171.

Winslade, J. 2009. "Tracing Lines of Flight: Implications of the Work of Gilles Deleuze for Narrative Practice." *Family Process*, 48 (3): 332–346.

X, A. 2001. "Give Up Activism." *Do or Die* 9: 160–166.

Young, D. J. 2005. "Writing Against the Native Point of View." In *Auto-Ethnographies: The Anthropology of Academic Practices*, edited by A. Meneley and D. J. Young, 203–215. Peterborough: Broadview Press.

Young, I. M. 1990. *Justice and the Politics of Difference*. Princeton, NJ: Princeton University Press.

Young, I. M. 1995. "Together in Difference: Transforming the Logic of Group Political Conflict." In *The Rights of Minority Cultures*, edited by W. Kymlicka, 155–176. Oxford: Oxford University Press.

ZAD partout. Zone à défendre à Notre-Dame-des-Landes. 2013. Paris: L'insomniaque.

Zibechi, R. 2010. *Dispersing Power: Social Movements as Anti-State Forces*. Oakland, Baltimore, Edinburgh: AK Press.

Index